Ewart Brookes

DESTROYER

With additional material by
Douglas Reeman

ARROW BOOKS

Arrow Books Limited
3 Fitzroy Square, London W1

An imprint of the Hutchinson Publishing Group

London Melbourne Sydney Auckland
Wellington Johannesburg and agencies
throughout the world

First published Jarrolds Publishers (London) Ltd
Revised Arrow edition 1973
Second impression 1977

Made and printed in Great Britain
by The Anchor Press Ltd
Tiptree, Essex

ISBN 0 09 906800 1

DESTROYER

The torpedo: developed in the 1870's into a successful weapon; at first seen as a defensive weapon, but soon realised to be an attacking threat that could revolutionise naval warfare.

The torpedo-boat: a completely new sort of ship, developed specifically to launch the new weapon; fast, highly manoeuvrable, lightly armed, designed for the quick, sudden sortie against the slow, ponderous battle fleets.

The torpedo-boat destroyer: the fleet's riposte; rather larger, but still small, very fast, able to outpace and sink the torpedo-boat, yet with the range to accompany the big ships.

Soon the two functions were combined in the one ship and the destroyer was born; and with it, a new kind of sailor; men whose motto was 'Seek out the enemy and attack', men whose loyalty to the destroyer remained, no matter where promotion or chance might take them.

To Peter, my son,
who now understands
the meaning of tradition

'So, reader, if this tale has seemed repetitious with shock and gore, exploding magazines, burning and sinking ships, plummeting planes—that is simply how it was.'

S. E. MORISON. *The History of United States Naval Operations*, V, 315

Illustrations

Javelin, from the same stable as *Kelly*
Bedouin, one of the redoubtable 'Tribals'
Daring, 1952
London, 1963
Bristol, 1972

Author's Note

About six years ago I was holidaying in Gower, that imperious finger of bold cliffs and golden sand which probes out into the Bristol Channel just west of Swansea.

One night there was a bit of a lick of a gale, enough to make the hotel windows rattle and to whip the spray from the tops of the breakers to come slashing against those windows.

It was a night to make one feel glad that eight or ten hours on the bridge was not for me.

At breakfast, when the tail of the blow was still roughing up the bay a little, the chatty waiter told us that a ship had gone ashore in Rhossili Bay. That same bay, three miles or so of firm sand, is the finger-tip of the Gower peninsula. His next words awakened my interest.

'She's a warship of some sort. She was being towed to the breakers' at Llanelly.'

I still remembered *Warspite*'s prolonged defiance off Penzance, her adamant refusal to round Land's End en voyage to a last rendezvous with a breaker's glowing, cutting flame.

I had trodden the red, gaunt remains of *Warspite* a year or two before and with a mixture of impractical resentment against sheer economics and a nostalgic flashback to a couple of visits on board *Warspite* during the war I was guilty of a whispered word or two in salutation and admiration for her defiance.

So, this new victim we must see. Off we went, my wife and son and I.

And we found her. A mile or two more and she would have been round the corner, into the Burry estuary, and the breakers would have had their will.

But, in a gale—a brief summer blow she would have snorted through in her heyday—she calmly smashed the two tows, left the tug handling her floundering around with solid water aboard and drove in on the top of the tide, deep into the sand.

She was a destroyer.

I could almost imagine her coming to a secret agreement with the seas. 'I've fought you, and fought you fairly, for many years. You will ultimately win, but no breaker's yard will get me. If you'll help I am content to stay here.'

And there she stayed. In succeeding weeks the tides failed to reach high enough to shift her and when bulldozers and lorries tried making a channel in the sand the sea kept its part of the bargain and promptly filled it in again.

That bay, Rhossili Bay, is a graveyard of ships. Many a tall-masted windjammer ended her days there, and east of where the destroyer went in, a galleon is reputed to have been driven ashore and finally engulfed by the sand. People still find authentic Spanish doubloons after winter gales have churned up the beach.

My holiday came to an end and I paid a last visit to her. The sea was glassily whispering around her with not enough depth to float a matchbox.

When the harassed foreman of the frustrated breaker's yard wasn't looking I gave her reddened side a little pat and wished her well.

Now, my son at that time was one long interrogative. 'Why?' started practically every sentence. I had outlined in detail why the tides were not high enough to reach her in depth, what she had been, guessed at what she had seen, given him her probable armament, speed, complement—and why I was on her side.

He now enthusiastically, almost arrogantly, wears the light-blue uniform of the Junior Service and answers questions for me.

But, leaving that bay for the last time at the end of my holiday, he posed a question. 'Why is she called a destroyer?'

It has taken me six years and 80,000-odd words to tell him.

I hope he appreciates it.

EWART BROOKES

Prologue

Towards the end of the American Civil War the great naval powers of the world were searching fervently for an entirely new form of fighting ship. Warships had grown heavier, more unwieldy, more ponderous.

First one then another power would increase the bore of their guns, giving them a mile or so extra range for their heavy guns. The form of warfare remained basically that of the Nelsonian period. Light, scouting ships and cruisers had taken over the role of frigates. Their task was to search for the enemy battle fleet, inform their heavier ships, which would close the enemy to slug it out solidly from these floating gun platforms which were not far removed from the grotesque monitors, the boiler-plating-protected monstrosities evolved in the American war.

Somehow, and the greatest naval brains of the world worried at the problem, an entirely new weapon would have to be produced. It would be one which would alter naval warfare.

Within a few years of the surrender of the Confederate forces under Lee to General Grant at Appomattox Court House two revolutionary weapons emerged, and their origins lay in that war which had raged for more than four years, setting brother against brother, father against son.

The submarine and the torpedo.

Primitive underwater craft had been tried in desperation in the Civil War and had been laughed out of court for their dismal failures. So had crude torpedoes—merely explosive charges fastened to the end of a roughly made raft. They, too, were ineffective. But the germs of the two ideas survived.

No naval weapon produced since the days of Drake had a more marked effect on the evolution of warships than the torpedo.

With the torpedoes came new types of ships to carry them and use them, new forms of defence in the construction of larger warships had to be evolved.

New tactics had to be studied and developed.

And, most of all, a new breed of men began to emerge from this fluid period, a breed of men who in the space of two generations have written largely and indelibly in the pages of British naval history.

Destroyer men.

This is the story of them and their ships.

I

A chill wind off the Thames whipped a scurry of rain through the streets of Woolwich as an ancient brougham drew up to the sombre gates of Woolwich Arsenal.

The cabby waited with stolid patience as his passenger climbed from the vehicle and reached into his pocket for the fare.

The cab wandered off, and its late passenger, completely disregarding the rain, stood before the gates, one hand in his pocket jingling some keys and small change.

Beyond those grey gates waited his destiny.

He would make himself both famous and rich behind them, or if failure was his fate he would wander off into obscurity.

A couple of years back he had been the manager of an engineering works in Fiume, Austria. He had been introduced to a retired Austrian naval captain who had had an engineering problem connected with some form of naval weapon, and with his knowledge of engineering he had been able to partially solve it. With his business training he had also discerned the vague outlines of something bigger, something as immense as the evolution of the big gun.

The Austrian's weapon, as yet crude, was something which could proceed under the water carrying an amount of explosive in its head sufficient to damage any warship it would strike.

A torpedo.

For two years he and the naval man had experimented, held trials, had their failures and had their successes, until eventually there was produced a weapon which could proceed at eight knots, driven by compressed air, and could travel nearly 1,000 yards.

But the supply of money for experiments, meagre to begin with, completely dried up and it had seemed as if all their work had gone for nothing.

Then the Admiralty, which had been making discreet inquiries about this formidable weapon, stepped in. It had appointed a committee of naval officers to inspect this weapon and to report back their view on its potentialities.

The committee's report was enthusiastic.

The engineer was invited to bring two of the weapons to England, together with their launching apparatus, for long trials.

The trials were carried out at Sheerness from the bows of an obsolete ship and were sufficiently successful to influence the Admiralty to bring immense pressure to bear on the Government to purchase the rights of manufacture in England.

They were promptly bought for £15,000. Roughly the cost of three modern torpedoes!

Included in the deal were various clauses which ensured that nobody else in England would have access to their manufacture and that a number of naval officers would be trained in their construction.

The next step was to provide the engineer with a workshop where he could labour to perfect his weapon without the worry of finance and where his efforts could be shrouded in complete secrecy.

Such room was arranged at Woolwich Arsenal.

So the engineer had arrived. He stood for a few minutes with complete disregard for the rain which had put a glisten on his shoulders and was turning his tall beaver hat a silver grey.

Finally he moved up to the gate, rapped on it with the heavy bronze knocker and waited.

A small doorway in the larger gate opened cautiously and a head peered forth.

'I am expected. My name is Robert Whitehead.'

Within minutes zealous officials were guiding him to the workshop and drawing office provided. He thanked them and with a wave of his hand dismissed them, so that he was alone among the new and glistening machines, the still-clean work-benches and the as yet tidy drawing office.

Tomorrow, men would crouch over those benches, would work those machines and would spread rolled blue prints over the drawing boards, striving with Robert Whitehead, and under his direction seeking to improve and perfect the revolutionary weapon he had laboured to produce.

There were already in existence weapons described as torpedoes, in other words weapons designed to lay alongside a surface ship an explosive charge heavy enough to damage her seriously if not sink her.

There were two main competitors.

There was the spar torpedo, a long spar protruding from the bow of a steam cutter with an explosive charge at its end. The cutter would then attempt to place the charge against the ship's side. A suicidal mission.

Then there was the Harvey torpedo, invented by a naval commander of that name, by which an explosive charge was towed on a line across the bows of an anchored ship and would explode on contact with the ship's side.

Others had been invented and had proved dismal failures.

So the spar and the Harvey were Whitehead's principal rivals. The Harvey torpedo was, by then, already becoming obsolete, as it was so limited in its use.

A two-headed problem began to assert itself. Firstly the difficulty of keeping a torpedo on a straight track when it was launched, and secondly devising a proper launching ship to carry it within range. The first problem was Whitehead's. The second problem lay on the Admiralty table.

As Whitehead and his staff worked laboriously to solve their difficulty so did the experts at the Admiralty argue the pros and cons of their headache.

In three or four years of trial and error Whitehead eventually provided a partial solution by introducing two small propellers operating from one shaft in opposite directions and driven by compressed air, and by 1875 the Whitehead torpedo was reasonably successful. It was a weapon which could be taken out against a blockading squadron or a bombarding fleet and could be expected to hit something. In any event, the threat of it would be enough to turn the surface ships away.

It was still a defensive weapon when it was fired, but from what could it be fired?

Several ships were adapted, or built, to provide a platform or cradle for the launching, none of them with any success, until some mute, inglorious naval Milton suggested why not a small, fast ship fitted with Whitehead torpedoes? It would have to be strong enough to dash out into the open sea to fire torpedoes, and fast enough to evade any ponderous gun-fire at her, and could then dash back into harbour for another load of torpedoes.

The midnight oil was burned in the Admiralty's Naval Architect's rooms and, behold, the first torpedo boat was the result.

HMS *Lightning* was launched.

She had an overall length of eighty-four feet and was designed to do around twenty knots. Although a spar torpedo was provided in her original design, her main threat was two Whitehead torpedo tubes.

HMS *Lightning* was a success. In her trials she did all that was asked of her. Twisting and squirming like an eel, she could speed out to sea, get within the theoretical range and get away again.

Immediately an order was placed with various builders to construct twelve more, and one or two, profiting by minor errors in *Lightning*, reached the then phenomenal speed of more than twenty-one knots.

But still they were visualised as nothing more than extended shore defences.

One problem produces another and the new problem facing

the Admiralty was the question of defending the large and cumbersome surface ships against the attacks of the venomous mosquito craft.

The obvious solution was to provide anti-torpedo nets strung along the sides of the ships from stout booms, but the loss of speed when steaming was almost disastrous. It was an effective answer if the large ships were moving slowly in front of a harbour on a bombardment mission, or if they were anchored somewhere near as a potential blockading squadron.

But both those forms of naval warfare were rapidly being expunged from naval tactics.

Again, somebody who has never been named, or maybe the genesis of the idea came up in some prolonged wardroom discussion, produced the simpler answer.

To meet these swift little craft which would dash out from harbour all that would have to be done was to design—and build—bigger craft, faster craft and arm them with a gun. When the torpedo boats sallied forth the faster ship would intercept them and would destroy them.

A new name crept into naval design.

Torpedo-boat catchers.

The Admiralty ordered two, and HMS *Gossamer* and HMS *Rattlesnake* slipped into the water just sixteen years after Robert Whitehead had arrived at Woolwich to revolutionise naval warfare with his equally revolutionary weapon now recognised as the only effective torpedo.

On paper the defence against the torpedo boat was solved. But only on paper. In theory the torpedo boat approaching a fleet would be threatened by the torpedo-boat catcher, possibly caught and sunk.

A year after she was launched, HMS *Rattlesnake* took part in some extended trials in the Channel and theory was tried in actual test.

And it was disappointing.

Rattlesnake had a slim margin in speed over the torpedo boats of a little more than two knots and her ability to intercept the torpedo boats shrank down to almost zero.

Desperate efforts were made to improve the speed of the torpedo-boat catchers and *Rattlesnake*'s design was accepted as a basis for prolonged experiments without success. As the builders of the catchers strove for that extra two or three knots, so the builders of the torpedo boats also searched their designs for more speed, and the latest type being built could reach twenty-four knots.

Who then to approach to produce a catcher which could keep the sea and could achieve at least a three-to-four-knot superiority?

Somewhat ironically, the Admiralty, working on the theory that the best gamekeeper is the ex-poacher, approached a man who had achieved a world-wide reputation as a builder of fast torpedo boats, Mr William Yarrow.

'Build for us,' said the Admiralty, 'two ships of 250 tons displacement which will carry not only guns with which we can destroy the torpedo boats but will carry torpedoes, and build them so that they can do at least twenty-seven knots. Other navies have the torpedo boats, we must have the means to meet their threat.'

And Mr Yarrow built two: HMS *Havock* and HMS *Hornet*. They were successful. They were armed with a twelve-pounder gun and three six-pounder guns, all capable of seriously damaging a torpedo boat, and their final distribution of torpedoes was from beam tubes.

On their speed trials they went up to twenty-seven knots with comparative ease—and went over it by a then secret and comforting margin.

It was around then that the term 'torpedo-boat catcher' disappeared and the more arrogant title 'torpedo-boat destroyer' crept into common usage.

It was around then, also, that a new breed of naval officers began to emerge. Destroyer men. Dedicated young men who would think of no other ships but their beloved destroyers. They still exist today.

Yarrow's destroyers were sent out to sea to test their sea capabilities and the tests were passed with flying colours.

Comfortable? Never. Habitable? Barely. But despite the buffeting of the open sea they could still steam at high speed.

While all these problems of ship and counter-ship were being met—and solved—Whitehead's torpedoes were being improved so that they could extend their range, their speed and the amount of explosive they could carry.

Once the problem of keeping a torpedo accurately on its course for 1,500 yards was solved, the torpedo-boat destroyer carrying it would emerge as a really formidable ship not merely for defence but for offence.

But a few more years were to elapse before the experts finally solved that problem.

Naval architects were also deeply engrossed in the problem of gaining speed and still more speed without having to put increasingly powerful engines into fragile hulls which would shake to pieces or hammer themselves into cripples in anything of a sea.

A piece of blatant advertising gave them the answer, even if it produced red faces at the Admiralty and on the bridges of the fleet assembled at Spithead for Queen Victoria's Diamond Jubilee Naval Review in 1897.

The immense British fleet was anchored in review order with room between the lines for the royal yacht to steam past them. Suddenly a little boat steamed down the almost sacred waters between the warships. Picket boats and duty torpedo boats set out after her to peremptorily usher her away.

They had as much chance of catching her as a lumbering old English sheepdog has of catching a hare. The chase went on, with the little craft impudently allowing the pursuers to close up to her then racing off again, leaving the naval craft behind as if they were steaming at slow speed.

It was Mr Charles Parsons demonstrating the power of his steam-turbine engine and demonstrate it he did in no uncertain fashion. An engine which could drive a boat at that speed just had to be investigated, no matter what opinions might be held as to the good or bad taste shown by the inventor in crashing the Review.

Turbinia, as Parsons' little boat was named, had been built and engined by R. and W. Hawthorne, Leslie and Co. Ltd. of Hebburn-on-Tyne.

This firm had been building ships, torpedo boats, for years, so they were well aware of the speed problems involved in producing a bigger and better torpedo-boat destroyer without having to fit impossibly large and powerful engines.

While Robert Hawthorne and Andrew Leslie might have looked askance at Charles Parsons' impudence, they were shrewdly aware that his steam turbine was the immediate answer to the problem facing all the builders of the small, fast craft.

Thirty knots had been reached three years before.

Cammell Laird, Thornycroft and Yarrow, names to conjure with then, and still famous names, had each been commissioned to build torpedo-boat destroyers which could touch thirty knots, and they succeeded.

Thornycroft's first one, the *Boxer*, did better than twenty-nine knots, and Cammell Laird's *Quail* did the required thirty knots. But to achieve it the triple expansion engines of 5,000 horse power or so had to turn at 400 revolutions a minute.

The machinery must have been a blur of light at that speed and the engine room a terrifying place.

Parsons' turbine engine had proved itself in a highly irregular style, but it led to an order for a torpedo-boat destroyer being placed with Hawthorne, Leslie, and two years after the blatant exhibition at the Naval Review, the *Viper* slid into the water at Hebburn fitted with Parsons' steam-turbine engines. She was a typical torpedo-boat destroyer of the era. Low, long and lean, with practically no freeboard, a small bridge well forward overlooking a turtle-backed bow and three squat funnels.

But she could move.

On her trials she touched thirty-seven knots with a bland assurance from her builders that in a real emergency she could produce a couple more for a short burst.

In anything of a seaway *Viper*, and her sister *Cobra*, which shortly followed her also equipped with steam-turbine engines, were dirty ships. Comfort was something one longed for once harbour was reached.

Viper was wrecked a year after her launch and *Cobra* developed inherent weakness in hull design, not surprising when her slim length was considered.

Surprisingly, after these two fast ships the Admiralty reverted to reciprocating engines once more and at the same time demanded larger ships and a design which would make them less wet in a seaway.

The turtle-back bow disappeared and the raised foredeck established the traditional destroyer silhouette which basically remains today.

The new ships were around 600 tons and more than thirty of them joined the fleet from various builders in the next two or three years.

They were slow. Their maximum speed was around twenty-six knots, but they could keep the sea under almost the worst conditions and men could live in them with some degree of comfort. They could steam with the fleet, although nobody could quite designate what their job was except to combat a threat from darting torpedo boats.

Nobody, as yet, visualised a swarm of them racing in to attack large ships, firing their torpedoes and racing away again in a white-foamed turn.

Officially at least, such thoughts amounted almost to treason, but no doubt somewhere among the breed of men growing up with the small ships were some young commanding officers who secretly toyed with the idea.

Along with the development of the torpedo boat and the torpedo-boat destroyer, Whitehead's torpedoes—the origin of it all—had also developed. From the modest twenty-pound charge, Whitehead now produced a twenty-one-inch-diameter torpedo with a truly formidable charge in its blunt nose and one which could reasonably be expected to keep a straight course for more than two thousand yards.

Queen Victoria's sixty years' reign came to an end and her son Edward, Prince of Wales, ascended the throne. The canker of jealousy in the soul of the German Kaiser, thwarted in his ambition to be King and Emperor of Great Britain and the Empire, began its painful, tragic course.

The Admiralty, although it had ordered more than thirty of the new 600-ton-class destroyers, was not happy about their speed.

More virile flag officers came to senior command and to the Board of the Admiralty, officers who had grown up with the experimental years when little ships had been tried out and when speeds more than twice that of their existing destroyers had been reached.

It was recognised that if there were to be bigger torpedo-boat destroyers, up to 600, 700 or even 800 tons, then the reciprocating engines would have to give way to the steam-turbine engines. And it was so.

In 1904 Admiral Sir John Fisher, 'Jackie' to every man in the Navy, was appointed First Sea Lord. By a curious twist his appointment started on the anniversary of Trafalgar Day.

The winds of change were not long in blowing through the corridors of the Admiralty. 'Jackie' Fisher wanted more ships, faster ships, bigger ships, particularly torpedo-boat destroyers.

As he visualised them as carrying torpedoes to attack, the term 'torpedo-boat destroyer' began to disappear and the description 'destroyer' came into common use. It remains today, though what some of the early destroyer men would say of the 5,000-ton destroyers now being built would be illuminating.

2

Over the years it has been claimed—with justification—for a number of officers that they were both architects and builders in that small but immortal band which laid the foundations of destroyer tactics, and established the beginnings of destroyer traditions.

To no man can be given better credit for these achievements than to Admiral of the Fleet Lord Keyes of Zeebrugge and Dover, GCB, KCVO, CMG, DSO.

Yet his entry into the Navy came about through the merest chance. His family tradition, going back for generations, had been in the Army. He spent the first half-dozen years of his life in a fort—Tudiana Fort—on the North West India frontier, where his father, Brigadier-General Sir Charles Keyes, commanded the Punjab Frontier Force.

General Keyes retired from the Army in 1884 and gathered around him his family for a holiday in a house on the shores of Lough Swilly.

The fleet was carrying out exercises from Lough Swilly, and General Keyes and his son Roger went aboard one of the heavy cruisers on a social visit. Within a short period of that visit Roger, then rising twelve years, dogmatically announced that he wished to enter the Navy and calmly added that it was his intention to become an admiral.

Rather reluctantly, his father capitulated and the future Admiral of the Fleet was presented to the three barriers he would have to surmount.

The first was a nomination for a cadetship, the second was a medical examination which demanded 100 per cent physical fitness and finally a competitive examination equally demanding.

The first obstacle was an easy one. Lord George Hamilton, First Lord of the Admiralty, was a friend of the Keyes family and provided the necessary recommendation.

The physical examination was considerably stiffer. The Indian climate had taken its toll of the puny boy. He was frighteningly underweight—his official statistics at entry were 4 ft 10 in. height, 5 stone weight and chest expanded 25 in. Besides which, he had the shadowed eyes and thin, gaunt outlines which spelled 'delicate'.

But again his guardian angel hovered over his shoulder.

The doctor knew Roger Keyes' father very well, had met him in India, and with but a cursory examination passed the boy.

Two obstacles surmounted. Nobody could do anything immediately about the third. Roger Keyes was singularly inept at spelling. A short, stiff course under a Greenwich crammer packed enough into him to enable him to scrape through, which he did, twenty-fourth out of a class of thirty-eight.

The undersized wisp of a boy, with a slightly crooked arm caused by a badly set fracture, joined *Britannia* in 1885.

Two years later he was sent to join HMS *Raleigh*, a full-rigged frigate of 5,200 tons, flag-ship of the C-in-C Cape of Good Hope and West Africa station, later joining the *Turquoise*, a barque-rigged corvette of 2,200 tons of the East India squadron, serving mainly against slavers off Zanzibar.

He returned to this country, serving on various classes of ships, including the royal yacht *Victoria and Albert*, without any hint that his predilections lay towards the small, lean boats. That came after he had left the *Victoria and Albert* and was serving on a recruiting corvette, the *Curaçao*, under Commander Martin Jerram.

Up to that point, with the exception of the period he served in the royal yacht, Keyes' whole sea career, of about ten years, had been served in that hard school of sailing ships.

Then, during the Diamond Jubilee Review at Spithead, a very junior lieutenant watched the early torpedo boats and tiny torpedo-boat destroyers racing about, and when one came alongside *Curaçao* on an errand he went aboard—and came back fascinated.

There was a *command* for a young officer, a command which offered scope for initiative and dash.

But he was very junior and the most he could hope for was appointment as first lieutenant on one.

Commander Jerram, who thought highly of Keyes, agreed sympathetically with his ambitions and passed along a glowing recommendation.

To Keyes' intense joy his lack of seniority was overlooked

and he was appointed to command a destroyer in the Devonport Instructional Flotilla, the *Opossum,* with *Ferret* and *Decoy* completing Keyes' division. The senior destroyer of the flotilla was *Bat,* a new 360-ton, thirty-knot ship commanded by a commander. Keyes' command and the two others in his division were 260 tons and capable of twenty-seven knots.

In later years, apart from minor differences, destroyers conformed to shape and style, but *Opossum, Ferret* and *Decoy* were markedly different in appearance. *Opossum* had a high freeboard, with three tall, thin funnels; *Ferret* was long, low and squat, with four stumpy funnels; while *Decoy* had but two and an even lower freeboard than *Ferret.*

Work in the Instructional Flotilla consisted of the simple task of teaching stokers how to handle the high-speed engines and polishing up officers' training.

As for any tactical exercises, they were non-existent.

At that time our traditional enemy was France and the accepted task of the destroyers was simple. Should war break out, the French ports were to be blockaded immediately by cruisers with the heavy ships in the offing.

If and when the swarms of French torpedo boats emerged with the intention of attacking the blockading cruisers with torpedoes, they would be attacked and sunk by the destroyers. Just like that.

But in the tiny wardrooms where the pros and cons of defence and attack were repeatedly thrashed out, elementary division and flotilla tactics were outlined and planned.

With a few boxes of matches, a tobacco pouch or two, a salt-cellar and empty coffee-cups the tactics began to take shape. If only C-in-C could be persuaded to let the destroyers practise occasionally with the larger ships. But conservative views still reigned strong in the higher levels. Circumstances might compel the fleet to accept destroyers, but as yet there was to be no expansion of the elementary task foreshadowed for them.

Before this fundamental victory could be achieved Roger

Keyes was appointed to the destroyer *Hart* on the China station in 1898, only to find that she was to be decommissioned when he arrived and his command transferred to one of the latest types of destroyer, the *Fame*.

Even out there, destroyers were looked upon as glorified picket boats, tenders to the flag-ship. Their errand-boy journeys were longer than in England, but the principle was the same.

Young Roger Keyes, however, found one marked difference. The Instructional Flotilla had been run on rather slap-happy lines. A certain amount of night sea-time had to be put into each three-week period of training. This requirement was met by night trips from one port to another. Furthermore, the ships had been painted in the dingy grey of the Channel Fleet.

Fame, with her white topsides and polished-copper cowls, looked more like a yacht than a destroyer. Keyes, with his life-long friend and his then first lieutenant Sub-Lieutenant Wilfred Tomkinson, proceeded without delay to make the ship's company as smart as the ship. He took her and her sister ship to sea for gunnery, torpedo and various other exercises, and in her later inspection by a senior officer he received his deserved praise.

Round about that time the Chinese were beginning to build up strong anti-British feeling, and when agitators incited the crowds to burn British police huts in Kowloon, Sir Henry Blake, Governor of Hong Kong, decided to go to Canton to read the Riot Act to the Chinese Viceroy.

He was given *Fame* in which to make the journey and she did the eighty-six miles in four and a half hours.

On the return journey, made in darkness, *Fame* repeated that time. Incidentally, it was a wasted journey because the Viceroy broke his promise within hours of making it.

So a firmer hand was applied. A couple of companies of the Hong Kong Regiment were sent to take over the head of the beach in Mirs Bay, that happy hunting ground for junk pirates, while *Fame,* with a military party of Signals, sailed for the same spot.

The Chinese appeared to be massed on the hill overlooking the spot manned by the soldiers. When *Fame* arrived Keyes promptly went ashore with the soldiers and was given command of the left flank, while a Major Long commanded the right flank and centre.

Tomkinson, on *Fame*, had a busy half-hour shooting with considerable accuracy from the destroyer's guns, while his commanding officer equally enjoyed the short but brisk fight ashore—incidentally, that was his first experience of Combined Operations, a command he was to hold many years later.

Roger Keyes had nearly all the excitement he wanted while at Hong Kong, as during his stay the Boxer Rebellion smouldered, then broke into fierce flame.

His destroyer, together with *Whiting*, raced with other units of the fleet to become part of the international fleet off the mouth of the Pei-ho River. The river was virtually the sole means of communication with Tientsin, thirty miles inland, and with the besieged Peking ninety miles away.

At the mouth of the river was Taku, with the only telegraph contact with Peking.

Taku was guarded by two heavily armed forts on the north bank and one on the south. The guns, about seventy in number, were Krupps, and the Chinese gunners had been trained in their use by experts from that same philanthropic organisation. Adding to the fire power protecting the mouth of the river were four modern Chinese destroyers—also German-built—moored near the northern forts.

A number of times *Fame* was ordered to take ashore to the telegraph terminal at Taku long signals for Peking. Each time Keyes sailed into the river he could see the five-inch and eight-inch guns in the forts following him around on their swivels.

Keyes developed an active dislike for those guns and at the same time cast an avaricious eye at the destroyers. To Sir

James Bruce, acting C-in-C, Keyes submitted a plan which was the essence of simplicity by which the forts and the destroyers would be taken.

At the same time Sir James was told that it was suspected that the Chinese were mining the river.

He approved Keyes' plan and submitted it as part of a larger plan to the chiefs of the international force lying off Pei-Ho. It was agreed to issue an ultimatum, to expire at 2 am the next day, to the Chinese commander of the forts, demanding immediate surrender.

Keyes was delighted. It was a cutting-out expedition in the classic naval style. The four destroyers lay astern of one another moored to the wall, so Keyes planned for *Fame*, towing a whaler full of armed men, to run up abeam of number one destroyer, *Whiting* to do the same only abeam of the third ship, then both would turn sharply in, slip their whalers, which would board and attack numbers two and four.

But the Chinese commander of the forts jumped the gun. At 1 am, an hour before the ultimatum expired, the forts broke into stabbing sheets of fire.

Framed in water-spouts from the shells, *Fame* and *Whiting* slipped and moved upriver. To the disappointment of the destroyers' crews, the Chinese manning the four ships put up but little fight against the cutlass-and-pistol-armed bluejackets. Once they were captured, Keyes took them, with *Whiting*, upriver about seven or eight miles to be out of range of the Taku forts. When daylight came he hurriedly retraced his course, hoping to have a hand in capturing the forts, but the international force had completed that part of the task.

But he had his chance, which he created by directly disobeying an order to reconnoitre another heavily armed fort twelve miles upriver—Hsi-Cheng—but which under no circumstances was he to provoke or come under fire.

Keyes learned that the fort was virtually unarmed, as the bulk of the garrison had gone racing off to Tientsin and Peking.

Keyes led a charge by thirty sailors and melted a small number of Chinese soldiers like snow in the sun. Then he blew up the fort with a roar which was heard twenty miles away.

He also succeeded in getting himself attached to a military unit relieving Peking, leaving his first lieutenant in command to do the ferry and picket-boat duties which seemed to be the fate of destroyers.

For his pains Sir Edward Seymour, back at his post as C-in-C, informed Keyes that he was to be replaced as commanding officer of *Fame*, in fact a new captain was on his way out from England.

Rather dramatically, Keyes collapsed with diphtheria and for a time his life hung in the balance; on recovery he was sent home to England. He was allowed a short period of command on *Fame*, taking her and one of the captured destroyers from Taku to Hong Kong, incidentally battling through a typhoon which partly wrecked the harbour.

For his efforts in planning the capture of the destroyers and other escapades he was awarded fifteen pounds! The grounds were that Britain and China were not officially at war.

After some home leave, to Keyes' unqualified delight he was appointed first as second-in-command of the Devonport Instructional Flotilla, and after a few months to command of it.

During his service on the China station Keyes had never ceased to harp on his variations on a given theme: i.e. that destroyers were better sea boats than they were given credit for, and properly handled could be a threat to major war vessels if they could be used as a flotilla or division.

Fortunately for Keyes, he had a man who thoroughly approved of his ideas in the newly appointed Commander-in-Chief at Plymouth.

Keyes ran his flotilla from *Bat*, a 360-ton boat, and in a few short months he rubbed the rough edges off the flotilla. When he took over command of it he found that the word 'instructional' meant exactly what it had three years previously when he served in it. A few days' exercise, a night passage or two, sufficed.

His C-in-C approved all the programme that Keyes outlined and gave him *carte blanche* to go ahead. First the officers had to be instilled with the enthusiasm for whipping their ships into shape, then they were introduced to Keyes' ideas on destroyer warfare.

One of the officers who absorbed Keyes' ideas completely was a young commander, Walter Cowan.

They remained intimate friends throughout their lives. In the last war Keyes, sixty-eight years old, brought endless drive to the newly formed Combined Operations, while Walter Cowan, at seventy-three, was operating with Commandos and in the African desert, where he was awarded a bar to a DSO he had won forty-eight years back.

Keyes had his chance to prove his theories.

A fleet exercise was to be carried out with the fleet sailing from Lough Swilly to the Channel ports. Admiral Sir Gerard Noel, commanding the Home Fleet, was quite frank. He was prepared to allow Keyes to test his theories on destroyer tactics, but he, personally, attached little importance to them or their war value,

Keyes hid his destroyers in ambush in Milford Haven waiting for the fleet to sail from Dublin Bay. A strong gale was blowing when he received information that the fleet had sailed. His little flotilla, five destroyers, slammed out of Milford and in darkness located the cruiser screen of the 'enemy' fleet. He wriggled past them without being discovered, approached to within two and a half cables of the battleships (500 yards), took his rolling, pitching, little boats on a parallel course, as often as not taking solid water over their tiny bridges, until each destroyer was abeam of a capital ship, then he turned them in to attack.

The surprise was complete and dramatic. Very lights curved upwards to simulate torpedo attacks. In weather which was beating the big ships unmercifully and which was considered impossible for the small boats they had come out of the darkness and had struck.

The rear-admiral acting as umpire had no hesitation in ruling that a devastating blow had been struck against the fleet, and Admiral Gerard Noel generously incorporated the terms of conversion in his report.

'It was', he wrote, 'a good example of how a battle squadron can be practically annihilated by a group of destroyers on a dark night, if well commanded. . . .'

The traditional enemy, France, had ceased to be that. An arrogant, jealous monarch, jealous particularly of the mighty British Navy, had almost eagerly taken over that role. Keyes was quick to perceive that destroyer warfare would be in the open waters of the North Sea, not off blockaded ports.

And young officers serving in the flotilla were to command destroyers just over ten years later in the Heligoland, Dogger Bank and Jutland battles.

Well and truly had Keyes laid his foundations.

For the next five years he served in command of a cruiser and as Naval Attaché in Rome, and was confidently expecting a heavy-cruiser command when out of the blue he was given command of another part of the Service involving another type of small ship, submarine, which was still held suspect by very senior officers. Keyes threw himself into the task with enthusiasm, although somewhat craftily he acquired a destroyer, *Lurcher*, in which to go to sea, as he had been forbidden to do any sea trips in the submarines.

When war broke out Keyes found himself at Harwich with his submarines and a kindred soul in command of the destroyers in the base, Commodore Reginald Tyrwhitt.

'What wouldn't I give for a command consisting of a few light cruisers, destroyers and submarines supported as necessary by cruisers at a distance,' he wrote to a friend at the Admiralty.

He had the next-best thing, a fertile imagination and a wealth of dash. He and Tyrwhitt between them concocted a scheme by which they could deal a resounding blow at the

Germans. They learned that German destroyers were patrolling minefields in the Heligoland Bight with a covering force of light cruisers.

A combined destroyer and submarine force, with a couple of light cruisers, were to descend on this force. It nearly came off as they planned, as told later in this book. As it was, they shook the Germans badly.

Keyes served throughout the Dardanelles and returned to this country to find it in dire straits. The submarine war loomed menacingly and looked like beating Britain to its knees.

Keyes was severely critical of the Dover Patrol and its anti-submarine measures. They had been devised by Admiral Sir Reginald Bacon, who considered them effective and at the same time frowned heavily on suggestions that in addition to improving the Dover barrage the submarine nests in Zeebrugge and Ostend should be attacked and blocked.

Keyes produced figures extracted from Intelligence reports, including documents recovered from a sunken German submarine, showing that far from being effective the barrage was not causing submarines any great inconvenience. They were slipping through at night on the surface to create havoc in Western Approaches.

Keyes hammered away, almost demanding a more aggressive patrol at Dover—and found a supporter in Admiral Sir Rosslyn Wemyss, First Sea Lord.

He sent for Rear-Admiral Keyes and said: 'You have talked a hell of a lot about what ought to be done in the Dover area. Now you must go down and do it all yourself.'

On New Year's Day 1918 Keyes took over command of Dover and at the same time was promoted to vice-admiral, aged forty-five.

Within twenty-four hours of taking command he sent for all the available captains and told them that in his opinion the anti-submarine measures were utterly inefficient. In an atmosphere of coolness, almost hostility, the officers demurred.

Keyes silenced them with cold, hard figures. In the past ten months 253 German submarines had passed through the Straits, nearly all at night, and not one had been sunk or attacked.

He added that he proposed to alter all that.

And he did. It was no use an officer exclaiming that some task was beyond his boat. Keyes knew all about destroyers, what they could do and their limitations. He had helped to lay the foundations of the Service.

The minefields were extended, patrols doubled and trebled—few ships had a night in harbour unless they had defects and the Straits were flooded with light.

Submarines had either to risk being attacked on the surface, which they inevitably were, or submerge and risk the minefield, which they did and were sunk.

In less than two months the chagrined Germans abandoned the Straits and took to the longer voyage round Scotland. Then Keyes elaborated his scheme for blocking Zeebrugge and Ostend, to make them impossible for the Germans to use as submarine nests.

That story, too, is part of history and has no place in this book. But we have seen Keyes as a destroyer captain, seen him evolve and push to success entirely new destroyer tactics. Young men who had served with him served also to fight in the three North Sea battles with distinction.

Turbulent, aggressive, at times unshakably dogmatic, he had helped as much as any man to mould destroyer traditions from the days when they were considered to be little more than glorified picket boats until the day came when a destroyer command was considered to be the acme of service for a young man. The tradition was simple. 'Seek out the enemy and turn to attack never counting the weight of the opposition.'

In destroyers they learned that the improbable was done; the impossible, too, was done, although it might take a little longer.

That was the heritage left behind by Admiral of the Fleet Lord Keyes of Zeebrugge and Dover, GCB, KCVO, CMG, DSO.

3

Admiral Fisher worshipped speed. Speed in building, speed in decision, speed in action. And he lived up to it.

All the principal destroyer-builders were told tersely what he wanted and were told to go ahead and build. He left the design mainly to them so long as they produced the ships he wanted.

And he got them.

The Board of Admiralty, driven along at break-neck speed by Fisher, required two classes of ships. A smaller class around 250–300 tons, capable of doing twenty-six knots, glorified torpedo boats in fact, and larger craft of 600–700 tons, capable of speeds up to thirty-six knots.

The smaller boats were produced in some numbers—between thirty and forty—but were not very successful. They might have justified themselves if some maritime nation had had the temerity to attack this country and had laid a fleet alongside one of our naval bases. They were capable of coping with any torpedo boats owned by any other navy. Beyond that they were of little use, although a number of them remained in service up to the outbreak of war in 1914 and served as stop-gaps until the larger destroyers began to arrive. They also served as a hard training school for men and officers who later went on to serve in larger destroyers.

A fascinating hour or two can be spent perusing old volumes of that unique book *Jane's Fighting Ships* between 1907 and 1910, some of the years when Admiral Fisher was at the helm.

There are names which are now famous but which began then to appear for the first time.

There is a whole retinue of 'Tribals': *Afridi*, *Amazon*, *Cossack*, *Gurkha*, *Zulu*, *Tartar*, *Saracen*, *Mohawk*, *Crusader*, *Nubian* and others.

It is interesting, too, to study their lines from the photographs and to compare them with destroyers of a later generation.

They varied in size from 900 tons to 1,000 tons, all of them capable of doing upwards of thirty-four knots, fitted as they were with Parsons' turbines. According to the figures provided, Thornycroft built the *Tartar*, which could top thirty-seven knots, and Samuel White's *Mohawk* could do thirty-five knots.

Some were armed with twelve-pounder guns and carried the eighteen-inch torpedo, while others had four-inch guns. The 'Tribals' of the last war, built thirty years afterwards, could not have beaten them for speed.

For comparison purposes compare, say, a 'Battle' class destroyer of the closing years of the last war with the *Swift* of the Fisher era.

Swift was 2,170 tons, armed with four four-inch guns and two torpedo tubes. Her turbine engines were 30,000 horse power, and although her specifications called for thirty-six knots, she actually reached nearly forty knots on her speed trials.

She was a beautiful ship. She had a long raised foredeck, by now the conventional destroyer design, tall raking masts and three squat funnels situated over her lean hull, which was surpassingly clean in design.

Unfortunately, she was considered largely as an experimental job, and her cost for those days was astronomical. It was nearly £300,000. But what would any flag officer not have given a few short years onwards to have had a flotilla or two of *Swifts* to add to his strength?

The storm-clouds of war were massing darkly when Admiral Fisher's term of office as First Sea Lord ended, but his reign had laid a solid foundation. In addition to the dreadnoughts and cruisers he had demanded, and had forced through, a stream of real destroyers began to flow off the stocks. When Admiral Fisher closed his desk for the last time there were upwards of forty destroyers on the stocks and plans in hand for another forty. So by 1912 there was a welcome addition of more than eighty destroyers added to the fleet.

They were of a standardised design around 1,000 tons, armed with four-inch guns and carried four torpedo tubes.

The twenty-one-inch torpedo had also arrived in numbers and was therefore standard equipment. As one destroyer slipped smoothly into the water so another was laid down. The advantages of standardisation were speed of planning and building and the production of a class of destroyer which could work as a flotilla, the leader knowing within reason what all the ships were capable of.

A flotilla in those days consisted of a light cruiser as leader with twenty destroyers in attendance. Although this had certain advantages—a light cruiser throwing twenty hell-for-leather destroyers at a fleet was something to make larger ships turn rapidly away—it had disadvantages, too, and later it was changed to eight with a destroyer leader.

Admiral Fisher, in his term of office, had to force his claims for more ships through Parliament and was more than once attacked as a warmonger, was accused of dragging his naval coat-tails in front of Germany's nose when all the Germans wanted was to be recognised as a great power and to be left alone to expand their modest empire.

But by 1913 few people of any note believed anything other than that war was almost inevitable. The grand naval strategy was based on the assumption that no matter what form the war on land might take, at sea there was but one thing for Germany to do with its swiftly growing strength. Take it to sea and subject it to the stern test of action.

The natural cockpit for such a fight would have to be the North Sea, and to be ready to enter that fight the fleet would of necessity have to be close at hand. It would also have to have eyes. There would have to be ships scouting, light cruisers and destroyers; there would have to be destroyers to accompany the fleet.

There would have to be more and more destroyers.

And there were never enough.

The pattern is familiar. It has come down through the years with us. When there is uneasy peace any suggestion of large-scale building of destroyers is frowned upon. Naval Estimates have to be trimmed and pruned. Then dark clouds of war loom on the horizon, lightning flashes ominously from them and the bolts strike right and left.

The thin grey line is stretched to breaking point trying to do all the tasks it is called upon to do. There are losses of ships in convoy, somewhere the enemy breaks through the line and petulant voices are raised: 'What is the Navy doing? Why didn't it stop the enemy? Why didn't it catch the enemy? No longer with reluctance, a large building programme is approved, but has to take its turn with other accelerated demands. Building takes time.

And the thin grey line is stretched until it is but hairline in thickness.

It was so in 1914 when war broke out.

Again perusing the pages of *Jane's Fighting Ships* published in 1914 reveals that there were available about 200 destroyers, of which roughly half were comparatively modern, the result of the drive by Admiral Fisher. The others were older ships, glorified torpedo boats.

With the exception of one flotilla which was in the Mediterranean, the available destroyers were positioned so that they were virtually guarding the whole of the east coast from the Orkneys to Dover, one half of them—four flotillas with their cruiser leaders—with the Grand Fleet in that grim grey bastion Scapa Flow.

Hard work faced them. Patrolling off enemy coasts, constantly watching for the heavy ships of the German fleet, guarding against minelaying forays; in short, keeping the sea.

Another factor had come into naval warfare and after initial teething troubles threatened to become a real menace. At the turn of the century and early in 1914 another class of small ship had been evolved, tested, derided, encouraged and had finally emerged. The submarine.

In its original conception it had been visualised as a defensive weapon. Like the torpedo boat it was to be a potential threat to any blockading or bombarding fleet, relying on stealth of approach to do its work.

But the young men in command of these small submarines very rapidly evolved their own tactics and switched from defence to attack. In manœuvres in the Channel and off the Irish coast more than one choleric flag officer had to submit with ill-concealed bad grace when a submarine suddenly popped up in a clear sea and suavely informed the flag officer that in theory he was swimming for his life, as the submarine had, also in theory, torpedoed his ship.

Such unorthodox tactics might be mentioned with rancour during the second round of port, but it had to be recognised that what a gay young spark in his submarine could do in theory he could equally do in fact against an enemy. So, equally, could a German submarine!

Another job was created for the destroyer.

In addition to patrolling and searching for the enemy fleet, searching for minelayers and raiders, it had also to screen the capital ships and the heavy ships from submarine attack with singularly few weapons for the job.

There were no means of detection other than lynx-eyed look-outs who were expected to sight the periscope of the submarine as it was poked above the water for a quick look. Then it would be attacked by gunfire. Or rammed. The depth-charge was yet to come.

Destroyer tactics had begun to take shape in the early years of the century. The somewhat haphazard form of attack visualised for the original torpedo boats was to race out of harbour in a swarm, pick their victim, wriggle and twist into range, fire their primitive torpedoes and race back to harbour, possibly for another load of torpedoes.

But as the destroyer began to emerge as an offensive weapon and the range of torpedoes improved from the original 500 yards to 1,000 yards, more agile brains began to think out forms of correlated attack by flotillas.

It was very soon recognised that no squadron or fleet of

heavy surface ships would have the temerity to thrust on regardless with a flotilla of destroyers racing to meet it, each loaded with torpedoes. The fleet would be compelled to turn away in self-preservation. The same agile brains worked it out that if two flotillas, or more, attacked from each side whichever way the heavy ships turned they would run into trouble.

In manœuvres, working to a set plan, it came off.

In actual warfare it seldom occurred. The enemy, too, had swarms of destroyers bent on doing one of two things, if not both. Force the attacking destroyers to fight and at the same time try to get in a similar position.

In fact, in both wars only a few such perfect occasions arose. One was when the *Scharnhorst* was trapped by the *Duke of York* off North Cape in December 1943.

The destroyers *Savage* and *Saumarez* slammed through a snow-riven gale to get on one side of the fleeing *Scharnhorst* and the Norwegian destroyer *Stord* and *Scorpion* hurled themselves at her other side. No matter which way *Scharnhorst* turned she would be threatened.

And they hit her with three torpedoes which spelled her doom.

But by 1914 destroyer tactics had taken definite shape, despite the rather primitive forms of signalling. With twenty ships working as two divisions of ten—and seldom did the cruiser leader have a full flotilla—by the time flag hoists passed down the line and had been acknowledged, or had been passed by winking light, the situation demanding a certain manœuvre had altered in complexion.

In many respects the arrangement of twenty destroyers to a flotilla, with the leadership vested in a light cruiser, was excellent. There were sufficient officers on the cruiser to handle the destroyers, limited only by the speed which signals could be passed, and a flotilla of destroyers led by that cruiser was a formidable weapon.

But when war started the eight-ship flotilla with a destroyer leader had been tried out with success.

War was but a few hours old when the first naval shots were fired. And to a destroyer fell the credit for that historical fact.

With the cruiser *Amphion*'s flotilla was the destroyer *Lance*, one of the Laforey class which had commissioned only a few weeks before the outbreak, and the *Landrail*. They were out from Harwich searching for a suspected minelayer. They found her. It was the German ship *Konigen Luise* and *Lance* opened fire followed by *Landrail*.

In no time at all the minelayer was a sinking wreck, but it is ironical that while returning from the sweep the cruiser *Amphion* struck one of the mines laid by the minelayer.

War was not twenty-four hours old when 151 men died.

After all the pre-war drum-beating and flag-waving and arrogant threats made by the Germans, it was accepted that sooner or late the Germans would send a powerful fleet to sea to try their strength against the British Navy.

It was anybody's guess when, where and how they would do it, but when they did, it was accepted that destroyers would play no mean part in any such fight.

In the meantime there had to be the interminable patrols, the nightly probes off the enemy coast, so that if there was any large-scale sailing of the German fleet the Grand Fleet, disposed at Scapa Flow and Rosyth, would have ample warning.

There were nights of boredom patrolling the empty sea, or standing by at immediate notice for steam as part of a striking force down the east coast.

Others, hastily adapted, were given the task of minelaying to cope with the ever-increasing campaign of laying minefields where they would do the most harm.

As for destroyer tactics in a large-scale battle, they were yet to be tried. True, there had been manœuvres, with meticulous umpires marking 'yea' and 'nay' on dummy attacks and winnowing out rather outrageous claims made by both sides.

But in the heat of battle, when men's courage was to be

tested, many things could happen. Ships could be sorely stricken, men could fall wounded or dead.

Nevertheless, the basic element of destroyer tactics had become thoroughly engrained in the minds of the young and enthusiastic commanding officers. It was 'turn to meet the enemy, race in, force him to turn away at least, torpedo him if possible'.

In essence this was Nelson's dictum: 'No captain can be far wrong if he places himself alongside an enemy.'

Given a chance, the breed would show through true.

Rarin' to go, also, were the submarines of Commodore Roger Keyes at Harwich. They, too, had been keeping watch off the enemy coast in the region of Heligoland, and by degrees, from their reports, it was gathered that the Germans, expecting some action of some sort, had got into the habit of sending out a destroyer patrol into the North Sea.

Working with them were German light cruisers and at dawn they all returned to their anchorage.

A trap was planned. The destroyers were to be enticed out to sea, using submarines as a lure, then two flotillas of British destroyers under their light-cruiser leaders would swoop down behind them to bar their way home, and if all worked out a sharp lesson would be taught to the Germans. In the event of a fight developing it was not beyond possibility that heavier German craft would sail to rescue their own destroyers and cruisers.

To meet that contingency two battle cruisers, the *Invincible* and *New Zealand*, were to steam to support.

So when the detailed plan was complete the orders were that some of Keyes' submarines were to surface, draw the destroyers westwards and when the cruisers sought to join in with the German destroyers an inner ring of submarines would be waiting for them.

Commodore Reginald Tyrwhitt's Harwich striking force of light cruisers and destroyers, around thirty or so in number, would be waiting in the wings for their cue to join in this deadly naval ballet.

The submarines sailed, those which were to be the bait and those which were to attack the German cruisers, so did the cruisers *Arethusa* and *Fearless* and the destroyers.

To lend weight to the argument should heavier German ships sail, the Admiralty decided at the last moment to augment the strength of the two battle cruisers. Vice-Admiral David Beatty in *Lion*, leading the 1st Battle Cruiser Squadron, sailed from Rosyth, so there were, with *Lion*, *Queen Mary*, *Princess Royal*, *Invincible* and *New Zealand*. In addition, Commodore Goodenough went to sea with the 1st Light Cruiser Squadron.

Unfortunately, the signal ordering Beatty's battle cruisers and Goodenough's light cruisers to sail reached neither Commodore Tyrwhitt nor Commodore Keyes, whose respective forces were rendezvousing about eight miles or so off Heligoland to trap, if possible, the German destroyers and a couple of German light cruisers. So far as they were concerned there would be only the battle cruisers *Invincible* and *New Zealand* in the offing should the Germans sail anything heavier.

So, shortly after dawn, a haze promising a day of heat, there was no mean naval force at sea proceeding towards Heligoland.

First there were the two flotillas of submarines, the bait and the trap, then the Harwich cruisers *Arethusa* and *Fearless* with their destroyers. Unknown to them, about ten miles astern were Goodenough's six light cruisers, and parallel to the Harwich cruisers and destroyers and about twenty miles to seaward was Beatty with his battle cruisers.

Arethusa's destroyers were the first to sight the enemy. A slight darkening of the morning mist took on sharper outlines and became a German destroyer. *Laurel* opened fire and turned to chase the German, followed in quick succession by the remainder of her division, *Lysander*, *Laertes* and *Liberty*, twin sisters of the destroyer which had fired the first naval shot of the war a couple of weeks back against the minelayer.

Off they raced after the shocked German ship, which disappeared into the haze with the British shells steepling up columns of water around her.

Tyrwhitt, in *Arethusa*, rapidly lost touch with his destroyers. All he had received was a brief sighting signal from *Laurel* before she and her consorts disappeared into the haze, and now all he had to go upon was the sound of the guns.

He turned the remainder of his champing flotilla to steam towards the gun-fire, and the cruiser *Fearless*, two or three miles astern, did likewise.

In a few minutes they were racing through a ring of German torpedo boats, which they brushed aside, hitting some of them before they, too, took refuge in the morning mist which cut down visibility to little more than 3,000 or 4,000 yards.

The sharp turn eastward after *Laurel* brought some more German destroyers into view, they, too, being equally confused by the sound of gun-fire somewhere in the haze and to the east of them.

A few shots were exchanged with them without any material damage being done to either side. The destroyers were racing hard to close the range before the Germans could escape and they ran into an impromptu ambush.

Something larger than destroyers loomed up in the mist and were soon recognised as enemy cruisers.

The *Stettin* and *Frauenlob*, detailed to cover the German destroyer patrol's return to harbour, heard the sound of gunfire and steamed to investigate.

As they appeared, so did some German destroyers, and it ceased to be a chase and the action became general.

It was to be the first time destroyers had been in any sort of general action and a lot of questions remained to be asked —and answered.

4

Bear in mind that this battle, afterwards to go down in history as the Battle of Heligoland, started off as a punitive foray against German destroyers which were patrolling off

Heligoland each night and it was hoped to bag a cruiser or so if they came out to cover the destroyers.

Signalling, by modern standards, or even by later standards in the First World War, was almost primitive. Wireless was the spark gap, Morse code, flags often could not be read through the haze of smoke from funnels and there remained the signal searchlight.

But, all things being equal, the sudden appearance of the *Stettin* and *Frauenlob* was not unexpected. It had been hoped that the inner ring of submarines would have had an opportunity to attack them with torpedoes and had the opportunity gone when they sailed they would still be vulnerable on their return if they were not sunk by the British cruisers.

Both *Arethusa* and *Fearless* opened fire first on *Stettin*, forcing her to turn away as much from the gun-fire as from the threat of the destroyers crowding around the British cruisers.

Fearless and her rampant destroyers turned to follow *Stettin*, and *Arethusa* concentrated her force on *Frauenlob*, which sturdily fought back. *Arethusa* had not long been in commission and she took a considerable beating from the German cruiser, whose gunnery was excellent.

She scored some hits on the German cruiser, but she herself was hit repeatedly. At one period only one gun could be brought to action. Fortunately, her destroyer screen slammed into *Frauenlob* with their four-inch guns, and two of them, *Lance* and *Lawford*, raced in and made a torpedo attack.

Wisely, the German cruiser turned away into the mist and in pursuing her the British destroyers gained a consolation prize. A couple of forlorn German torpedo boats hove into sight and were severely handled by the destroyers, although not disabled enough to have to stop.

The destroyers now grouped themselves around the limping *Arethusa*, which could creep along at only about eight knots.

The attack had split the German destroyer patrol into splinters. While *Arethusa* and her flotillas were engaged with

Frauenlob, farther north in the morning mist *Fearless* and her destroyers were hammering away at *Stettin*.

A lone German destroyer slipped out of the mist, stayed in sight long enough for the destroyers *Goshawk*, *Lapwing Lizard* and *Phoenix* to engage her, then she turned back into the mist slap into the arms, figuratively speaking, of two of Commodore Goodenough's cruisers, *Nottingham* and *Lowestoft*, who were hastening to *Arethusa*'s assistance.

They opened fire on her and forced her back on the pursuing British destroyers. She was trapped. She fired torpedoes at the *Nottingham* and *Lowestoft*, more in desperation than with the hope of hitting them, thus forcing them to turn away.

The trapped German raced past her pursuers, receiving some hits from them as she tried to wriggle once more back into the mist, only to find another division of four more British destroyers, *Ferret*, *Forester*, *Druid* and *Defender*, barring her path.

In a few moments she was on fire, disabled and obviously doomed, but fought on to the last, finally turning turtle.

Rescue boats were lowered from the British destroyers, but while they were engaged in this merciful task, *Stettin* reappeared and opened fire on the ring of destroyers.

One of the destroyers fired torpedoes at *Stettin* while the others recovered their life-saving boats and slipped into the haze away from *Stettin*'s accurate fire, which they returned, hitting her two or three times.

The threat of torpedo action forced *Stettin* away once more.

For the next couple of hours the action became extremely confused and it was more by luck than judgment that friend did not fire at friend or even torpedo one another.

Commodore Keyes in a destroyer had made contact with his ambushing submarines and was hoping that they would come across at least one of the supporting German cruisers. He still had no knowledge of the augmented force, Goodenough's light cruisers and the remainder of Beatty's battle cruisers. Momentarily he sighted two cruisers and reported them as enemy and added that he was shadowing them. This he did until he saw them rejoin the light-cruiser force, and still under the impression that they were Germans he signalled *Invincible* that he would try to draw them towards her.

Fortunately, before any shooting could occur, the error was corrected. *Arethusa,* still limping along at less than ten knots with only a couple of guns available, had around her a crowd of destroyers. *Fearless* and her destroyers, while still searching for the scattered remnants of the German patrol, were not far away in support.

In the meantime intense activity was taking place in the German naval bases. The signals from their destroyers and the cruisers showed that this was more than a mere affair of destroyer patrols clashing.

The cruisers *Ariadne*, *Köln*, *Mainz*, *Kolberg*, *Stralsund* and *Strassburg* sailed immediately to join *Stettin* and *Frauenlob*, which, with the remainder of the German destroyers, were still probing the mist.

The fight was still very confused. *Stettin* and *Frauenlob* were playing a jack-in-the-box game in and out of the mist, each side trying to draw their opponents into a trap.

The sadly battered *Arethusa*, surrounded by destroyers and striving desperately to repair the extensive damage done to her by *Frauenlob*, turned wearily eastward once more when garbled signals came through that destroyers somewhere east of her were engaged in a fight with cruisers.

That confusion in time was cleared up, fortunately without harm being done by friend to friend.

So *Arethusa*'s bow was turned westward. But her share in the fight was not finished. A German cruiser slipped out of the mist. *Frauenlob* again? Or *Stettin*?

Arethusa's and *Fearless*'s destroyers raced to meet the new threat, identified the enemy cruiser as yet another opponent. It was the *Strassburg*, but torpedo threats forced her to turn away into the mist. The destroyers were reluctant to pursue too far in case they left *Arethusa* and *Fearless* unscreened.

So back they steamed to do a sheepdog act. Yet again a vague shape loomed up in the mist. *Strassburg* once more? No, this time it was the *Köln* seeking her consort and, she hoped, a protecting screen of destroyers.

Instead she blundered into the British destroyers and the two Harwich cruisers. She was rapidly accommodated with a fight.

Again there was the classic torpedo-threat attack which forced the newcomer to retreat into the covering mist. As she disappeared, another German cruiser came probing through, steaming for the sound of the gun-fire. *Strassburg* had come back into the fight and she concentrated on the limping *Arethusa*.

Fearless turned to meet this threat, and the destroyers, released from their close-herding act around *Arethusa*, read a flag signal from her yard-arm: 'Attack with torpedoes', and away they raced joyously.

It was too much. *Fearless* was slamming at *Strassburg* and between them was the best part of two divisions of destroyers, the formidable and latest 'L's': *Lark*, *Lance*, *Landrail*, *Lookout*, *Legion*, *Lennox* and two or three more. They closed to about 4,000 yards and fired their torpedoes at the already turning *Strassburg* and gave her the benefit of an invigorating gun-fire. The torpedoes were still running when out of the confusing mist came more British destroyers: *Archer*, *Acheron*, *Attack*, and two or three more of *Fearless*'s destroyers, including *Ferret*, *Defender*, *Phoenix* and the remainder of the L's: *Laurel*, *Liberty*, *Lysander* and *Laertes*.

So in this mist-covered cockpit, less than ten miles from the German island of Heligoland, there were now assembled more than thirty-odd British destroyers, eight light cruisers and five battle cruisers and a then unknown number of German torpedo boats, destroyers, cruisers and heavy cruisers.

Could these forces be marshalled into some coherent order, then there were, laid out, all the ingredients for a delectable naval fight, with the destroyers playing no mean part.

Up to this period damage in the confused fighting had totalled a German torpedo boat or two blasted out of the water and the momentary appearance of isolated German cruisers steaming out of the mist, slamming at *Arethusa* and *Fearless*, then retreating once more back into the mist, being repeated *ad lib*.

In return, *Arethusa* had been severely damaged but by no means was she *hors de combat*.

But once get all these units on both sides into some sort of correlation, then naval history would turn a new page. From the days of the wooden-walled ships of the line there had been no pattern in real battle. The Japanese slaughter of the Russian fleet offered no blue print, neither did the clumsy ship-against-ship fighting done in the American Civil War. All that had come out of that tragic war from the naval side had been the monitors and the very inefficient spar torpedo, now with the limbo of the past.

So far as the fight had gone, the destroyers had proved something. A heavily armed ship, or for that matter a squadron of heavily armed ships, could be forced to turn away at the threat of a torpedo attack made by destroyers resolutely handled.

It had been proved to the complete satisfaction of the small-ship men in the cold examination room of manœuvre in peace-time. It had been proved over and over again in the heat of the first naval action of the war.

Strange as it may seem, there were still senior officers of flag rank who doubted. They claimed that a skilfully handled cruiser or heavy cruiser would be able to blast a destroyer out of the water with her secondary armament before it could get into effective torpedo range.

This August morning of 1914 was proving otherwise, despite the confused position. There was no doubt left. *Stettin*, *Frauenlob*, *Köln* and *Strassburg* in turn had been forced to break off their action against *Arethusa* and *Fearless* and retreat into the mist. Not by weight of gun-fire, because they had proved superior in that, as *Arethusa* could show.

What would have happened had all the German cruisers joined up and had launched a concerted attack must always remain a matter for conjecture.

A truly awesome picture presents itself. Seven German cruisers steaming into action screened by a couple of divisions of destroyers against two British light cruisers and thirty-odd destroyers.

Would the Germans have been prepared to risk losing a cruiser or two and a few destroyers to smash the comparatively light British forces, and could they have done it before Goodenough's cruisers and Beatty's battle cruisers could steam into the fight?

It must always remain an argument for the theorists.

But to return to the fight which was taking place.

Some of *Fearless*'s destroyers, steering south seeking their leader, ran into a three-funnelled cruiser, her outlines not very distinct.

It was *Mainz*. The destroyers, coming under an accurate and sustained fire, turned north again after launching torpedoes which *Mainz* avoided.

Then to the north of the fleeing destroyers four more indistinct outlines darkened the mist. Four cruisers. For a few minutes the racing destroyers thought they had run into an ambush, but the newcomers were cruisers of Goodenough's squadron, who wasted no time in letting *Mainz* know their intentions.

Mainz, heavily outnumbered, was no longer the pursuer, she became the pursued. She swung away south, but not before some hits were registered as she disappeared into the exasperating mist and blundered into the limping *Arethusa*, *Fearless* and screening destroyers.

Immediately the destroyers with *Fearless* went into the attack, inserting themselves between the German cruiser and the crippled *Arethusa*.

Mainz thrust on resolutely, damaging *Laurel*, *Liberty* and *Laertes* before *Fearless* and *Arethusa*, with the remainder of the destroyers, could concentrate on her. One of the torpedoes launched at her hit *Mainz* and slowed her down.

She could neither steam hard to the attack nor could she escape back into the mist.

The end for *Mainz* was not far away.

In hot pursuit of her came Goodenough's cruisers. They steamed out of the haze about 4,000 yards from her and at that range made every shell effective. In a few minutes she was a blazing wreck and all that remained was for some of the destroyers to go alongside and rescue the survivors before she went down bow first.

The confused fighting had been going on for more than six hours practically on the German Navy's doorstep and the list of cripples was growing. *Laurel* and *Liberty* could limp along slowly, so could *Arethusa*, but *Laertes* could not move. She was taken in tow by a sister and once more the painful course was set west.

And once more out of the mist steamed two German cruisers, *Strassburg* and *Köln*. In front of them they had a crippled British cruiser, only two of her guns effective, and three disabled British destroyers. Sitting targets.

Once more poor *Arethusa*, who had had more than her share of hard knocks, came in for more despite the attempt made by *Fearless* and some destroyers to draw the enemy fire on themselves.

Somewhere in that August-morning haze, somewhere to the north, were *Invincible* and *New Zealand*, and just those two so far as the Harwich force knew, and now was the moment for them to lend their immense weight and gun power to assist the hard-pressed *Arethusa*.

It was a possibility, too, that somewhere in that same haze would be some heavy German ships. The German Commander-in-Chief had known for nearly six hours that a British force of undetermined strength was operating virtually on his doorstep and it was a reasonable assumption that he would send out heavy cruisers to investigate, and castigate, the enemy.

Some of *Fearless*'s destroyers which had been screening the cripples tore into *Strassburg* and *Köln*, determined to extract a maximum price before they could sink *Arethusa* and her accompanying cripples.

As they raced threateningly to meet the two German cruisers, the mist thickened, showed a bulk. And what a bulk it was. Out of the mist, thrusting aside tremendous white bow waves, came battle cruisers.

Friend or foe?

A few seconds were enough to identify them.

It was the British battle cruisers. Not two, as the Harwich force had expected, but five. First in line was *Lion*, flying the flag of Vice-Admiral Beatty, then in quick succession, as if they were parting a curtain to take the centre of the stage, came *Queen Mary*, *Princess Royal*, *Invincible* and *New Zealand* in majestic line ahead.

In station astern of the battle cruisers were Goodenough's light cruisers.

Strassburg, with a desperate wriggle and turn, succeeded in retreating into the haze, her escape being hastened by a salvo from *Lion* which framed her in towering columns of water. *Köln* was not so fortunate. She was trapped inescapably and was soon being hammered to a shambles by the 13.5-inch guns of the battle cruisers. *Köln* reeled away, hoping that she could retreat into the covering mist. For a few brief minutes it looked as if she would do so. Another German cruiser, the *Ariadne*, probing into the mist towards the sound of the gun-fire, blundered into the massacre of *Köln* and received a battering from *Lion* and *Queen Mary*.

She, too, tried to reach the refuge of the concealing haze. With furious fires raging on her and a heavy list, she lasted very little longer, finally rolling over and sinking.

The battle cruisers now turned to search once more for *Köln*. And found her. She was barely creeping along, hoping that some consort would again help or that a heavy German ship would show up to engage the attention of the British battle cruisers.

It was a vain hope.

Lion, at the head of the line, sighted her and hit her with successive salvoes. It was the end. Destroyers who closed in around the pathetic wreckage found not one survivor.

The Battle of Heligoland was over.

German battle cruisers did race to the area but they were too late. The British force, the limping *Arethusa*, the triumphant destroyers, and the other ships, were well across the North Sea, heading for safety.

Now what of the destroyers in this somewhat confused fight?

The young commanding officers of the small ships had every reason to congratulate themselves. Time and again they had forced German cruisers to turn away from punishing the crippled *Arethusa* by either threatening a torpedo attack or actually carrying out one. True, some of their collective efforts lacked a certain amount of direction due to the limitations of signalling. In addition, they had damaged a couple of German torpedo boats—which incidentally never appeared again—and had sunk a German destroyer.

Mainz was hit with torpedoes, slowed down and eventually was sunk as a direct result of their work. Five British destroyers were hit, four of them while attacking *Mainz* in protection of *Arethusa*. It is possible that between their leaders, *Arethusa* and *Fearless*, and the dozen or so destroyers attacking *Mainz*, they might have finished her off by themselves had not Goodenough's cruisers arrived.

From that August day onwards even the most carping and doubting critics were forced to admit that the destroyer had arrived as a formidable fighting force.

From the early 1870's, from the first hesitant and groping attempts to evolve a ship which could carry torpedoes to the enemy, through the torpedo-boat catcher period, on through the torpedo-boat destroyer to the true destroyer—the small ships which had met and played a substantial part in beating a German force in the first full-scale destroyer action in August 1914—had taken less than forty years.

5

When the coded signal 'Commence hostilities against Germany' was decoded on board the Grand Fleet flag-ship *Iron Duke* shortly before midnight on August 4th, 1914, the Grand Fleet was already at sea, plugging the hole in the northern part of the North Sea.

The German Army Staff's plan for a mighty sweep through Belgium and northern France had been broadly appreciated for some time.

But what of its navy?

Would it be committed to full-out, hell-for-leather effort in support of an invasion from the Lowlands? Or would it be move and counter move until the High Seas Fleet and the Grand Fleet met in one almighty clash?

There were new and untried tactics at sea, there were new weapons of which nobody had a full assessment.

And among the new elements were the destroyers. The disposition of the destroyers to their war stations emphasised the deplorable shortage of this class of ship.

By the end of July the Grand Fleet had earmarked seventy-odd of the latest type to be based at Scapa. Another four flotillas were spread out, and thinly spread at that, down the coast from the Tyne to Dover. But quite half of them were older ships, some having been built as early as 1900. One veteran, *Lightning*, a turtle-backed bowed warrior, had slipped down the launching ways in 1896.

She did sterling service in her patrol flotilla until she struck a mine in 1915. But her age serves to exemplify the shortage of destroyers at the outbreak of war.

To these older destroyers fell the mundane task of nightly patrols against minelaying ships and patrols far out in case a German squadron essayed a dash across the North Sea. As the first autumn of the war crept into the cold winter months, theirs was a task which brought little glory and a maximum of hard work under most exhausting conditions. In many cases they had not even the pleasure of a consort. They had about twenty to twenty-five miles of bitter North Sea to patrol, often with visibility severely restricted.

But for the patrolling destroyers there were hectic moments, too. Such a one was the first raid the Germans staged on the east coast.

By an odd coincidence, as the German raiding squadron steamed west in the darkness—four battle cruisers, four cruisers and some smaller ships—two British cruiser leaders, with four destroyers each, steamed east, bent on seeking out and destroying some German minesweepers which were assiduously and efficiently undoing all the good minelaying our layers had done.

This comparatively small punitive force steamed on a reciprocal course to that of the German squadron, at one time being less than ten miles away from them in the darkness.

It fell to the hard-worked patrol destroyers based on Yarmouth to discover the enemy. They steamed out independently, each with a patrol to do: *Halcyon, Lively, Leopard* and *Success,* resigned to a night of plugging up and down in the darkness, investigating suspicious ships, always on the alert, fighting against the weariness which boredom drags along in attendance.

Suddenly out of the darkness there loomed up a cruiser. *Halcyon* challenged, but the reply forthcoming was a salvo uncomfortably accurate. Then the lone cruiser was joined by the German squadron. So the four destroyers were facing the battle cruisers *Seydlitz*, *Moltke*, *Blucher* and *Von Der Tann* and the light cruisers *Strassburg*, *Stralsund*, *Kolberg* and *Graudenz*, three of the latter still smarting over the severe handling they had received in the Heligoland fight.

The British destroyers lay over at an acute angle as they turned away from heavy fire from all the German ships. *Halcyon* was hit, not severely, but the Germans had the range and the chances were that the next salvo from any of them would blow *Halcyon* out of the water.

She disappeared behind a forest of towering splashes as shells plunged into the sea all around her. *Lively*, racing behind *Halcyon*, turned to meet the German squadron, an incredibly courageous act, swept between them and the harassed *Halcyon* and laid a thick, concealing smoke-screen to cover her. Although this had been tried in manœuvres in peace-time, it had never been attempted against a heavy and accurate gun-fire. To *Lively*, then, falls the honour of making the first smoke-screen behind which *Halcyon* withdrew.

Lively's courageous turn towards the German ships made them hesitate and turn away, first against the possible threat of a torpedo attack—and the light cruisers had had some experience of the British destroyers tearing in to fire their torpedoes—and secondly Admiral Hipper in command suspected that no lone ship would risk that unless not far behind her were heavier ships hurrying to profit from any damage done to his ships by this dare-devil lone destroyer.

To be caught off the English coast with a lame duck or two was unthinkable. Hipper turned away from his original plan to bombard Yarmouth from three or four miles' range and contented himself with throwing a few shells from 20,000 yards, which blew up a lot of Gorleston beach. Then he went home.

Incidentally, farther north, just in case the raid provoked any of our battle cruisers or battleships into sailing, the Germans had disposed four battleships to meet them.

So there were all the ingredients for another fairly large-scale fight. None of our big ships sailed and Hipper had to increase speed to get away from the wasp-like *Lively*, which persisted in shadowing him and reporting his course and speed.

Altogether a night far removed from boredom.

Then followed weeks of patrolling, investigating ships acting suspiciously, sweeping up an occasional minelayer, the nightly round, the common task, until a bitterly cold December was two weeks old.

Shrewd Intelligence, plus eavesdropping on the almost

incessant, high-pitched German wireless, led to the assessment that something was cooking.

It was.

Some time in the very near future the Germans, aware that our battle-cruiser strength was reduced by a third by the dispatch of the *Invincible* and *Inflexible* to avenge Cradock's defeat off South America, would try once more to come to grips with the Grand Fleet in an all-out fight.

Uncanny timing suggested that the next forty-eight hours from December 13th would be pregnant with possibilities. But where would the Germans strike?

They had the whole of the North Sea, at least the eastern part of it, in which to dispose their striking force.

From Harwich to Scapa, ships came to immediate notice for steam, and on midnight, December 14th, they sailed. More than fifty of them.

Six battleships and four light cruisers steamed from Scapa Flow, the four remaining battle cruisers and attendant destroyers sailed from Cromarty Firth, four heavy cruisers departed from Rosyth and from Harwich, Commodore Tyrwhitt and his light cruisers with twenty-odd destroyers turned their bows east.

It was the destroyers from Cromarty who made first contact. In the Indian hour of the early morning of December 15th the destroyer *Lynx* sighted a destroyer, received no reply to her challenge and opened fire.

The German destroyer turned sharply and raced away.

Contact had been made and the first night action by destroyers was on.

Lynx and *Ambuscade* were damaged in the first exchange of shots and *Hardy*, racing after *Lynx* and *Ambuscade*, blundered into a cruiser and was also promptly hit, fortunately not seriously, and *Hardy* drove the cruiser into a violent turn with a torpedo attack.

Ambuscade, *Lynx* and *Hardy* were out of the fight and turned for home, with *Shark*, *Acasta* and *Spitfire* zealously shepherding them.

Then five German destroyers, shadowy in the first pearl-grey dawn, sliced in towards the British division. Three of the British destroyers swung away to attack them and found themselves being drawn into an ambush with a German cruiser in the offing. There was scarcely time to get in one salvo at the cruiser before withdrawing when three more cruisers were sighted—and reported.

That was too much metal even for the British destroyers. Unfortunately, the sighting report was not transmitted to Beatty in *Lion*.

Visibility deteriorated with daylight and remained poor throughout the day. The High Seas Fleet, and the Grand Fleet, although catching occasional glimpses of each other, never came to grips.

It must be admitted that the British destroyers who had made contact with the enemy returned home in a chastened mood.

Three of the Cromarty force of destroyers had been hit without scoring any tangible reply and they had learned that while the German destroyers had not been evident in the Heligoland battle, when contact was made they were not averse to a fight—and their gunnery was good.

Taking it at its true valuation, it was but a brief high-lit episode in an endless round of monotonous patrols in mainly vile weather. And during them there were losses. *Maori*, *Lynx* and *Velox* were sunk by mines, as was the veteran *Lightning*. Another veteran, the *Recruit*, on patrol off the Galloper Light, was stalked and sunk by a German submarine.

A dreary, gale-lashed December wore into January before any more real action came the way of the destroyers.

A sudden increase in the German radio signals spelled activity of some sort and once more the British cruisers and battle cruisers sailed to investigate and if possible bring the German ships to a decisive action.

Beatty's battle cruisers steamed down from the bleak north, Commodore Goodenough's light cruisers steamed to rendezvous with them and from Harwich went *Arethusa* with *Aurora* and *Undaunted*, leaders with the destroyers.

Under Tyrwhitt's broad pennant were the latest type of destroyers, the 'M' class, which had been laid down just before the war broke out and were now effective. They were powerful little ships, armed with three four-inch guns, four twenty-one-inch torpedoes, were about 1,000 tons and were designed to do a speed of thirty-five knots. With *Aurora*'s and *Undaunted*'s flotillas they numbered more than thirty destroyers.

It was *Aurora*'s destroyers who first sighted the enemy shortly after dawn. They made contact with an old antagonist, the light cruiser *Kolberg* with a screen of destroyers. There was a brief exchange of salvoes at four miles' range, then *Kolberg* turned away eastward.

The leaders and their destroyers pursued her into the pink-tinged dawn and ran slap into the German battle cruisers with light cruisers and a cloud of destroyers in close attendance. At the same time Goodenough's light cruisers made contact and reported course and speed to Beatty's heavy ships, which were steaming full speed on a south-easterly course.

By eight o'clock Beatty had the enemy in sight and action was joined. *Seydlitz*, the German flag-ship, was set on fire and *Blucher* lost heavily in a duel with *New Zealand*.

Then the German destroyers did what was expected of destroyers. A flag signal fluttered to Hipper's ship's yard-arm and the German destroyers tore into a torpedo attack, forcing Beatty's battle cruisers to turn away. *Seydlitz*, although fighting a fire, hit *Lion* as she turned away. A few moments later *Derfflinger* also registered hits on *Lion*'s water-line and slowed her down.

Unfortunately, a misunderstanding in signals led to the remaining four battle cruisers concentrating their fire on *Blucher* instead of chasing the retiring German battle cruisers. By the time that was rectified, when Beatty transferred his flag to a destroyer, the German squadrons had escaped.

The British destroyers of the Harwich force closed in to

finish off *Blucher*, which had been taking a terrific hammering from the British battle cruisers. *Meteor* paid for her temerity. *Blucher* concentrated her secondary armament on *Meteor* and hit her five or six times. It was a last gesture, however. *Arethusa*'s destroyers closed in like wolves and torpedoed her. Slowly, she rolled over and sank.

It was an inconclusive end to what might have been a full-scale battle and the British destroyers, due partly to the fact that they had to drop back because they fouled the range for *Lion* and her ships, never came to grips with their natural enemy, the German destroyers, and apart from finishing off *Blucher* had no opportunity to attack with torpedoes.

Then it was, once more, the daily (and nightly) round, the common task, a saddening one because faithful *Arethusa* hit a mine early in February and was lost. Commodore Tyrwhitt's broad pennant was hoisted in the cruiser *Conquest*. The other leaders at Harwich were *Cleopatra* and *Penelope*.

The Harwich force, now quite a formidable one, including some of the latest destroyers to join the fleet, had high hopes late in April 1916 that they would have an opportunity of engaging in a full-scale fleet action.

Admiral Scheer sailed his battle cruisers on a raid on the east coast with the whole German fleet in support.

Shrewd, almost uncanny, deduction by Intelligence had led to the confident belief that the Germans were staging a major naval operation of some description and the Harwich scouting force, as always, was sent to sea to probe, to find and to report the enemy.

So *Conquest*, *Cleopatra* and *Penelope* sailed at midnight on April 24th, steering a ruled-edge course for German-claimed waters.

As light forces went at that time, it was a fairly formidable one. There were some of the latest 'M's', who had already been blooded: *Manly*, *Meteor*, *Mastiff*, *Miranda*, *Mentor*, *Matchless*, *Mansfield*, and the redoubtable 'L's', some of which had already met the Germans two or three times. They included *Lasso*, *Legion*, *Laertes*, *Linnet*, *Lochinvar*, *Lysander* and *Lightfoot*.

On a purely personal note, which has nothing to do with this narrative, nearly twenty-seven years later, after two busy years in command at Dover, I was pulled out, sent on leave before joining a ship to command at Freetown, Sierra Leone. While on leave I was informed the appointment had been cancelled, the ship had been lost after an action with a submarine on the way to Lagos.

She was HMS *Laertes*, a smaller and fairly new escort ship, but I feel a proprietary interest in ships of that name.

To return to the search: Tyrwhitt's assessment, based on Admiralty Intelligence and his own deductions, was impeccable. The dawn was no more than a pale-grey promise, with sky and sea just lighter than darkness, but with the eastern horizon a clear-cut line in the limitless visibility.

The Harwich force sighted some light cruisers and destroyers, obviously screening some larger metal, and on investigating closer, although still out of range, they saw a squadron of four German battle cruisers.

Tyrwhitt, aware that some British submarines were on patrol in the vicinity, tried to draw the German squadrons over them, but the Germans maintained course and speed.

Commodore Tyrwhitt knew, too, that somewhere north of him was Beatty racing southwards, exactly where he did not know. Neither did he know that the German battle cruisers were bent on bombarding Lowestoft.

It was an odd point, this persistent raiding on east-coast fishing ports, one which was never completely cleared up, even after investigation into German naval records after the war.

It is a reasonable presumption that German agents, not well versed in naval matters, attached far too much importance to the presence of a few minor war vessels in Lowestoft, Yarmouth and other ports. One would have thought that a German squadron of battle cruisers would have collected a bigger dividend by appearing out of the morning mist and bombarding Harwich, where there was a fairly formidable array of destroyers and light cruisers.

So to Lowestoft went the German battle cruisers, leaving the light cruisers and destroyers to deal with the Harwich force. *Conquest* and rampaging consorts opened fire on the German light forces at extreme range, forcing them to turn away, and, incidentally, forcing the German heavy ships to break off their bombardment of fishermen's cottages to steer south to their aid.

The light forces on either side were approximately equal and had they been left to enjoy their own fight probably another page in destroyer history would have been written.

It was not to be.

Admiral Boedicker's battle cruisers slammed into the Harwich force, hit *Conquest* and *Laertes*, and the remainder of the destroyers had to make a smoke-screen behind which *Conquest* and the others retired.

Although the German battle cruisers and their light cruisers and destroyers, as yet undamaged, knew that supporting them were twenty-odd German battleships, they refused to be drawn into pursuit through the smoke-screen, but turned east at high speed.

In all it was highly unsatisfactory from the British point of view, and abortive from the Germans' aspect.

There were German battle cruisers and cruisers, with a destroyer screen, solidly backed up by the High Seas Fleet, faced only by the Harwich light cruisers and destroyers in the immediate vicinity, Beatty's battle cruisers somewhere north ploughing through hard weather with his light cruisers and destroyer screen trying hard to keep up, and nearly 200 miles farther north was the Grand Fleet hammering into even worse weather.

It was Heligoland Bight in reverse, with the advantage well over towards the Germans.

Possibly, the thought of having two or three, or more, lame ducks limping about too near the British coast, to be at the mercy of the British destroyers and cruisers, acted as a deterrent.

Had, of course, a full battleship, battle-cruiser, light-cruiser and destroyer action taken place on that April day it would have meant that the Battle of Jutland would not have been fought.

6

It was almost inevitable that sooner or later the two greatest fleets in the world would ultimately come to grips.

Admiral Scheer had taken command of the High Seas Fleet early in 1916 and from his handling of the submarine warfare it was realised that he was an all-out advocate of ruthless action.

He had tentatively tried his hand in the abortive Lowestoft raid and after due consideration of the errors of omission and commission of that affair he was convinced that given a second opportunity he would materially improve on the result.

By late spring he and his staff had evolved a bait which they felt would entice the Grand Fleet to sea. The bait was to be a sortie with the High Seas Fleet into the North Sea, while his submarines, stationed off the known British bases, would wait in ambush to collect their toll as the British ships sailed.

Scheer had the submarines available because he had been compelled, by diplomatic pressure, to ease up on his submarine warfare after the sinking of the hospital ship *Sussex*, which created a tremendous wave of indignation throughout America.

The submarines were sailed to their allocated areas and a few days later, accompanied by an intense increase in the wireless traffic among the German ships, the High Seas Fleet began assembling at Wilhelmshaven.

That was enough for the Admiralty.

Jellicoe and Beatty were ordered to sea.

The ring was set.

Before midnight on May 30th the Grand Fleet, with its cloud of destroyers screening it, was clear of Scapa. A submarine fired torpedoes at one of the destroyers, but missed.

Farther south the 2nd Battle Squadron and the 1st Cruiser Squadron steamed out of Invergordon. If a submarine on aggressive patrol saw them depart it took no action. So, two comparatively minor factors in Scheer's plan went awry. The battle squadron and cruisers, with their destroyer screen, sailed for the rendezvous with Jellicoe unscathed. Screening them were more destroyers.

The 5th Battle Squadron, and the battle cruisers, with three light-cruiser squadrons and a screen of more than thirty-odd destroyers, cleared the Firth of Forth shortly after eleven o'clock.

One submarine tried a long-range shot at *Galatea*, missed, and found the sea too intensely populated to risk surfacing to signal Scheer of the departure of the fleet.

Hundreds of thousands of words have been written about the Battle of Jutland in both languages and even today for every 'pro' that can be produced somebody will produce an equally vehement 'con'. All this book is concerned with is the action as it affected the destroyers.

They were to come into their own as a tangible, recognised weapon in a major fleet action. A lot of questions were to be asked and a lot of answers were given in the next twenty-four hours or so.

The destroyer, as a weapon, had had a trial run in the confused hurly-burly of the Heligoland fight and several of them had earned laurels in the German raids on the east coast and in the Dogger Bank battle.

There were destroyers at sea on that May night which were going to make history, were going to establish in capital letters destroyer traditions which will travel down the ages so long as destroyers are built.

They numbered among themselves the latest classes of

destroyers to roll off the stocks under the concentrated building programme.

Among them were names which were passed to other ships twenty-five years later. *Obdurate*, *Onslow*, *Acheron*, *Defender*; and the 'L's': *Laurel*, *Landrail*, *Liberty*; and the 'M's': *Morris*, *Moorsom*, which had had their baptism with the Harwich patrol.

Beatty's battle cruisers, with their screen of light cruisers and destroyers, steamed south-easterly, the light cruisers probing outwards and searching. At two o'clock in the afternoon or thereabouts *Galatea* turned away to investigate a small merchant ship which was stopped with steam escaping from its safety valve. Actually that small coasting ship was probably stunned at the sight of so many warships astern and ahead of her that her captain considered it wiser to stop and let them go about their business.

At the same moment a German light cruiser, the *Elbing*, and a couple of destroyers steamed to investigate the same ship. Contact!

Within a few minutes after signalling to Beatty that enemy ships were in sight *Galatea* and *Elbing* were shooting at each other.

Shortly before 4 pm *Lutzow* and *Lion* started exchanging shots. The Battle of Jutland had begun.

The destroyers' part in that first phase was little more than occupying a grandstand view, but their turn was to come. Ahead of them they could see the German battle cruisers 15,000 yards away, slivers of flame and billowing smoke rippling along their sides as they fired salvoes at the British battle cruisers.

Astern of them Beatty's ships were replying.

Lion was badly hit, so was *Tiger*. *Lutzow* and *Derfflinger* were severely punished by *Princess Royal*; *Indefatigable* disappeared in one tremendous sheet of flame, the blast of the explosion momentarily drowning out the heavy boom of the big guns.

Still the destroyers were no more than privileged spectators. But Beatty was not unaware of their advantageous position.

To leader *Champion* he signalled: 'Attack with torpedoes.' The flag signal all the destroyers with *Champion* were waiting for slammed up to her yard-arm. As one ship, the destroyers turned to port—to meet the enemy—their sterns squatted low in the water, the bow waves climbed higher than the foredeck. *Nestor*, *Nicator*, *Turbulent*, *Petard*, *Obdurate* and *Nerissa* strove desperately for the last fraction of a knot.

Admiral Hipper, commanding the battle cruisers, saw the threat developing and ordered his own destroyers to steam to meet the British small ships to endeavour to break off the attack. They streamed through the flame-girdled battle cruisers, supported by light cruisers, opening fire as soon as they were in range.

As the heavy ships fought it out grimly, in between them the destroyers of both fleets staged their own fight. Racing to meet one another at a collective speed of nearly seventy knots, the range dropped from thousands of yards to hundreds in a few minutes. The German destroyers fired their torpedoes at the battle cruisers at an impossibly long range, faltered under the concentrated fire of the British destroyers, turned back to the protection of their larger sisters.

Petard gained the first victim. Lieutenant-Commander Evelyn Thomson slammed a torpedo into a German leader, hit her amidships, closed in, deluged her with rapid salvoes and left her sinking. *Petard* then joined in the race to the east towards the German battle cruisers behind which were steaming the German destroyers.

Another German destroyer lay stopped after several hits in her engine room. As the British ships raced past, each of them poured in a salvo or two, leaving her sinking behind them.

On the other side of the picture *Nomad* lay stopped from a hit in her engine room. Slowly she was sinking, alone; astern of her, thousands of yards away, were the British battle cruisers, ahead were the Germans, and little more than dark blobs on the water were *Nomad*'s consorts, still racing hell-bent-for-election after the German destroyers.

Lieutenant-Commander Paul Whitfield realised that his ship was sinking and prepared to destroy his confidential books.

Suddenly to the south of him he saw a vast cloud of smoke and below it a dozen or more big ships. It was the German battleships, the High Seas Fleet. His wireless room was a wreck. There was no way he could pass a signal to *Lion* or to Jellicoe three hours' steam to the north-west.

There was one thing he *could* do. And he did.

Grimly his torpedo-tube crews closed up—and waited. The moment the first of the battleships came into range he fired. No hits. Such courage deserved a better reward.

In the meantime the other British destroyers, having chased the German small ships into the protection of their cruisers and battle cruisers, concentrated on their main task, which had been only slightly interrupted by the destroyer fight in the no man's sea between the two forces of battle cruisers.

That task was to attack with torpedoes.

At a range of a little over 5,000 yards *Nestor* fired her torpedoes at *Lutzow*, followed a moment or two later by *Nicator*. But *Lutzow* turned away and the torpedoes sped on harmlessly.

Petard, flushed with her success over the German destroyer leader, fired at the *Seydlitz* and scored a hit, blowing a large hole in her side.

Nestor and *Nicator* once more turned east for another attack and twisted and wriggled through columns of water thrown up by the salvoes fired at them by the German battle cruisers. *Nestor* pressed in until the range was less than a mile and a half, fired torpedoes, but suffered the mortification of seeing their target, the leading battle cruiser, turn away.

As they turned away, *Nestor* was hit twice, and reeling from the heavy blows in her engine room rolled to a stop.

For a brief while she was able to raise enough steam for six or seven knots, but the effort was too great for her damaged boilers.

So, little more than a mile apart, both stopped, lay *Nestor* and *Nomad*, right in the path of the High Seas Fleet. These little destroyers had, like their kind, harried and threatened the big German ships and had chased the German destroyers right back to the protection of their own ships.

Petard, racing for safety, closed *Nestor* with the intention of passing a tow, but *Nestor*'s captain realised that if *Petard* delayed long enough to pass a tow and tried to steam at slow speed three destroyers would fall victims to the Germans, not two.

Petard steamed away, her own personal triumphs tinged with sorrow and bitterness at leaving behind her two sisters.

At point-blank range the German battleships wiped *Nomad* off the face of the water in a minute or two, leaving only a few survivors in floats and boats to watch her go.

A savage fire next demolished *Nestor*.

Not far away, *Nerissa*, *Termagant*, *Moorsom* and *Morris* were under fire from the big ships as they strove desperately to get in torpedo attacks. *Moorsom* in particular made two attacks on the battleships, came under heavy fire and was damaged, but managed to steam clear.

A little accountancy will show that so far as the destroyers were concerned they had a substantial credit balance.

They had forced Hipper to turn his ships away when he was leading on points, to use a boxing phrase. He had sunk *Queen Mary* and *Indefatigable*, had heavily hit *Lion* and was hammering at the others. It was no fault of the men on the small ships that the weapons they had were not good enough.

Even so, they had sunk two destroyers, one by torpedo, one by gun-fire, and had damaged two or three others.

They had, in addition, hit and damaged a battle cruiser, unfortunately not vitally.

Furthermore, they had met and licked the German destroyers in a purely destroyer fight when they came racing through to attack the British battle cruisers.

As the evening wore on, Beatty's battered battle cruisers led the Germans into the trap waiting to be sprung by Jellicoe. In the meantime the cruisers were still taking a severe mauling. *Defence* and *Warrior*, hammering at the cruiser *Wiesbaden*, were caught in this task by the High Seas Fleet.

Defence disappeared in one sheet of flame, *Warrior* was sadly crippled and with *Warspite* came under heavy punishment. They had to leave *Wiesbaden*. But, screening *Lion*, among other destroyers, was *Onslow*, commanded by Lieutenant-Commander John Tovey, a ship and a man to make naval history in years to come. From his position off *Lion*'s bow he raced in, opened fire with his four-inch guns and slammed a torpedo into *Wiesbaden*, coming under heavy fire from the German battle cruisers as he did so. A salvo from one of them hit and slowed down *Onslow* until she could steam at only ten knots. It looked as if she would suffer the same fate as *Nestor* and *Nomad*. Scarcely moving through the water, her engine-room staff striving desperately to give her a few more knots, *Onslow* turned and attacked the German battle cruisers with torpedoes, forcing them to turn away. Into Tovey's view rolled the ponderous bulk of the battleships. *Onslow* had only two torpedoes left and those she fired at the High Seas Fleet. Scheer also turned his fleet away from the torpedo attack.

Onslow, crawling along at less than ten knots, impudently, almost arrogantly, showered *Derfflinger* with some long-range shots from her four-inch guns. Then she limped away, eventually breaking down altogether until another lame sister, *Defender*, took her in tow and in bad weather towed her for nearly two days before reaching a Scottish port.

Farther east other destroyers were showing just the same spirit. *Shark*, *Acasta*, *Christopher* and *Ophelia*, with the light cruiser *Chester*, came under fire from the German battle cruisers which were hammering away at *Warrior* and *Warspite*. *Chester* was hit almost at once and had to withdraw.

Shark, *Acasta* and the other two sighted three German light cruisers and tore into the attack.

Then, behind the three cruisers, Commander Loftus Jones, in *Shark*, sighted yet another cruiser, the *Regensberg*, surrounded by a cloud of destroyers.

A formidable force to attack with four destroyers. There were four cruisers and ten destroyers, the latter some of those mauled in the earlier destroyer fight.

A British light cruiser blundered through the evening mist and for a time drew some of the fire away from the four destroyers until she disappeared, pursued by the German cruisers.

The German destroyers moved in for the kill.

Shark was hit almost immediately. Her bridge was wrecked and she could bring to bear only one gun. Even the *Shark* showed her teeth. Although Loftus Jones was mortally wounded with one leg shot off, he still commanded his ship, and a German destroyer, moving in too confidently, was hit and sunk. The end was near. *Shark* waved away any offer of help from the crippled *Acasta*, who had been severely mauled. Accompanied by *Ophelia* and *Christopher*, *Acasta* drew sadly away, limping back to the shelter of the larger ships.

From the ring of fire-girdled destroyers around the *Shark* a destroyer broke away, raced in and fired two torpedoes at close range. Both struck. *Shark* rolled over from the impact and went down, getting in just one more shot at the destroyer which had mortally wounded her.

The few survivors, taking with them the dying Loftus Jones, got away in a carley float and were picked up the next morning. By then Loftus Jones was dead.

He was awarded a posthumous Victoria Cross, one of the first of many to be awarded to destroyer men through the years.

Acasta, limping away escorted by *Ophelia*, had yet one more task to perform, and a vital one.

Between Scheer and his bases lay the Grand Fleet. Somehow he had to break through that ring of fire and steel, with or without a fight.

Through the evening mist loomed Hipper's battle cruisers, probing for a gap.

Acasta, with *Ophelia* following, did not hesitate. They turned and attacked with torpedoes. Neither scored a hit, but nevertheless they had forced Hipper to turn towards the High Seas Fleet. He reasoned that two lone destroyers would not have the incredible temerity to attack alone. Therefore they must be part of a screen for a larger force, either Beatty's rampaging battle cruisers or Jellicoe's Grand Fleet—or both. As the destroyers were coming from an easterly direction, Scheer accepted that reasoning and did not try a break-through when actually the way was virtually open to him. Jellicoe was not so far south-east as to be in a position to bar him from his home bases.

It was late in the afternoon when the battleships of the Grand Fleet and the High Seas Fleet finally joined in action. Scheer, still to the westward of Jellicoe's ships, finally decided to hammer a hole through the British line with his battle cruisers and then to thrust his battleships through that hole.

In the evening shadows loomed first Scheer's sadly mauled battle cruisers and behind them the battleships clearly visible against the setting sun, while the British fleet was merged into the haze to the east.

To Scheer's horror, he found himself steaming for the centre of the British line of battleships, with the Grand Fleet crossing his 'T'. There was no hole.

Under a merciless bombardment, which virtually demolished the battered *Derfflinger* and *Seydlitz*, the High Seas Fleet faltered under the lash and once more turned away to the west. The German destroyers streamed into a torpedo attack, which they failed to carry out, but they forced Jellicoe to turn away from his task of demolition and provided an opaque smoke-screen, behind which the High Seas Fleet escaped, except for a brief flurry when Beatty's battle cruisers caught a fleeting glimpse of the tail-end of the procession and hammered two or three ships before they disappeared into the mist.

Jellicoe, still unaware that *Queen Mary* and *Indefatigable* were lost, had every reason to be satisfied with the battle so far as it had gone. To the best of his knowledge a light cruiser and a battle cruiser had been sunk and others had been hit, but the Germans had suffered heavily and he still held the key position. He was to the eastward of the High Seas Fleet and on the morrow, with the whole day before him, he would make Scheer pay heavily for any further attempts to break through to his home bases.

So he steamed through the night with the battle cruisers ahead, the Grand Fleet following and the destroyers a few miles astern, where they could swing into action immediately against any threatened torpedo attack.

Unfortunately for Jellicoe, the Germans had broken down the British code and were able to decipher Jellicoe's night-disposition signals. Scheer slowed down his fleet, allowed the battle cruisers and battleships to pass, then shaped a course to take him astern of them for Horn's Riff.

All that stood between him and safety were the British destroyers. And they were to see some action. Confused action, with friend and foe mixed up.

The fleet had scarcely settled down to their positions for the night when the destroyers astern were in action.

7

The position affecting the destroyer flotillas guarding the stern of the fleet was briefly this. They knew that ahead of them were the battle cruisers, followed by the battleships steering a southerly course. Of the disposition of the light cruisers they were rather hazy. So any light cruisers appearing close to starboard might be British cruisers screening the fleet. Or they could be Germans. Pay a penny and choose.

Castor fell into that trap.

The Germans had possession of the challenge for the night and when the dark bulks of three cruisers loomed up in the darkness they flashed the challenge to *Castor* and her destroyers and a moment or two later flooded her in light from their searchlights and opened fire. Two of *Castor*'s destroyers opened fire on the searchlights on the cruisers and fired torpedoes to save *Castor* from further damage. The other destroyers, having seen the challenge made, felt that a ghastly error was being made and that friend was hitting friend.

The German cruisers, apparently part of the port screen for the High Seas Fleet, withdrew with the valuable knowledge in their hands that, knowing Jellicoe's night dispositions, they had struck the weak link in the British line: the destroyer flotillas astern of the Grand Fleet. The way was open for Scheer.

His south-easterly course was a converging one on that of Jellicoe's and was still full of danger for him. Were his speed a shade faster he would run into either the battle cruisers or the battleships, or both, and his nose would be severely blunted. Furthermore, he would still be barred from his home bases.

Jellicoe's 'Tail-end Charlie' destroyers steamed on after the Grand Fleet, as touchy as gunpowder and tensed up. Among them were destroyers with names which were to be handed down to a later decade with lustre and tradition already established. There were names such as *Broke*, *Achates*, *Garland*, *Ardent* and several others led by the leader *Tipperary*.

Twice shortly after eleven o'clock the destroyers sighted the vague outlines of cruisers to starboard but assumed they were light cruisers of the Grand Fleet screen. But shortly before midnight three of the cruisers closed in to less than 1,000 yards, illuminated *Tipperary* and slammed her with several broadsides, setting her on fire.

Spitfire, next in line, swung into a torpedo attack followed by two or three more of the flotilla, all of whom fired torpedoes, some of which hit a German light cruiser so heavily that later she sank.

After hitting the German cruiser, which was *Rostock*, *Spitfire* turned away to reload and found herself right in the path of two big ships. *Spitfire* had run smack into the two leading battleships of the High Seas Fleet, *Westfalen* and *Nassau*, which promptly turned on their searchlights. The British destroyer fired directly at the searchlights on one, extinguishing them, then wriggled past the bow, evading an attempt to ram by using rudder hard over and full speed.

The battleship trying to ram, *Nassau*, fired her guns, but could not depress them enough to hit *Spitfire*, but blasted her bridge and funnels to smithereens, setting her on fire.

Eventually, after a lone journey, *Spitfire* reached port.

Behind her was confusion. *Broke* was being hammered; her bridge and steering gear wrecked, she was out of control and what was worse she was involved in a collision with another destroyer, *Sparrowhawk*, which in turn was rammed by yet another British destroyer.

All three limped painfully away, *Sparrowhawk* ultimately to be sunk by our own gun-fire at daylight, she was so badly damaged.

Achates, *Ardent*, *Ambuscade*, *Garland* and two or three others, steaming southwards in the wake of the Grand Fleet, ran slap-bang into a whole line of vague, bulky shapes which eventually took the form of two cruisers, four battle cruisers and the van of the line of German battleships.

Any impression the British destroyers may have had that for some reason they had overrun the Grand Fleet was rapidly demolished. *Fortune* was smashed in a few minutes by devastating fire and lay a helpless hulk. The same plunging salvoes also damaged *Porpoise*, but she managed to creep away into the darkness. *Ambuscade* and *Garland* each fired torpedoes, then with *Achates* made their escape from the fury of fire, pursued by German light cruisers.

Ardent found herself alone facing the battle cruisers and battleships of the High Seas Fleet. She fired her one remaining torpedo, but scarcely had the torpedo left its tube when the leading battleships slammed *Ardent* and reduced her to a smoking shambles. Past her streamed ship after ship of the line of battleships and each one hammered poor little *Ardent* and it was a miracle that she still floated when the last of the battleships steamed on into the darkness.

Alone, on fire, wrecked, two-thirds of her crew dead, she slowly rolled over and sank.

Nearly twenty-five years later another destroyer *Ardent* was to face the might of a German battleship's fire and was to go down fighting to the last.

Such was tradition carried on.

Scheer risked the very thing which had prompted Jellicoe to wait for daylight before rejoining action, i.e. a night action and a threat of torpedo attacks by destroyers, and, aided by perfect knowledge of the Grand Fleet's night disposition, had smashed one frail barrier of destroyers. Not without cost. He had lost two cruisers, a fair price to pay for an open path to safety.

Now facing him was another barrier of British destroyers, most of whom had been in action in previous battles with the Germans. Their names have occurred before this page.

There, barring the passage of the High Seas Fleet, were *Lydiard*, *Laurel*, *Landrail*, *Liberty*, *Morris*, *Termagant*, *Nicator*, *Narborough* and *Petard*, with the scalp of a destroyer and a hit on *Seydlitz* to her credit; possibly the cream of British destroyers and destroyer men to face the might of the German battle cruisers and battleships. Farther east of them were still more British destroyers of the same calibre.

The 'M' class: *Marvel*, *Moresby*, *Marksman*, *Maenad*; the 'O's': *Obedient*, *Obdurate*, *Onslaught*—more names to be passed on to ships a decade later for more glory to be added to their scrolls of courage. Also there were the latest 'N's': *Narwal*, *Nessus*, *Noble*, *Nonsuch* and half a dozen others.

Lydiard and her consorts tried to get ahead of the German fleet to attack it from the west, the disengaged side. Had she succeeded she might have forced Scheer into a drastic alteration of course, driving him into the waiting flotillas of destroyers and creating such confusion that the High Seas Fleet might yet have been trapped when the Grand Fleet turned about at daylight.

Lydiard and her companions barely scraped past the bow of the leading ship, and *Petard*, tragically out of torpedoes, was hammered by the German ship's secondary armament until she escaped westward into the pre-dawn darkness.

Turbulent, astern of her, was not so lucky. She was smashed, disabled, on fire, when a German battleship rammed her and rolled her over.

The 'O's', the 'M's' and the 'N's', unknown to themselves, were steaming on a course which converged with that of the High Seas Fleet. Just before dawn, about two o'clock, when *Faulknor*, leading, estimated she was ahead of the German fleet, and in a sound position to attack, the latter loomed up to south-west of her.

Throughout the destroyer actions of the night, when the destroyers realised that they were in contact with considerable forces of the German fleet signals had been passed to Jellicoe in *Iron Duke*, leading the Grand Fleet southwards. At least, signals had been made, but even as the Germans had the night dispositions, so they had the wavelength of the destroyers and most effectively jammed any signals they made.

Tragically, Jellicoe never received them and when he did eventually turn to deal with the High Seas Fleet at daylight it was to find that the enemy had slipped behind him in the night, hammering his slender barrier of destroyers.

Faulknor's sighting signal suffered the fate of the other signals through the night. The battle squadrons were little more than ten miles ahead, less than half an hour's steaming, and could have turned to smite the enemy while the Germans were still turning from the destroyer attack.

So the destroyers had to bear the brunt of the attack and

could not be expected either to halt, turn or seriously damage the German fleet.

As it was, *Faulknor* and her consorts forced the High Seas Fleet to turn south of their south-easterly course for a while.

Faulknor, *Onslaught*, *Marvel* and *Obedient* fired torpedoes at the German battleships and hit the battleship *Pommern.* It was a vital blow. The battleship faltered, a pillar of vivid flame climbed skywards and she ceased to exist.

Again and again the destroyers raced in to fire torpedoes, *Onslaught* being heavily hit during the attack.

Such courage deserved a better fate. But courage was not enough. Virtually nothing existed now between Scheer and the open sea back to his base. He could afford to lose another ship or even two to the destroyers.

In his path lay the leader *Champion* and two destroyers, opponents to be brushed aside with barely a gesture.

With *Champion* were *Obdurate* and *Moresby.* Shortly before three o'clock they sighted four cruisers with an attendant destroyer screen. *Moresby* closed in to attack and got away her torpedo, which hit and sank a German destroyer.

It was the last attack to be made in the Battle of Jutland.

Many gallons of ink and thousands of reams of paper have gone to analyse the Battle of Jutland, its mistakes, its errors of over-caution; wise-after-the-event critics have dogmatically tried to place the blame here and there, have announced in loud, brazen voices what should have been done.

All we are concerned with is what the destroyers did.

Of courage there was more than enough to spare in the small ships. In material matters they had sunk a battleship, two light cruisers and five destroyers when they battled as the only barrier between Scheer and his homeward race.

They had sunk or seriously damaged other ships in the earlier part of the battle during the afternoon. Time and again they had flown the flag of courage and had raced in to force the German battle cruisers and battleships to turn away.

There had been individual instances of lone ships facing

the might of the High Seas Fleet. With the proper support from the big ships they could have played a material part in rewriting naval history.

And the price they paid?

Eight destroyers rested on the bottom of the North Sea. Others, limping away from the holocaust behind them, had to draw deeper on their wells of courage and stamina to get their ships back to port.

Those sunk were *Ardent*, *Fortune*, *Nestor*, *Nomad*, *Shark* *Sparrowhawk*, *Tipperary* and *Turbulent*, but each and every one had extracted a full price. The Germans lost five destroyers, V4, V27, V29, V48 and S35. Seven more were hit and severely damaged.

In case anybody should want to draw a comparison from those figures, it is as well to remember, with emphasis, that there were few occasions when the German destroyers were involved in action with our larger ships, whereas there were several occasions when British destroyers faced up to the enormous gun-fire of the German heavy cruisers and battleships in their efforts to get in an attack.

There were lessons to be learned from the three fights the destroyers had been engaged in—Heligoland, Dogger and Jutland. They were learned and were embodied in designs already in being and appeared in later ships.

To begin with, the weight of gun-fire carried by a destroyer, even the latest ones to appear at Jutland, was woefully light. They carried too small an allowance of torpedoes, most of them had four only, and after one or two brief actions, when their torpedoes were expended, there was little they could do except fight enemy destroyers.

The torpedo was not the unqualified success against battle cruisers and battleships it was expected to be. Against lightly armoured cruisers and destroyers it was effective.

One other point emerged with emphasis. It was an aspect that had not gone unnoticed prior to Jutland. That was the unwieldly size of the flotillas. It took far too long and allowed too many openings for error for one ship, even a light cruiser as a leader, to control sixteen or more destroyers. By the time a flag signal passed down the line the opportunity for some phase of attack had passed. It was argued that seven or eight destroyers under a destroyer leader was a compact size and so it became. In fact, there were already destroyer leaders in being and it merely required the formal adoption to make it fact.

N.B. For the earnest student of naval warfare I would suggest a prolonged visit to the Imperial War Museum in Lambeth Road—only a few hundred yards from Waterloo Station—as a must. In one corner, to which a member of the staff will conduct you, the whole of the Battle of Jutland is laid out. On the wall are admirable graphs showing the sailing of the two fleets—the Grand Fleet from Scapa, Cromarty and the Firth, and the German High Seas Fleet from its bases. Succeeding graphs follow the fortunes of the two fleets through the afternoon, the night actions and the escape of the High Seas Fleet across the Grand Fleet's stern in the early hours of the morning.

The student, too, will see what the destroyers did and will appreciate how narrow was the margin by which the High Seas Fleet escaped.

An even better appreciation of the battle may be gained by the round-by-round detailed log set out on the wall from the time Beatty delayed his turnabout at 2.15 pm and so made contact with the German battle cruisers up to the time that Lieutenant-Commander Roger Alison in *Moresby* fired what were virtually the last shots in the battle to sink the destroyer V4 just before 3 am.

Having assimilated graphs and logs, turn to the glass cases set out nearby. Every destroyer engaged is reproduced in models, named, described and with the name of her commanding officer. All to scale.

Then will be realised the courage of the destroyer men in their frail craft and with their puny armament and limited supply of torpedoes in hurling themselves at ships capable of blowing them out of the water with one shell.

The foundations of the destroyer-man heritage had already been laid. In the Battle of Jutland those foundations were strengthened, for all time.

Incidentally, in my visits to the Imperial War Museum I asked for no special concessions or treatment. Any books I asked for, or photographs, were produced forthwith, as was permission to copy the graphs and to take extracts from the minute-by-minute log. The policy is: 'You ask for it, we'll produce it.'

On one of my visits I was busy taking notes of an early type torpedo and became aware of somebody standing near, apparently equally interested in the weapon of bygone days. That frequently happened and I went on with my notes for a while. Then I looked up to meet the eyes of probably one of the most famous destroyer men of both wars.

It was Earl Mountbatten of Burma. We smiled, then he went on his nostalgic tour and I went on with my notes.

E.B.

8

The battles of Heligoland, Dogger and Jutland were breathless, even audacious, episodes in destroyer history, but elsewhere round the coast destroyers were carrying an ever-increasing burden of patrol, ever on their guard on the east coast against any further raids by German light forces, and against submarines.

They had to guard against the minelayer, nearly always a night-time job, intercept ships at sea and either order them to an examination port or escort them there.

In short, practically any monotonous job calling for a fast ship fell to the destroyers.

Once the Germans had overrun Belgium and had established bases at Zeebrugge and Ostend, they wasted little time in funnelling their submarines from those ports into the Channel and thence into Western Approaches.

There was no need for the submarines, somewhat primitive as were the early types, to range far afield. They knew full well that merchant ships coming to the end of an ocean voyage would have to make a landfall at Ushant, Land's End or the Irish coast, and all the submarine need do was to wait in ambush for an almost certain victim.

Then, too, there were the coastal lanes. Coasting ships bound from the Tyne south-about, ships from the Bristol Channel ports and Liverpool, were streaming along in an almost endless procession.

Victims were easy to find and comparatively easy to sink.

The Germans did not embark on an all-out sink-at-sight policy until the end of 1916 and early 1917. Nevertheless, their submarine warfare became a real threat. Ships were sunk at an alarming rate—were being sunk so extensively that by 1916 the country was in real danger.

At the outbreak of war, and for the first year or two, there was no real form of defence against submarines, or for that matter any real form of attack. The depth-charge, the dreaded wasserbomb, was yet to come, as was any form of underwater detection.

Patrolling destroyers, most of them the older ships of 1904–7 vintage, patrolled ceaselessly at the points where the ominous sinkings were taking place until they received a plaintive wail from a merchant ship that it was being attacked by a submarine. The destroyer would tear off at full speed to arrive in time to pick up survivors from a ship which had been stopped and sunk by a bomb or had been torpedoed.

The destroyer was blind. All it could look for was a wisp of white water as a periscope bobbed up—a task which reduces the proverbial haystack search for a needle to simplicity itself—or optimistically hope to catch the submarine on the surface.

The only weapons the destroyers had were their guns, useless until they had a target, and some primitive stick bombs, a thirty-five-pound charge on a pole for which the destroyer was expected to slam herself alongside the submarine and hurl the bomb at the submarine's hull.

One can scarcely imagine a destroyer captain, coming across a submarine on the surface, closing her closely enough to use that bomb. Long before that eventuality arose the destroyer would have been spitting fire at the sub or would turn to ram.

Various methods were tried in desperation. Explosive charges were towed under water and were fired by electricity, and yet another system was an explosive towed under water and angled out from the destroyer's quarter, rather like a modern Oropesa minesweep.

They achieved few, if any, successes until the depth-charge, with a thumping load of a couple of hundred pounds of explosive, was eventually evolved.

But the problem still remained.

First find your submarine.

There must have been some exasperating moments—and nerve-tingling moments, too—on the scanty bridges of some of those patrolling destroyers.

In response to an urgent SOS in their patrol area they would surge into top speed, race to the place, to find the sea cluttered with wreckage and a pathetic boat-load or two of survivors. Somewhere in the vicinity was a submarine. Maybe even at that moment cautiously peeping at the destroyer and working her into range.

Then would start the feverish guesswork on the bridge. Had the submarine departed, satisfied? Or was she still close to the remains of her victim, waiting for another to turn up?

On the off-chance, the destroyer might race around and would drop a charge or two, hoping to keep the submarine submerged long enough for the survivors to be picked up.

And probably another SOS would come sharply over the ether.

Eventually a hydrophone was evolved, or adapted, and was gradually fitted to destroyers—like everything else, having to take its turn in production. The hydrophone, located on the ship's bottom, was connected to headphones and would pick up the beat of the submarine's propeller.

The combination of hydrophone and depth-charge began to show results.

The hydrophone reduced the groping in complete darkness to a search in a certain murky direction. It could not give a range, unlike the Asdic of the last war, and the bearings were rather rough and ready. By turning the hydrophone to and fro in an arc until the sound picked up was at maximum strength the destroyer had, at least, an approximate line of attack.

Patrol trawlers of the last war on the east coast and in the Channel were fitted with the same type of hydrophones and they were reasonably effective in detecting the high-speed beat of the E-boats.

But with ten times the number of destroyers the task of reducing the sinking of merchant ships would still have been formidable, especially when the Germans finally adopted unrestricted sink-at-sight-without-warning warfare.

It has always been a source of wonder to students of naval warfare why the convoy system was not adopted far sooner than it was.

It was not a new form of protection. Throughout the days of the wooden-walled frigates, they had sailed and protected convoys of merchant ships, driving off attempted raids by French privateers.

Spain had to do it with its treasure-laden ships to save them from Elizabeth's captains.

Yet it was only after three years of war that the convoy system was finally introduced, and having in desperation introduced it, the next step was to provide ships for the protection of the convoys.

Destroyers, of course.

And there were not the destroyers available, at least not without drastically raiding the flotillas with the fleet, reducing the east-coast and Dover patrols so that those who remained were driven to their maximum, one ship having to do the work of three.

The destroyers withdrawn from the patrols and the fleet were also worked almost to destruction.

They shepherded their convoys of merchant ships; cajoled, bullied and sometimes prayed at stragglers to keep closed up; battled with merchant-ship captains, who were frankly terrified at night-time at the proximity of so many ships around them; battled against bad weather, limited visibility and with engines which constantly complained that they were doing their rapidly reducing best.

Finally the convoys were more or less safely delivered by the hard-worked destroyers to a rendezvous point somewhere west of twenty degrees west where an ocean escort of cruisers or armed merchant liners took them over and at the same time either handed over an east-bound convoy to the destroyers or the small ships went off to another meeting place to pick up another convoy.

There were other convoys in operation also. Those bound for the Mediterranean, West African ports and from the far north, where ships with valuable iron ore and timber sailed from Norwegian and Russian ports. The destroyers escorting them had not only the submarines to contend with but there was the constant threat of a swift raid by a German cruiser or two. A German raider could nip out, locate a convoy, hammer it and would be back in base before any of our cruisers could reach the spot.

Such a raid happened to a convoy escorted by two destroyers in the autumn of 1917.

Strongbow and *Mary Rose* were escorting a convoy when two German light cruisers located it. *Strongbow* came under immediate and heavy fire and in a few minutes was a sinking wreck. *Mary Rose*, some way astern with the stragglers, ordered them to scatter, then steamed full speed for the sound of gun-fire. The German cruisers were preparing to slaughter the ships *Strongbow* had been shepherding.

To go in was almost certain destruction, but *Mary Rose*

maintained full speed, opening fire with her three four-inch guns against the weight of the two German cruisers armed with 5.9-inch guns.

In she raced, torpedo tubes at the ready, until the fight was being fought at less than 3,000 yards.

The end was inevitable. *Mary Rose* was hit amidships and her engine room was reduced to a smoking shambles. Her forward guns were out of action, she lay rolling in the sea, just one gun spitting defiance at less than a mile range. *Mary Rose* was buying time for the convoy, by now racing away under clouds of smoke.

Unfortunately, tragically, she could not buy enough time.

The cruisers closed in to less than a mile and deluged her with salvoes.

Then when she disappeared beneath the water after one last shot from the defiant after gun, the cruisers set off in pursuit of the convoy, sinking ten of the ships.

It was not the last time the bleak, cold northern waters were to see British destroyers throwing themselves at a far superior enemy in protection of a convoy of ships.

But it was in the tradition by now firmly established.

There are still pundits who argue that convoying is a mixed blessing, that a group of ships sailing in company is a magnificent target for a resolute enemy who could sink a large number of them, whereas were they sailing independently a lot of them would reach port.

That was one of the arguments used against convoying in 1914–17 and again in the last war when wolf-packs of U-boats ambushed Western Ocean convoys and convoys to Gibraltar and decimated them.

They could take the tragic convoy which *Strongbow* and *Mary Rose* were escorting and could quote it as an instance. But it is a fallacious argument.

The key to it all lies in the fact that in both wars, due to a short-sighted policy, there were never anywhere near enough destroyers to do the multifarious tasks demanded of them.

The fleet and destroyer bases on the east coast and south

coast were almost denuded of destroyers to meet a clamorous demand, mainly from Admiral Sir Lewis Bayly, who was fighting a ruthless, no-quarter battle against an ever-inreasing number of German submarines in his area. His headquarters were at Queenstown, south Ireland, and his anti-submarine forces consisted of a number of drifters armed with three- or six-pounder guns, some armed yachts and later on some of the now famous Queenstown 'Flower' sloops.

Although German submarines were operating in the North Sea, the main weight of their onslaught was falling in Western Approaches, the Irish Sea, Bristol Channel and western end of the English Channel.

The larger submarines were finding it no difficulty to sail round the top of Scotland, outside the Western Isles and down into St George's Channel to reach their happy hunting grounds.

They were fast enough to run away from the drifters, even from the sloops, for that matter, and were armed heavily enough to stay on the surface and outrange the auxiliary ships based at Queenstown and Bantry.

It had to be destroyers.

And to provide them, Harwich, Dover and the fleet flotillas had to be reduced.

Nobody at that time could foresee that never again would a mighty German fleet sail to do battle. At any time the Germans, with the High Seas Fleet virtually intact, were a constant threat, and should the Grand Fleet have to sally forth for the return match there would have to be destroyers with the fleet, and many of them.

Reluctantly, and only after prolonged protests, other commands released their precious destroyers and stretched those which remained to thread-thin proportions. One had to do the work of four.

For a while a complicated game of robbing Peter to placate Paul went on and destroyers circled the British Isles temporarily on loan to some base or other which had a sudden emergency.

The *Mary Rose,* whose gallant end has been described, was a typical example. She had been attached to the Harwich flotillas for a time, moved north, served with the fleet at Scapa, back to Harwich and eventually, in answer to the incessant demand from Queenstown for modern destroyers, she arrived there.

Before leaving once more for northern waters, *Mary Rose* took part in an historic event. She was at sea with another destroyer, *Parthian,* on May 2nd, 1917, when out of the morning haze steamed a flotilla of strange-looking ships. They were long, lean, four-funnelled American destroyers, of which more anon.

Signals of welcome passed between *Mary Rose* and the senior American ship, *Wadsworth.* Shortly afterwards, as the Queenstown base's destroyer strength was augmented by more four-funnelled destroyers flying the Stars and Stripes, *Mary Rose* was one of those released to do convoy work in the North Sea. Her fate, escorting a Scandinavian convoy, we know.

The three other modern destroyers which had arrived to strengthen the Queenstown Command were *Parthian, Peyton* and *Narwal.* The latter, together with *Mary Rose,* had fought in the night action at Jutland when the destroyers strove to block Admiral Scheer's escape astern of the Grand Fleet.

Although comparatively new ships, they were veterans in battle, but valuable as they were they were but a drop of water in the proverbial ocean.

To this point ships were still sailing independently and were being sunk at an appalling rate. Scarcely a day passed when a ship was not attacked and often sunk.

Bayly's mixed bag of ships, sloops, trawlers, yachts, M.L.s, 'Q' ships and the few destroyers he had managed to acquire could do comparatively little. In fact, some of them were either sunk or damaged in combat with U-boats. And in any event they could not be at three or four places at the same time.

A chart of the Queenstown Command, that is right round Ireland, and including the entrance to the Bristol Channel and English Channel, carrying the ominous dots where ships had been sunk in 1916–17, shows them clustered mostly off the traditional landfalls: Fastnet, Land's End, Scillies and at the south end of the Irish Sea.

Fifty destroyers based at Queenstown could have only reduced the number of sinkings, not stopped them.

The answer, of course, was to sail ships in convoy and to augment the escorts with hunting patrols, 'Q' ships, 'P' boats, sloops and destroyers when the convoys reached their landfall.

When at long last that was eventually done the sinkings decreased appreciably, and submarine sinkings increased.

But before that was driven home to a reluctant Admiralty a large number of ships were sunk or damaged, and it is now history that in late 1916–17 the submarine menace was so great, and the rate of sinking of merchant ships had reached such catastrophic proportions, that the nation was virtually on its knees.

The war was nearly lost in the Western Approaches in those few months before the first tentative convoys were sailed and were found to be effective.

But before that happened the U-boats were to collect a formidable harvest, particularly in the Western Approaches.

The Germans had well realised that it was in those waters lay their most fruitful fields. They knew, too, from various factors that there was a woeful shortage of destroyers in the Queenstown Command.

In February 1917 Germany inaugurated her unrestricted submarine campaign. Any ship, regardless of nationality, would be sunk without warning. Britain was to be ringed by submarines and was to be brought to starvation point within six months. How near to success Germany came is now history.

Admiral von Capalle, Secretary of the German Navy, giving evidence at a German Parliamentary Inquiry into Germany's naval failures during the war, gave some illuminating evidence on the submarine warfare from that period on and during the two years or so that he was Secretary.

It appears that Admiral von Holtzendorff, author of the six months' campaign, based his claim on the resounding successes to date of submarine attacks.

Admiral von Capalle said the German Naval Staff regarded the southern entrances to the Irish Sea, the approaches to the English Channel and Bristol Channel and an area to about fifteen degrees west of Fastnet as the decisive U-boat theatres.

It was known to the German Naval Staff that despite an accelerated building programme there was still a shortage of destroyers in the British Navy and the main defence against submarines still rested on auxiliary ships.

The Dover barrage was not an effective deterrent to submarines and there was no effective barrier in the St George's Channel.

So the main weight of the submarine attack was to be concentrated in the areas mentioned. Three patrol areas were designated to cover those waters and for each area it was considered that a minimum of five submarines per patrol would be required, allowing for outward- and homeward-bound sailings. In actual fact, although fifteen was the considered minimum, Admiral Capalle related that the submarine warfare was conducted with not less than twenty-five submarines and occasionally forty boats.

In addition to attacking ships with torpedoes, some of the submarines were equipped as minelayers, which would lay their deadly eggs in a well-known channel before lying in wait for a lone merchant ship.

The German Naval Staff had accepted an estimated loss of three submarines a month.

In actual fact, in the next nine months from February 1917 to the beginning of November 1917 submarine losses were more than double that figure and climbed steadily once the Queenstown forces were augmented by a large number of destroyers.

It is an extraordinary facet of the German character that in war they devise weapons, or a campaign, then launch it while the nation's production is not up to the demands to be made on it. In other words they go off at half-cock.

Their poison-gas attack was made in France without adequate supplies to maintain it.

In the last war they laid mines of a type which defeated us for a while, but again the Germans were not prepared for an all-out onslaught. The magnetic, the acoustic, the magnetic-acoustic and the pressure mines were laid when supplies were sparse and they were unable to maintain the terrific pressure of the first attack.

So it was with the U-boat campaign launched in 1917. Even with losses twice what was estimated, i.e. losing six U-boats a month, the campaign could have been maintained at a high pressure, even increased, if the building programme had been continued.

Instead, Admiral Capalle stated, the U-boat construction immediately prior to the all-out declaration in February 1917 was actually slowed down as the German dockyards were engaged in the then considered urgent and vital task of repairing the damage done to the High Seas Fleet in the Battle of Jutland.

U-boat building had to take second place. At the peak of construction the output was between ten and twelve a month. Therefore around half a month's buildings were being sunk and more than that figure of submarines returned to harbour damaged and requiring extensive repairs.

What was of equal importance was the effect on the morale of the crews.

Admiral Koch at the same inquiry admitted that the losses of submarines were due primarily to the increasing strength of British counter-measures, 'an imperfect estimate of British endurance', fast surface craft equipped with depth-charges, which forced submarines to remain submerged for long periods up to exhaustion point, and the destroyer-escorted convoy system.

9

Within a month of the outbreak of war and the overrunning of Belgium, the Germans were in possession of two valuable bases for their light ships. They had Zeebrugge and Ostend, less than a couple of hours' steaming from the Dover Straits.

The Straits, a bottle-neck between the Goodwin Sands and similar sandbanks off Calais and Dunkirk, provided a short cut for U-boats sailing for the English Channel and Ireland and also provided happy hunting grounds for raiding German destroyers.

Any night and every night there was the possibility of a raid on Ramsgate, Margate, and for that matter on Dover and Folkestone, from which sailed the nightly troopships for Calais and Boulogne.

The Dover naval forces, immortalised as the Dover Patrol, consisted, in the early days at least, of a large number of drifters, armed with three- and six-pounder guns, half a dozen of the 'Tribal' destroyers, armed trawlers for inshore patrols and minesweeping and a few auxiliary yachts.

Across the Straits, from the Goodwins to the Ruytingen Bank, stretched a submarine net held in place by a line of buoys.

It was the primary duty of the drifters to patrol this net to detect, if possible, any submarines attempting to 'jump' the net to sail westward.

Let us establish the point at once that despite the drifter patrols the submarines never found the net defences any serious obstacle. They either waited for a west-going tide at night and, keeping close inshore on the French side, got through safely into the Channel, or wriggled through the net, tearing it with a serrated cutter fitted to their bows.

It was not until a mine barrage was laid that the Dover Straits were virtually closed to submarines.

What was of greater menace at the time was the almost

perpetual threat of a raid by a flotilla of German destroyers from Zeebrugge.

There had been some half-hearted attempts at demolition of that port when the Germans overran Belgium, but it was not long before it was established as a valuable springboard from which to launch raids.

Dunkirk was our nearest base to German-controlled Belgium and for naval purposes it was part of the Dover Command. The destroyers, the old 'Tribals', had all the monotony of patrols, even into enemy waters, occasionally breaking the common round by a few night bombardments of German positions close to the Belgian shore.

A few long-range shots were exchanged with probing German patrols, but nothing of any great account happened throughout the winter of 1915–16 and their main job was the patrols, intercepting shipping and diverting it to the Downs for examination, bolstering the drifter patrols along the net barrage and providing a nightly escort for the troopships sailing from Folkestone to Calais and Boulogne.

It was confidently expected that sooner or later the Germans would send a raiding force west, either to bombard our ports or to attack the transports, or both.

It was felt that against a possible raid in strength the old destroyers of the Dover Command would be at a decided disadvantage. They were strengthened by a couple of divisions of destroyers from Harwich, including the 'L' class *Laforey*, *Liberty*, *Lucifer* and *Laurel*, some of which had covered themselves with glory at Jutland and Heligoland.

Even with the addition of eight destroyers the Dover Patrol was by no means strong enough numerically to face a resolute raid. Fortunately, the first raid was not thrust home with any degree of resolution, although in weight of numbers the advantage lay with the Germans, as did the element of surprise.

Towards the end of October 1916 the Germans sailed more than twenty destroyers marauding into the Straits. They sailed in two forces, one to attack the patrols guarding the nets and the other to engage any of our destroyer patrols encountered. Such opposition as they expected to meet, old destroyers, were to be brushed aside, then the transports, heavily laden with troops, were to be hammered.

A real old-timer, the *Flirt*, ran into a line of German destroyers racing along without lights, but assumed that they were ships from Harwich. A net-patrolling drifter was sunk, and *Flirt*, turning to pick up survivors, again saw the destroyers and again assumed they were friendly. For her pains she was demolished by the German destroyers, all of which concentrated their fire on the sitting duck.

Another patrol on the net gave the alarm and the 'Tribals', at immediate notice for steam in Dover, slipped and sailed in two groups.

Nubian, heading the first trio, ran slap-bang into six destroyers, challenged and for her pains was shot at by them all at a range of less than 100 yards. Torpedoes were fired by the Germans but they missed. *Nubian*, alone, as *Cossack* and *Amazon* were somewhere astern in the darkness, turned to attack, and this time a torpedo struck home, blowing off her forecastle for one-third of her length. The German destroyers, partly because the element of surprise was gone, and partly because they did not know what opposition they would meet, left *Nubian* to her fate and raced on towards the transport lanes.

They bumped into *Amazon*, who also challenged, and she, too, was smitten by a short but concentrated fire and received damage in her boiler room.

This division of German destroyers decided that discretion was the better part of valour and turned about for home. For one or two of them to be crippled and unable to steam, and therefore perhaps discovered at daylight still in the Dover Straits, would mean being a sitting target for the incensed British patrols.

The other division, which had been busily sinking drifters along the net, turned for home also, to find *Viking* astride their path.

Viking, rightly enough as there were 'L' class destroyers in the area, challenged, and she and *Mohawk* were hit but were not badly damaged.

Regrettably, the Germans, all twenty-odd of them, escaped without a scratch. Their bag for the night, instead of a trail of sinking transports, was one old destroyer, the *Flirt*, *Nubian* seriously damaged and three more destroyers with scars.

Nubian, after some misadventures, including going ashore when bad weather parted her from the tugs, finally reached Dover. A little while later another 'Tribal', the *Zulu*, was mined and a large part of her stern was blown off.

In a spirit of economy the forepart of *Zulu* was married to the after part of *Nubian* and some humorist decided that a suitable name for the result of the marriage would be *Zubian*. Under that name she did a lot of sterling service under the White Ensign.

The Germans continued small-scale raids, occasionally sinking a drifter or two, then retreating at full speed into the darkness before a British destroyer patrol could get close enough to them to reply. Sometimes they varied the raids by throwing a few shells at Margate or Ramsgate.

The value of these raids, in terms of reward, were minute, and sooner or later one of these raiding parties would be bound to run into a destroyer force of ours and would have to pay for their temerity.

Early in 1917 eight German destroyers bombarded Broadstairs while another half a dozen lay off to cover them.

The lone British destroyer *Laverock* ran into them and escaped a torpedo fired at her, and when she turned to bring them to action the half-dozen German destroyers turned tail and raced off into the darkness. Understandable. They had no means of telling whether the British destroyer was alone or was one of a division.

Less than two weeks later, in yet another raid, in which Ramsgate was bombarded, *Paragon* was torpedoed by a destroyer covering the bombarding ships, and *Llewellyn* and *Laforey*, picking up survivors, were attacked by torpedo, and

Llewellyn was hit, not badly enough to sink her.

Despite impassioned appeals from other commands for destroyers, mainly from the Queenstown Command, where the submarine menace was assuming frightening proportions, some of the latest class of destroyers were sent to Dover.

It was felt that while the raids by twelve or fifteen or even twenty destroyers in which a drifter or two would be sunk, or a few shells hurled into sleeping towns, did not amount to a row of beans, sooner or later a determined raid in force would hit the nightly troopships.

Apart from the intrinsic loss, the spectacle of six or eight heavily laden troopships sinking in the Dover Straits, with perhaps diversionary raids on Dover, Calais and Ramsgate as 'noises off', would have a profound morale effect.

So the Dover Patrol was strengthened and among the ships sent there were *Broke*, repaired and now full of aggression after her part in the Jutland battle, and *Swift*, that generation-too-soon destroyer which had been built by Fisher. Commanding *Swift* was Commander A. M. Peck, and in command of *Broke* was Commander E. R. G. Evans, already famous for his part in Captain Scott's last and tragic Antarctic expedition.

The night of April 20th, 1917, was a moonless, dark night, heavy clouds overhead. Just the night for a raid.

By one of those odd coincidences that happen so frequently in naval life the midshipman mentioned later in this story of *Broke*'s and *Swift*'s fight, returned to Dover in 1940 as lieutenant-in-command of the minesweeping/patrol trawler *Sarpedon*, and I was in command of a ship in his group. On more than one night, when we were at immediate notice—which was nearly every night when we were not at sea—we heard the story of the fight at first hand sitting in *Sarpedon*'s tiny wardroom.

The normal drifter and destroyer patrols were sent out and *Swift* and *Broke* were sent to sea with a more or less roving commission to steam in those waters, which from previous experience it was felt that if there was to be a raid that would be the area.

Swift and *Broke* slipped through the water a couple of cables apart when they saw the gun-flashes off Calais and Dover. The two destroyers were to seaward of the Goodwins and to the east of Dover, therefore between the raiding destroyers and home.

Swift and *Broke* raced to intercept and ran into six destroyers racing eastwards at full speed with no lights. Powerful as they were, *Swift* and *Broke* stood a more than three-to-one chance of a severe mauling if they joined issue in a normal fight.

Peck, on *Swift*, had different ideas.

The German destroyers opened fire immediately without hitting, and *Swift* turned, fired her torpedo, hit a German destroyer and tried to ram. The blinding flash of gun-fire upset Commander Peck's direction and he went right through the line without ramming. But as he did so the destroyer he had fired a torpedo at shook to a tremendous explosion.

Commander Evans, on *Broke*, racing along on *Swift*'s port quarter, sliced into the last in the German line at nearly thirty knots, ramming her amidships. He kept his engines going at full speed and his midshipman manned the forecastle with a party of seamen armed with cutlasses, rifles and bayonets to prevent any attempt at boarding. The midshipman was of the opinion at the time, and was still firmly convinced twenty-five years later, that the Germans trying to clamber aboard *Broke* were bent more on saving their lives than any attempt to board her as an aggressive force.

A vignette he liked to relate was of an unofficial party of anti-boarders armed with iron bars and butchers' cleavers. One brawny seaman saw a German petty officer gaining a knee-and-hand hold on *Broke*, shifted his cutlass to the other hand, hauled off and dealt the German a devastating punch right between the eyes which knocked him clean off *Broke*'s forecastle down on to the deck of the stricken destroyer.

Broke, still boring into the German destroyer, forced her to lie over until her decks were flooded. It was like an enraged bull finally catching a matador. Her guns, depressed as far as they would go, slammed into the German destroyer, the flash being close enough to burn her paintwork. *Broke*, too, was on fire, illuminating her for the other German destroyers which had turned and were pouring shells into *Broke* and the destroyer she was fast into with impartiality.

Swift, in the meantime, had turned and once more attacked the surviving four German destroyers and drove them off.

Evans's victim finally broke in two, the halves sinking on either side of *Broke*. With her bow crumpled, a fire still raging, *Broke* turned to join the chase after *Swift*, who was still shooting at the fleeing German destroyers. But neither *Broke* nor *Swift*, both badly damaged, could raise enough speed and the Germans escaped.

Limping back to Dover, the two destroyers came across the destroyer *Swift* had torpedoed. She was sinking and Evans skilfully edged *Broke* up to her. When he was little more than 100 yards from her the German opened fire and hit *Broke* in the bridge.

Broke's forward gun replied and a torpedo set the German on fire. The savage mauling she had received when ramming and from the gun-fire of the German destroyers proved too much for *Broke*'s sadly abused engines. They stopped and *Broke* drifted down almost on to the burning German destroyer and for a time was in danger of hitting her. There was, also, the possibility that the German's magazine would explode and had it done so that would have been the end of *Broke*.

Eventually the engine-room staff managed to get some movement and *Broke* drew away to safety as the German finally sank.

Swift limped in under her own steam and *Broke* was towed in by another destroyer until tugs took her over for the final entry.

It was a sharp lesson. A raid on a coastal town in which a few shells were tossed indiscriminately into the sleeping

Torpedo boat No. 2, built 1882. Somebody loved her!

The Entire troupe. Torpedo boat No. 43, 1888
Bigger and better.

The shape of things to come. Torpedo boat No. 5, 1888.

Fame. Roger Keyes' China Station command.

Destroyer *Bat*. With this ship Keyes 'sank' the Home Fleet

Torpedo-boat destroyer *Albatross* experiments with smoke.

Cold comfort; no bridge. Torpedo-boat destroyer *Ferret*, 1893.

Fervent, 1895. Go-as-you-please design.

Long, low, lean and mean. Whaleback-bowed *Banshee*, 1896.

One of the last of the torpedo boats, 1892—with a real bridge!

Swift, Admiral Fisher's experiment, victor in Dover Straits night fight . .

. . . with Flotilla Leader *Broke*.

USS *Wadsworth*

USS *Conyngham* on trials, December, 1915

streets and the sinking of a few drifters by six or eight destroyers, with little or no damage in return, was vastly different to the loss of two destroyers and two or three severely handled.

Apart from a few nightly sallies to bombard shore positions east of Dunkirk, the Germans left the Dover Straits severely alone. The word had gone round that the command now numbered some of the latest and best of our destroyers.

It was almost a year before our destroyers came to grips with a German force in those waters.

The destroyer leader *Botha*, *Morris* and three French craft were off Dunkirk when they sighted the low outlines of enemy ships. *Botha* fired two torpedoes, then turned in to ram. At nearly thirty knots she cut clean through a German torpedo boat, swung round, leaving the two parts of the German boat to sink, with the intention of ramming another. She missed but opened fire at such close range that the German torpedo boat was virtually wrecked.

Unfortunately, one of the French boats following *Morris*, seeing a destroyer tearing *towards* her, fired a torpedo and hit *Botha* amidships, wrecking her engine room.

Dawn saw *Botha* lying low in the water and the smouldering remains of the torpedo boat *Botha* had smitten with gunfire.

A couple of salvoes from *Morris* finished her off, then came the dismal task of towing *Botha* to Dunkirk.

From then onwards, to the end of the war, for the destroyers of the Dover Patrol it was the monotony of patrol, convoying ships into and out of the Dover Straits.

It has always been felt that with the number of destroyers they had available the Germans could have exploited them a great deal more than they did, especially in the earlier days when the opposition was a few old torpedo boats and some small ten-year-old 'Tribals'.

By sending a mixed bag of their 'A' class torpedo boats and some of their heavier 'G' class destroyers marauding as far west as Folkestone, risking the loss of two or three ships to play havoc with the nightly sailings of transports laden with troops, they would have been bound to do at least two things. They would have caused Harwich and possibly Portsmouth to have weakened their destroyer forces to strengthen Dover, besides sinking a few transports and possibly catching a few merchant ships at anchor in the Downs.

Two raids a month would have caused considerable concern.

Instead, on one raid they sent twenty-plus destroyers into the Straits, lobbed a few shells ashore, sank a few drifters and returned home.

One is intrigued to visualise what might have happened had the positions been reversed. With men like Admiral Bacon, Commodore Keyes and Tyrwhitt in command there would have been more raids and more actions by those young men in command, exemplifying that destroyer dash and spirit which showed itself twenty-five years later in Norway, at Dunkirk, in the Mediterranean and on the Russian convoys. 'Fight, and count the odds later.'

10

From the late spring of 1915 Queenstown Command, otherwise Western Approaches, had become probably the most vital command in the war.

While the Germans were still infesting the North Sea and the eastern part of the English Channel with their smaller UC submarines, their larger U-boats, with an endurance of nearly 5,000 miles, were sailing round the north of Scotland to concentrate on those main entrances to our large ports, viz. English Channel, Bristol Channel, Irish Sea and farther west.

The ever-climbing list of ships sunk assumed desperate proportions even before the Germans embarked on their sink-at-sight, all-out submarine warfare.

The command had been given to Admiral Sir Lewis Bayly, KCB, KCMG, CVO, and if ever a man was tailor-made by his experience for such a command it was Admiral Bayly.

He had been Commodore of Destroyers around the time that Admiral Fisher was making his imperative demands for more and larger destroyers. In fact, it had been claimed for him that he was 'the father of destroyer tactics and organisation'. He knew the worth of the little ships, ill-equipped as they were to deal with submarines.

But he had no destroyers under his command.

In fact, it was at the time he took over command that the first of the famous Queenstown sloops arrived at the base. Nearly a year was to pass before he finally succeeded in obtaining a few destroyers which were filched from other bases. With them he had to be content to bolster up his auxiliary forces of drifters, trawlers and yachts plus the dozen 'Flower' class sloops.

But on the other side of the Atlantic events were moving swiftly for the entry of America into the war.

Admiral S. W. Sims, President of the United States Naval War College, sailed on the American liner *New York*, under an assumed name, for England—and had an alarming entry into the war.

A German submarine had mined the approaches to the Mersey and on April 9th, 1917, *New York* struck one of those mines when near the Bar Light vessel, and Admiral Sims, with other passengers, had to be transferred to a rescuing ship.

A 'Mr S. W. Davidson' and a 'Mr J. V. Richardson', two American business men, were quietly announced at the Admiralty, and Mr Davidson, otherwise Admiral Sims, and his aide, Commander Babcock, were soon discussing the problems of naval warfare, particularly as applied to the submarine threat, with Admiral Jellicoe.

Jellicoe put the case bluntly. At the present rate of sinking, even with our defensive forces going at full stretch, November would see us at the limit of our endurance. Defeat would be inevitable.

It did not take these two, Admiral Sims and the First Sea

Lord, Admiral Jellicoe, long to decide that the best weapon with which to fight submarines was the destroyer.

Admiral Sims sent off a coded message to the U.S. Naval Department to dispatch all available destroyers to Queenstown.

In anticipation of this signal, destroyers in America were being quietly brought to the 'ready'. Captain J. K. Taussig, commanding *Wadsworth*, collected five more of his flotilla, *Conyngham*, *Porter*, *McDougal*, *Davis* and *Wainwright*, bunkered and stored up at Boston 'for distant service' and sailed still under secret orders; until Captain Taussig opened his orders when he had been at sea for twenty-four hours, off Cape Cod.

Captain Taussig's orders were:

'The British Admiralty have requested the co-operation of a division of American destroyers in the protection of commerce near the coasts of Great Britain and France. Your mission is to assist naval operations of Entente Powers in every way possible. Proceed to Queenstown, Ireland. Report to Senior British Naval Officer present, and thereafter co-operate fully with the British Navy. . . .'

As already related, the six American destroyers made contact with the British destroyer *Mary Rose* on May 2nd, 1917, providing scope for considerable curiosity on both sides.

The crew of the *Mary Rose* saw slim, lean-flanked, four-funnelled ships with tall, raking masts, shorter foredecks than were characteristic of British destroyers, in outline looking like smaller editions of some of our light cruisers.

In turn, the Americans, scrutinising their hosts, saw a squat ship, already a veteran of several fights, funnels shorter and not grouped so closely together.

In one respect, however, they were the same. They were manned by men and officers of the destroyer breed.

The *Wadsworth* and her flotilla were the first to arrive, were given a few days in harbour, during which they housed their tall masts, then were sent out immediately to war.

Wadsworth and *Conyngham* were immensely pleased,

indeed honoured, when they found that the British captain who joined them to show them the ropes in this introductory period was the famous Captain Evans of the *Broke*, whose attack on the six German destroyers in the Dover Straits had made stimulating reading for them not long before they had sailed.

The American papers had carried extensively the story of *Swift*'s and *Broke*'s fight, and now here in the flesh was one of the two men who had tackled the German destroyers, to sail with them while his redoubtable ship was being repaired.

What made more sombre reading for them was the tale of ships sunk by submarines in the three months prior to their arrival.

In February, 86 ships had been sunk, in March, 103 and in April, 155.

Although May was but a few days old, the sinkings were already well into double figures and were increasing daily. And a substantial number were being sunk in the waters they were to patrol and search.

Although the American destroyers were to become an integral part of Admiral Bayly's Queenstown force, their first flotillas were followed shortly afterwards by a mother ship, the USN *Melville*, and a month later by the USN *Dixie*. They were equipped with everything and anything which appertained to destroyers and it is a tribute to their staffs that despite hard weather, collisions and other damage they kept the final number of destroyers, thirty-five, well up to scratch.

Following Captain Taussig's flotilla there came succeeding flotillas, many of them of *Wadsworth*'s type, 1,100 tons, 315 feet long, with a speed of thirty knots, and others of smaller tonnage, 750 tons, popularly known among the American ratings as 'flivvers', but all with a punch. They were equipped with twenty-four depth-charges in rails astern, and two throwers or 'Y' guns for throwing depth-charges out on either quarter.

They were armed with two three-inch or four-inch guns,

one forward, one aft, a pom-pom and four torpedo tubes.

They were incredibly lively boats and how they could roll! British ratings were to find out how much and how quickly they could roll twenty-five years onwards when some of those destroyers returned once more to help us in our hour of need.

Following *Wadsworth*'s flotilla in May succeeding flotillas of six arrived every ten or twelve days until there were between thirty and forty of them attached to the Queenstown Command which had by now assumed considerable proportions. In addition to the American destroyers there were nine sloops for escort work, seven for minesweeping (which could go on patrol at the drop of Bayly's hat), nine 'Q' ships, or mystery ships as they were called, and a number of trawlers, drifters and M.L.s. The smaller ships latterly worked from Berehaven, on the south-west toe of Ireland, and from Larne on the north-east corner.

Coincidental with the arrival of the valuable American destroyers, the first convoys were started, and *Wadsworth* and her sisters, in addition to undertaking long patrols, did their full share of meeting convoys at a rendezvous around twenty degrees west and escorting them almost to the doorsteps of their home ports.

It fell to six of the Queenstown American destroyers to provide the escort for the first six transports laden with American troops to arrive in France.

Cushing, *Cassin*, *O'Brien*, *Jacob Jones*, *Ericsson* and *Conyngham* were sailed from Queenstown around the morning of June 20th for a rendezvous with the convoy of fast transports which were being escorted across the Atlantic by the American destroyers *Wilkes* and *Fanning*.

Convoy and additional escort met on the dot and the six destroyers ranged themselves around the troop-packed ships after an exchange of signals between Commander Hanrahan in command of *Cushing* and *Fanning*, the senior ship of the escort.

The crews of *Wilkes* and *Fanning* regarded the joining six with some degree of awe. They had been in the submarine zone for nearly two months and although they had not as yet had any hot action, they had patrolled, had rescued torpedoed crews and had forced submarines to submerge. They had seen war.

The transports were safely delivered to St Nazaire, then the eight destroyers returned to Queenstown, where later *Fanning* was to have her crowded hour of glory. One of the same type of U.S. destroyers, *Campbeltown*, was to take her part—a sad but glorious part—in the raid on St Nazaire in March 1942 when, her bow packed with explosives, she was rammed against the lock gates.

That first convoy of American troopships was a tentative test of the value of convoys as opposed to sailing ships independently. It proved its value. Nothing deterred a submarine commander from thrusting his attack home more than half a dozen exuberant destroyers dashing around dropping depth-charges at the first suggestion of a periscope.

Admiral Sims, at his first meeting with First Sea Lord Admiral Jellicoe, had stressed and emphasised his views in succeeding meetings that convoys were the part-answer to the submarine menace, and a considerable part at that.

Subsequent convoys were escorted safely across the Atlantic with an escort of destroyers bound ultimately for Queenstown, and, as we have seen, the escort was strengthened when the transports were three or four days out from France.

No U.S. troopships were lost to submarines although it was known that submarines were operating at strength in the waters through which they had to sail at the end of their trip.

In July 1917 Admiral Sims, in a report to Washington, was optimistic enough to claim that the convoy system as operating would contribute largely to the defeat of the submarine campaign.

There was a risk, and a calculated risk, that a German raiding cruiser or two might break out and would descend on the lightly escorted troopships, or even an ocean-going U-boat might decide to explore the field farther west and even as far as the American coast.

The risk was taken and the fast convoys were never raided.

The American passion for formulas showed itself here. The experiences of the destroyers already working from Queenstown, plus any detail they could extract from Captain Evans and other British destroyer officers who worked with them, were analysed and subsequent escorts sailed equipped mentally and mechanically ready to meet any submarine attacks.

They were equipped with hydrophones and kept a constant watch on the U-boat wave-lengths, and from the chatter of the submarines at night-time obtained cross-bearings on them.

After that anything bigger than a floating box was shot at enthusiastically.

Within three months of the arrival of the first American destroyers, and the close herding of convoys of merchant ships by British and American destroyers, the first cracks in the submarine menace began to show.

Attacking a lone merchant ship or two was a vastly different proposition to attacking an orderly convoy with speeding, zig-zagging destroyers skirting it.

In the North Sea British destroyers were taking their toll of the coastal submarines. The inefficient net barrage at Dover had been replaced by a minefield on which some submarines had been destroyed trying to penetrate west while submerged and any submarine foolhardy enough to attempt a surface trip found that destroyers were waiting and eager.

By the end of September 1917 the totals of sinkings had shrunk to heartening proportions. Instead of the defeat which had stared us in the face six months back, the convoy system and the number of destroyers available to escort the convoys ensured that most of the ships were able to leave and arrive at their ports in comparative safety.

It was almost inevitable that sooner or later the American destroyers would have a casualty, apart from the collisions which were happening, due partly to their extremely wide turning circle.

The first victim was *Cassin*, one of the first four-funnel destroyers to arrive at Queenstown.

She sailed on patrol on October 15th, 1917, and when off Mine Head sighted a submarine on the surface about 6,000 yards away.

Cassin started a search and an hour later a torpedo slammed into her stern and blew away about thirty feet of it.

Cassin could steam, but only slowly, and her wound was aggravated by depth-charges blown off her stern chutes exploding far too closely. Ironically enough, the depth-charges kept the U-boat down for more than an hour until she cautiously surfaced about 4,000 yards away and was promptly shot at by *Cassin*.

Another U.S. destroyer, *Porter*, arrived, followed by two of those maids of all work, sloops, which in worsening weather passed a succession of tows and finally got *Cassin* into Queenstown.

Scarcely a month was to pass before the Queenstown/U.S. destroyers were to get their revenge.

On November 17th *Fanning*, *Nicholson*, three more American destroyers and the sloop *Zinnia* were escorting a convoy which had formed up at Queenstown to sail westward.

Fanning and the other ships had been warned that patrolling trawlers had sighted and had attacked a submarine off Daunt Rock, one of the portals to Queenstown, two hours before the convoy was due to sail, and had sighted it again, or another, as the convoy was emerging.

The lumbering merchant ships came out and were rapidly marshalled into columns by the destroyers which circled them.

An alert look-out on *Fanning* sighted a periscope briefly lifted ahead of the convoy about 500 yards away.

Fanning and *Nicholson* raced towards it and *Fanning* dropped a pattern of depth-charges more as a swift counter-attack with the intention of keeping the submarine down until they could range themselves for a deliberate attack.

To *Fanning*'s joy the submarine surfaced not more than 400 yards away, stern cocked up steeply right ahead of the racing *Fanning*. *Nicholson* got in three quick shots and as she raced past the porpoising submarine she, too, dropped some depth-charges almost alongside it.

Fanning turned helm hard over, as if to ram, firing rapidly as she did so, then came to a stop alongside the submarine, which was now on a level keel but awash, with her crew tumbling up on deck as fast as they could.

The submarine was U-58, capable of sixteen knots on the surface and nine knots submerged. She was armed with one four-inch gun, one twenty-two-pounder gun and ten torpedoes.

U-58 was a veteran of the attack on the Queenstown area with several victims to her credit. She had sailed from Wilhelmshaven, was one of the few to get through the Dover barrage before it was finally tightened up by steaming on the surface close to the French coast at night. Three days later she was off Queenstown to fall victim to *Fanning* and *Nicholson*.

Fanning tried to take her in tow but the Germans before surrendering had set off a scuttling charge.

It was the first American destroyer's official victim with something to show for their efforts: thirty-nine prisoners.

With autumn drawing to a close and winter savagely beating at the Western Approaches the first tragic total loss was suffered by the Queenstown Americans at the hands of a U-boat.

The destroyer *Jacob Jones*, returning from handing over a convoy at the western end of the English Channel, was torpedoed in the engine room and began to sink stern first. Her depth-charges started exploding, adding to the damage, and she went down in less than ten minutes with a loss of sixty men.

The survivors were picked up by the sloop *Carmelia*.

The submarine which sank *Jacob Jones* was U-53, sister

ship to *Fanning*'s victim, and was the U-boat which had crossed the Atlantic some months previously and arrogantly arrived at Newport, Rhode Island.

In succeeding months the American destroyers were to appreciate that U-boats were not the only enemy they had to face in Western Approaches.

During December, when the weather was the worst even old hands could remember off the south coast of Ireland, *Nicholson*, *Ammen*, *Duncan*, *Cummings*, *Trippe* and *O'Brien* all suffered damage from foul weather, *Ammen* and *Cummings* losing funnels and most of their boats.

Melville and *Dixie* were worked to the full extent to keep the destroyers in commission and it is a tribute to their fine work that in the main the destroyer force at Queenstown was nearly always up to full strength.

The Germans prepared for and launched a new submarine campaign in February 1918, but it was a campaign of desperation, the last throw of a gambler realising that his all was down on the board and the cards were falling dead against him.

So far as Western Approaches were concerned, the submarine menace had been met and defeated by the unquenchable spirit of the destroyers, sloops and auxiliary ships in the command.

Because of the thirty-six destroyers attached to that command the burden was lifted from British destroyers which were able to concentrate in the English Channel, North Sea and even in the Mediterranean.

And they were able to concentrate because belatedly the convoy system was finally adopted.

When the war ended Admiral Bayly's command came to an end. From it was born a Queenstown Association of Anglo-American officers which used to meet yearly.

Admiral Bayly, who had driven the men of both nations to the limit of their endurance, and beyond, was entertained to dinner in New York by the members of that association and was presented with a silver rose bowl and a silver model of a four-'stacker' American destroyer. Every commanding officer's signature was engraved on it.

It was named USS *Pulltogether*.

Somewhere there is a moral in that.

II

When the end of hostilities came in November 1918, the destroyer strength of the Navy stood at 350. At the head of the procession, the most modern destroyers in the world in service were the 'V's' and 'W's', their design based on wide and profound experience in the battles of Heligoland, Dogger and Jutland.

They were 1,300 tons, were armed with four 4.7-inch guns, six twenty-one-inch torpedo tubes, with a designed speed of more than thirty-four knots. Until a modest programme of building was embarked upon in 1925 there was nothing bigger or better at sea.

Together with their older and war-worn sisters, the 'M's' and 'L's', they did sterling work escorting and submarine hunting. It is significant that once the convoy programme was finally adopted in 1917, convoys lavishly escorted by destroyers, the sinkings shrank to comparatively small proportions.

Nearly 17,000 merchant ships were convoyed through the submarine areas with a loss of little more than 100 ships sunk in convoy. And a lot of them were the inevitable stragglers.

Very few submarines took the risk of running the minefield-destroyer patrol at Dover and those who did, paid for their temerity. And there were no more destroyer raids from Zeebrugge.

The submarines ranged far and wide, after making the long trip around Fair Isle, outside the Hebrides and into the Atlantic or the western English Channel or even as far down as the Azores or off Gibraltar.

Towards the end of hostilities the Germans had, in submarine strength, around ninety submarines of various classes. There were fourteen based at Brunsbuttel, eighteen at Heligoland, fifteen practically completed at Wilhelmshaven, twelve at Emden, ten of the ocean-going cruiser submarines at Kiel and twenty of the smaller coastal type at Zeebrugge.

With rather more than a third of them constantly at sea the submarine campaign was by no means a spent force and its limited success was due almost entirely to the counter-campaign of the destroyers.

Ironically, although they had been recognised and accepted as the best weapon against submarines, that was not the job for which they were evolved.

We have seen how the introduction of Whitehead's torpedo in 1870 had led to first the torpedo-carrying boat, then a torpedo-boat catcher, onwards to the torpedo-boat destroyer, and finally the destroyer.

They had proved themselves in fleet actions at Heligoland, Dogger and Jutland and, although there were never enough of them despite an accelerated building programme later in the war, they accepted the burden of anti-submarine warfare when for a long time they were not equipped for it.

They had known the heat and fire of action, they had suffered the soul-scarring frustration of fighting against an enemy who at the time held all the cards, or at least most of them; they had known the monotony of patrol in every sort of weather.

And from it all they had started an edifice of destroyer tradition which will never die so long as men sail the seas.

They had produced a breed of dedicated men who are men apart. Once a destroyer man, always a destroyer man at heart, even if the tide of events eventually places, as it has done in many instances, thick gold rings on the sleeves and command of squadrons of big ships.

Many a lonely admiral, austere, remote, has allowed a nostalgic gleam to brighten his eye when he has watched from his flag-ship the long, lean, lethal destroyers racing alongside him.

Some of the destroyer captains in the 1914–18 War were in high command when 1939 arrived, and their voices were raised, as they had been raised in the years past.

'More destroyers.' But, in the main, voices crying in the wilderness and refusing to be comforted by anything but 'more destroyers'.

In the passing years building, of course, had to be restricted. But destroyers were built. That fascinating annual volume, *Jane's Fighting Ships*, shows the modest but progressive path the building took.

Following the 'V's' and 'W's', which were really late 1914–18 War destroyers, came the 'A's': *Active, Amazon, Ambuscade, Acasta, Achates, Acheron, Antelope, Anthony, Ardent Arrow*. Remember those names. In the years ahead they were to add more lustre to destroyer history.

Their armament was the same as the 'V's' and 'W's', with an additional two torpedo tubes and a designed speed of thirty-seven knots.

Following them came the 'Admiral' class of destroyer: *Codrington, Exmouth, Duncan, Grenville, Hardy, Inglefield, Keith, Kempenfelt, Faulknor* and *Keppel*. In them, 200 tons larger than their predecessors, were four 4.7-inch guns and eight tubes.

From 1928 to 1929 about eight destroyers a year were added to the fleet: the 'Beagles'; the 'D' class: *Defender, Diamond, Decoy, Daring, Dainty, Delight, Diana, Duchess*. Those names have been handed on to destroyers of today, ships almost twice the size of the 'D's' built in 1931.

The years rolled on with the sky ever darkening as the war clouds rolled ominously across it. In half-dozens, in eights, fours and fives, more destroyers came out of the famous yards to be added to their sisters some of which were past the first flush of youth, but were still destroyers. The demand, too, grew. The Mediterranean Command, the Far East, the cry was for more destroyers.

By 1934, and in early 1935, only those who were wilfully blind to current events failed to recognise that war within the next few years was inevitable.

The Germans, with their curious valuation of treaties and promises, broke them willy-nilly to suit themselves.

Finally a vast, a frightening, rearmament programme for the next three years, plus supplementary Estimates, got under way to try to catch up with the years the political locusts had eaten.

Most of the destroyers built from 1927 to 1928 were of the same type, with comparatively minor differences. They were round about 1,400 tons, armed with four 4.7-inch guns and eight tubes in two quadruple mountings. Speed was thirty-five knots at their best.

But the 1936 Estimates called for destroyers which were markedly different. They called for sixteen destroyers to be of 1,900 tons, to be armed with four twin 4.7-inch turrets, but carrying only four torpedo tubes.

Destroyers were beginning to fringe on the light-cruiser class.

The names given to the latest-class destroyers were names which had already gained lustre in destroyer annals. The names were carried on from the little 'Tribals' built in 1904–7 and which had literally driven themselves to destruction. So *Ashanti*, *Bedouin*, *Cossack*, *Eskimo*, *Mashona*, *Maori*, *Mohawk*, *Nubian*, *Matabele*, *Punjabi*, *Tartar* and *Somali* were launched. The last of them to roll off the stocks commissioned just in time to go into war service, as did the first of the 'Javelin' class.

One of the young destroyer men of the 1914–18 War had forged ahead and a year before war broke out he hammered away at stressing the importance of destroyers for escort work. He remembered the invaluable work done by even the aged destroyers of his younger years; he remembered how half a dozen of them could escort a convoy of forty ships and could drive off—even sink—some of the submarines which attempted to attack the convoy.

That was Admiral Sir Andrew Cunningham, Chief of Staff to Admiral Sir Roger Backhouse, First Sea Lord.

Through his chief he badgered, bullied, cajoled, even begged, for a programme which would run parallel to production of the powerful fleet destroyers like the 'Tribals' and 'Javelins', and 'Kellys'. He wanted a smaller class of destroyer, something on the lines of the 'V's' and 'W's' of 1918, a destroyer of around 1,000 tons, armed mainly with depth-charges, three or four 4.7-inch guns and two pairs of torpedo tubes.

He wanted a lot of them, as many as could be built in the ever-increasing rearmament programme. But, try as hard as he might, he could not get the vocal politicians sitting in the House of Commons to agree to an expansion of the destroyer-building programme to include these smaller ships.

The bitter lesson was to come in little more than a year when valuable convoys had to sail the Atlantic with possibly one destroyer, a couple of corvettes and deep-sea trawlers armed with one four-inch gun and depth-charges.

And the inevitable losses, in the middle days of the war, provoked those same vocal gentlemen into acid criticism of the Navy—which was far too busy to reply, as it might have done, saying: 'We told you so.'

A programme of building of such smaller ships was started, they were described in the Estimates as fast escort ships. They were the 'Hunt' class destroyers, because they were small destroyers, named after famous hunts.

They were less than 1,000 tons, their speed was around twenty-five knots and they mounted two twin turrets mostly of four-inch guns.

And there were not anywhere near enough of them.

By an odd quirk, the 'Hunt' class destroyers, with some of the old faithful 'V's' and 'W's', completed the circle, living up to the name they had inherited as torpedo-boat destroyers. They were armed with a light gun right up in the eyes of the ship and used it with deadly effect against the German motor-torpedo boats—the E-boats which raided convoys in the North Sea and in the Channel.

Their actions were often fought at such close quarters that it was impossible to get the larger guns to bear. But many an E-boat, slicing across the bows of a 'Hunt' class destroyer, found itself threaded at the end of a stream of pom-pom shells.

The old business of robbing Peter to meet Paul's demands once again asserted itself. Fleet destroyers had to be detached for convoy duties, submarine hunts and patrols off enemy-held coastlines, and on occasions the 'Hunts', whose top speed was rather disappointing—well below thirty knots—became embroiled in fleet actions, particularly in the Mediterranean.

In the first few months of the war, until the mighty German military machine started rolling in May 1940, some inglorious—but not muted—American journalist, thwarted of stories, named those months 'The Phony War' and the phrase has passed into history.

Possibly, so far as the sister Services were concerned, there was not much action, but the small ships of the Navy deserved no such criticism. While the allied armies of France and Britain sat poised behind the spurious security of the Maginot Line, and the Air Force was compelled to restrict its raids to those ridiculous leaflet-dropping operations, the small ships were busily engaged.

When Mr Neville Chamberlain's weary voice came on the air on that fateful September Sunday to announce that we were at war with Germany the Navy was as ready as it could be.

Omissions there were, and a building programme was already in progress to offset that; in the meantime what ships there were, particularly destroyers, would have to bear the brunt.

In the somewhat accelerated building programme of 1938–9 the keel was laid of a destroyer which was, in less than two years, to pack into that period all the action, and adventure, all the drama and tragedy, ever likely to befall a destroyer again.

To begin with she was to bear the name of a famous admiral who had, in the grey days of depression, tied up the many and inglorious ends of what has been passed down as 'The Invergordon Mutiny'.

She was, also, to be commanded by a man who had watched her grow from skilfully drawn lines on paper; had in fact contributed much to her design, based on his experience as a destroyer captain.

He eventually took command and commissioned her literally on the eve of the outbreak of war and commanded her throughout her two years of life.

Finally, she undoubtedly symbolised all that was destroyers. She and her captain and her crew were truly what has been described somewhere as being 'true destroyer'; a state of mind, a state of being.

Such then was *Kelly*, and this tribute to her is a tribute to all destroyer men.

12

October 25th, 1938. A dreary grey drizzle of rain, occasionally given added malevolence by a gusty wind, soaked everything and everybody on the Tyne. It had done so since before dawn and the little group of people on the modest platform erected near the bow of a part-completed ship shrugged themselves closer into their coat collars.

Another destroyer was to be shortly launched from the Hebburn-on-Tyne shipbuilding yard of Messrs R. & W. Hawthorne, Leslie and Co. Ltd. Not a particularly exciting launch. Hawthorne, Leslie had been building destroyers and kindred craft for more than fifty years.

This destroyer, still with only a number, 'Job 615', would slip smoothly into the grey-black Tyne and almost before the ripples caused by her launching would cease to disturb the shavings and chips on the edge of the water the keel blocks would be ready for another.

A lady stepped forward on the platform, a serious-faced man in a bowler hat gave one last glance at the hull, nodded and the bottle of champagne swung in an arc and splintered against the knife-like stem.

'I name this ship *Kelly*. May God guide her and guard her and keep all who sail in her,' cried Miss Antonia Kelly, daughter of a famous admiral whose name the ship was to bear in her short but brilliant life.

And as the newly named *Kelly* slipped into the water a thin, pale sun struggled through the grey pall to shine on her just as if somebody had turned a spot-light on her.

Kelly was one of a class of destroyers included in the Emergency Programme of Naval Construction for 1937. The sixteen 'Tribals' had emerged from the 1935 Estimates in a quickening but vain effort to fill the obvious and ominous gaps in the destroyer strength. The 1937 Estimates sought to narrow those gaps.

Kelly and her sisters differed materially from the 'Tribals' not only in armament, but in design. Whereas the 'Tribals' had eight 4.7-inch guns in four turrets and one quadruple set of torpedo tubes, the *Kelly* and her sisters had two quintuple torpedo tubes and only six 4.7-inch guns in three turrets.

It was in hull construction, however, that the wide difference occurred. Her designer, Mr A. P. Cole, the naval architect who had designed all the destroyers built since 1934, had gone all out for greater longitudinal strength, something which was to bring lasting gratitude from her captain and crew before very long.

So *Kelly*, no longer just a job number, slid smoothly into the water and soon lay alongside *Jervis*, the other flotilla leader of the same design being built by Hawthorne, Leslie. Time was running out. The cynical Munich pact, never worth more than the paper on which it was written, was already tattered and the paranoic ex-house-painter was callously preparing his next flimsy excuse. The war clouds loomed more ominously on the horizon.

Almost as soon as she was secured alongside *Jervis* a swarm of men descended on her, and as time passed *Kelly* began to take full shape. In her silhouette she differed from the 'Tribals'. It was lower and she had one short, squat funnel raking sharply behind her tripod mast. It gave her an appearance of concentrated power, like a fighter's fist poised ready to unleash a devastating punch in a split second.

Work went ahead through an uneasy spring and into the summer and gradually, through dockside trials and tests, *Kelly* came to a degree of readiness, until on August 23rd she was commissioned. Her Chatham-mustered ship's company arrived to learn, for better or for worse, from the advance party what sort of ship was to be their home for immeasurable time.

Surveying the ship's company from the quarter-deck was her captain, probably with more conjectures running through his mind than were in the minds of any of the crew.

He was Captain Lord Louis Mountbatten, Captain 'D', captain of the Fifth Destroyer Flotilla, captain of a flotilla which was to include *Kashmir*, *Kandahar*, *Kelvin*, *Kimberley*, *Kipling*, *Khartoum* and *Kingston*.

Before many months were to pass they were to earn the title 'The Fighting Fifth'.

To the tall, distinguished captain who stood on the quarter-deck on that August day it was more than a routine commissioning of a destroyer. He had been in on the ground floor, as it were, from the first rivet driven home on *Kelly*.

He had commanded the destroyers *Daring* and *Wishart* in the Mediterranean before returning to London to a staff post at the Admiralty. As a destroyer man of long standing, his interest was inevitably directed towards the small ships, and before long his steps led him to the room where Mr Cole, the naval architect, was surrounded by all the paraphernalia of a drawing office, and as inevitably he started making suggestions and outlining ideas based on his long service in destroyers. That was when *Kelly* and her sisters were little more than tortuous lines on blue prints.

And his suggestions and ideas were gladly accepted. His interest in the design of the new class of destroyers was so profound that he frequently went from London to the Tyne to see 'Job No. 615' taking shape, to see in being the suggestions he had made.

Nobody, therefore, was unduly surprised when in the spring of 1939 he was appointed to *Kelly* and as Captain 'D' of the Fifth Flotilla. So much of him had been built into *Kelly* and into the other seven ships of his flotilla.

He stood on the quarter-deck of the ship which he had helped to mould near to his heart's desire, while on the quay, in serried line of blue, was the ship's company, which shortly would have to undergo a similar moulding. Before long every man in that company would stand eye to eye with him and would receive a handshake and a look which would tell the captain what sort of man he would have for a shipmate.

Kelly sailed from Hebburn to Chatham, her depot, where she took on the rest of her ship's company and main stores and ammunition. That was a normally mundane task taking anything from two to three weeks.

Kelly's captain, knowing that a finger rested on a trigger in Berlin, tackled it in a characteristic way.

The ship's company were mustered and heard their captain.

'I have always found that you cannot have an efficient ship unless you have a happy ship,' he said. 'And you cannot have a happy ship unless you have an efficient ship. That is the way I intend to start this commission, and that is the way I intend to go on. With a happy and efficient trip.'

Comforting words!

Then came the sting.

'We have to store and ammunition ship. Now, normally we are allowed three weeks to complete this operation. I have decided that it must be completed in three days. . . . We have a job to do. Let's do it.'

It was done in three days and three nights, snatching

moments of sleep when they could, but at the end of it *Kelly* was ready for sea and ready to meet the enemy. Six days after her commissioning she sailed, stored and munitioned, from Chatham for Portland for working-up trials, usually another long and detailed job with everything being done at slow time to begin with until the tempo was gradually quickened and every man knew his job at speed.

Kelly was at sea when the first hint of the impending outbreak of hostilities came in a warning signal to fuse all shells and ship all warheads on torpedoes.

Captain 'D' was lecturing all available officers and petty officers on the Mountbatten Station-keeper, an invention of his own which automatically keeps a ship in station with others. It enables the officer of the watch, or the captain in action, to concentrate on the task in hand while the ship virtually keeps herself in station on the next ahead.

Usually at the end of his lecture Captain Mountbatten would end his address by pointing out that having absorbed the basic principles of the Mountbatten Station-keeper they would know enough about it to set it working if war broke out.

As his lecture drew to a close a petty officer entered and handed Captain 'D' a signal. He paused in his lecture, read the signal, slipped it in his pocket and brought his talk to a close.

Then in level, unemotional tones he said: 'War has at this moment broke out.'

The signal read:

'From Admiralty to all concerned at home and abroad. Most immediate. Commence hostilities at once with Germany.'

They listened to the weary voice of Mr Chamberlain warning the nation that it was the evil things they would be fighting. It was the voice of a disillusioned man, a man broken by disappointment.

The next voice the ship's company heard was not wearied, neither was it a broken voice. Over the ship's broadcast system they heard *Kelly*'s captain say: 'Whenever we leave harbour we shall be right in the face of the enemy, who will be out to destroy us. We must find him and destroy him first.'

Within twenty-four hours *Kelly* was visibly and violently at war.

She went to sea with the destroyer *Acheron* on a two-ship anti-submarine exercise along with a motor boat. In the middle of the exercise two torpedoes flashed past *Kelly*. They were not dummies. They were from one of the many submarines the Germans had at sea ready and waiting for The Moment.

Kelly, *Acheron* and the Asdic-equipped motor boat went into action. *Kelly* got an almost immediate answering ping on her set and dropped depth-charges. *Acheron* followed suit and large patches of oil came to the surface. It was claimed as a 'probable'.

But *Kelly*'s crew earned no laurels from Captain 'D'. The Germans had got in the first crack and might have sunk *Kelly*. Lord Louis read the Riot Act and re-emphasised that *Kelly* should have hit first.

Like other destroyers, *Kelly* was overworked in the succeeding weeks, shepherding merchant ships, investigating submarine reports. Then came an incident which drove it home forcibly to *Kelly*'s crew that a submarine attack was not merely a question of dodging the torpedoes then dropping depth-charges and recovering the stunned fish.

The war was only a fortnight old when *Kelly*, in dirty weather, was patrolling off Land's End and received an S O S call from the aircraft-carrier *Courageous*. The carrier, with a screen of destroyers, was guarding the approaches to the Bristol Channel and had detached two of her screen to hunt a submarine threatening a merchant ship. At the same time she turned into wind to receive her Swordfish planes which were returning from a patrol.

By damnable luck a German submarine was there and fired two torpedoes into *Courageous*.

Kelly put her stern well down and her bow sliced through

the heavy seas as she went flat out to help. When she arrived *Courageous* had sunk and two merchant ships were picking up survivors. *Kelly* picked some from the sea then closed the heavily rolling and pitching merchant ships to take off the men they had rescued. Many of them were wounded, some were choking from the oil and aviation spirit welling out of *Courageous*.

To have attempted to go close alongside the merchant ships would have risked *Kelly* being ripped open like a salmon tin. Instead the motor cutter was lowered and painfully, with infinite patience and tenderness, the shocked and wounded survivors were ferried across to *Kelly*. It was an epic in itself. A dozen times through the night the tiny motor cutter came within inches of being smashed as the rolling high-sided merchant ships first towered above them then came lurching down a sea as if to crush and sink the motor boat.

Of the 1,260 men on the carrier 500 were lost.

Looking thoughtfully at the gasping, retching sailors from *Courageous*, some of them bleeding from oil-caked wounds, some of them gasping their lives away, brought it home to *Kelly*'s crew that war was not a glorious picnic consisting of a breathless dash to sea, a bout of catch-as-can with a submarine, then a swagger into a pub to retail, fall by fall, how it was done.

They saw death in all its ugliness for the first time. And not for the last.

Destroyers were more precious than large nuggets of gold and ninety per cent sea-time was considered nothing more than normal. Like others of her ilk, *Kelly* patrolled, escorted, dashed in to oil-up and collect more depth-charges and went out again to patrol and convoy.

Another 'probable' U-boat, leaning strongly towards a 'positive' came to *Kelly* (ultimately confirmed as a 'kill') bringing a substantial profit. Two submarines sent to the bottom and several others damaged in the first month or so of the outbreak of war was a remarkable achievement. *Kelly* had every right to feel proud.

But the penalty of doing a job well, at least in the Service, is that one is immediately given another job to do.

On the day that *Kelly* was collecting her second submarine, another U-boat, U-47, stole in through the incomplete Scapa Flow defences and sank the *Royal Oak*. The shock to the Navy was tremendous. Scapa Flow had been the safe haven for most of the First World War and nobody, from the First Sea Lord down, thought that a U-boat would have the temerity to risk almost certain death by entering the Flow.

But one did and the result of Lieutenant Prien's daring in getting in, sinking a battleship and getting out again forced the Navy to seek other shelter. Opinions at high level were divided. Some strongly pressed the claims of the Firth of Forth, others plumped for the Clyde, although this would mean at least another day's steaming-time to any operation in those northern waters. Eventually, despite an air raid on Rosyth in which *Southampton* and *Edinburgh* were hit and a number of men on the 'Tribal' destroyer *Mohawk* were wounded and killed, Rosyth was decided upon once its anti-aircraft defences were strengthened. In the meantime the Home Fleet used the Clyde and later Loch Ewe on the west coast of Scotland.

Having enjoyed the Indian summer in the south, *Kelly* steamed north, calling in at Loch Ewe and thence on to Scapa, where she stayed, throughout the long, cold winter. She patrolled, screened, steamed to the Norwegian coast, to Greenland in the sporadic searches for the German pocket battleships which were out somewhere in the wastes of the Atlantic laying death and destruction among merchant ships.

Lighter moments were few for captain and crew, but there was one which was retailed through many a wardroom and mess-deck when *Kelly*'s crew released it for general consumption.

Kelly, among other destroyers, had been pursuing a prize ship captured by the *Deutschland*—the prize, eventually harried and pressed, steamed into Bergen and allowed herself and her crew to be interned. *Kelly* strayed perhaps half a mile or so inside the three-mile limit in pursuit of the prize and a tiny Norwegian gunboat, small enough to be taken on *Kelly*'s foredeck, closed and threatened to open fire unless *Kelly* withdrew. An unknown humorist in 'B' turret yelled to the gunboat: 'Garn! Hit somebody your own shape,' and waited for the laugh, but his thunder was stolen.

Captain Lord Louis Mountbatten, related to half the crowned heads of Europe, leaned over the wing of his bridge and gracefully agreed to pull out.

Then, speaking through his loud hailer, he suavely added: 'Please give my compliments to my cousin, Crown Prince Olaf, and tell him I hope he is keeping well.'

Kelly's crew to a man felt that the last word had been with them.

During that patrol *Kelly* was badly damaged by an extra-heavy sea which swept down her starboard side, tearing off all the boats, twisting davits like paper, smashing part of her superstructure, taking with the wreckage a young rating.

Kelly struggled back to Scapa and after temporary patching she was sent to the Tyne for repairs.

Hawthorne, Leslie's welcomed her proudly, like a daughter who had covered herself with glory. They had built her and she had justified them.

In a month they made her as good as new. With *Mohawk*, which had been badly damaged in the raid on the Firth of Forth, she was detailed to sail for the bleak northern waters again.

The night before, somebody switched on the wireless and immediately the attention of everybody was intense. They heard the flat, harsh voice of the traitor Lord Haw-Haw on his nightly hate.

'. . . And where is your Lord Louis Mountbatten and his ship? We know. He is on the Tyne. But he will never leave it.'

There was nothing magic or mysterious about that snarled information. Neutral ships, with a strong leaning towards the

Germans, were steaming to and from the Tyne and *Kelly* was there for all to see.

And the day *Kelly* and *Mohawk* sailed the latest secret weapon boasted about by the Germans were laid plentifully in the mouth of the Tyne.

As they slipped smoothly towards the sea, the two destroyers received a signal that two tankers had been torpedoed or mined not far from the Tyne. *Kelly* and *Mohawk* increased speed, *Kelly* just missing a collision with a bulky merchant ship, and once into the open sea they raced for the spot where the two ships, both tankers, were in trouble.

They reached them to find one was burning furiously, both were sinking.

As *Kelly* ranged alongside the burning tanker, those on board felt a bump, then another, and after a heart-stopping pause yet another.

Then came a violent explosion under her stern and a tree-like column of water climbed upwards then fell on *Kelly* with a crash.

She had been mined.

The Germans, ever methodical, had mixed the mines, with magnetics lying on the bottom and moored mines laid around them to emphasise the trap.

And in all probability it was one of the moored mines which had hit and crippled *Kelly*.

Slowly she rolled to a stop, as helpless as the burning tanker she had striven to help, a perfect target for any lurking U-boat.

Kelly was laboriously towed back to the Tyne and upriver to Hawthorne, Leslie's. It takes a lot to jar a Geordie out of his phlegmatic calm but the arrival of *Kelly* with a twisted stern and wrenched propellers left them momentarily breathless. Then Hebburn gave tongue.

'This is getting to be a habit, chum. You only sailed yesterday afternoon,' was the general burden of the comment.

Most of the crew had been on leave for the previous repair and the 'ready' as well as travelling warrants had run dry.

But Lady Mountbatten paid all fares home, so the ship's company got two whacks of Christmas leave.

But for Captain 'D' and his staff there was no such luck. They went to Portland, where Lord Louis boarded *Kelvin*, which was equipped as a leader, and for two months he ran the flotilla from her.

Then back to *Kelly* and hard work in northern waters. It was then *Kelly* was in collision with another 'Tribal' destroyer, *Gurkha*. *Kelly* was escorting a north-bound convoy, *Gurkha* a south-bound one. The weather had been filthy for days on end. Snowstorm after snowstorm had cut visibility down to two score yards. The two ships saw vague bulks loom up, sweep down their sides, there was the wrenching scream of tortured metal. In turning away from *Kelly*, *Gurkha*'s propeller-guard had ripped into *Kelly*'s bow, making a gash more than twenty-five feet long.

Kelly had to swing away from the convoy to carry out repairs, and while the struggling, sweating, swearing ratings lashed a collision mat over the hole, Captain 'D' for once was thankful for a concealing snowstorm which hid him both from a U-boat or any ranging bombers.

So *Kelly* limped into Lerwick, in the Shetlands, to strengthen the temporary repairs, struggled to Scapa, where plates were welded over the gap, and eventually turned her bow south for yet another sojourn in dry dock.

But not to Hebburn this time. All the Tyne yards were filled to bursting point and Kelly had to steam south to a dry dock on the Thames.

Just one month after leaving Hebburn-on-Tyne in all her pristine glory and patched-up stern.

Nobody could truthfully complain that life had been monotonous for *Kelly*. In eight months she had collected two U-boats, besides seriously damaging several more, she had had a new stern fitted and now she was to have best part of a new bow fitted. She had steamed thousands of miles protecting convoys, she had saved lives and in performing those tasks had steamed right around the British Isles and had penetrated up into the frozen 60's and 70's.

And all this during a period which an American journalist, no doubt from the front line in Paris or in London, had sarcastically dubbed 'The Phony War'.

It was rather a pity that the Admiralty could not see the way clear then—as it did later—to allow journalists to sail on operations, in escorting destroyers, in corvettes, in minesweepers, which were fighting a desperate, and at the time losing, battle against a variety of mines, or with the ill-prepared, gallant, armed merchant liners who maintained a constant watch in Denmark Straits under almost impossible conditions.

The words 'Phony War' would have shrivelled and died in no time at all.

13

Kelly was in dock in London when the Germans, extensively aided by a powerful Fifth Column, smote Norway and Denmark. *Kelly*'s crew fumed and fretted. Ships they had sailed with, had fought with, had patrolled and convoyed with, were fighting heavily in Norway while their ship lay supine in dock in the hands of the dockyard 'mateys'.

They heard of destroyers fighting off enemy aircraft which were heavily bombing Norwegian towns at which British troops had been landed in a confused attempt to thwart the German invasion. They heard with pride of *Renown*'s battle with the *Scharnhorst* and *Gneisenau* in a raging snowstorm. They heard, too, with sorrow, of the destroyers' fight for Narvik, and for Lord Louis Mountbatten it was a personal grief. Captain Warburton-Lee's death in that fight brought to an end a long friendship not untinged with a friendly rivalry. They had been in command of destroyers in the uneasy days of peace in the Mediterranean, Captain Warburton-Lee in *Witch* and Captain Mountbatten in *Wishart*.

April drew to its closing days of tragedy. There was to be the first of the evacuations of British troops which somehow eventually became naval epics. It was the pattern to be followed again and again.

The Navy would put them ashore. The Navy would lift them off. In the terrible accountancy which followed the losses were tragic, almost disastrous.

Namsos, endlessly bombed by German aircraft, was in flames. The Germans virtually held Norway in the palm of one hand.

On April 29th a naval force, transports and escorting ships, sailed from Scapa to take off the troops there: French Foreign Legion, Chasseurs Alpins and British. Time was precious. Each hour saw the German ring closing in around the remnants of General Carton de Wiart's pathetic little force.

And the rescue task force ran into heavy fog.

The fog brought one blessing. The German bombers, which had been harassing the force as it steamed across the North Sea, could no longer find it. But, on the other hand, the fog slowed it down so the evacuation timetable was delayed.

On the quays at Namsos the weary troops waited, momentarily saved from the torture of bombing by the same fog which was holding up the ships which were to rescue them.

Then came the signal of the delay and the troops started to scatter to wait for the next night. If it came.

Although the town of Namsos itself was clear of fog, the narrow steep-sided fiord leading to the open sea swirled under a grey, writhing blanket.

As they started to dispersc, the weary soldiers took one last despairing look down the fiord and blinked. Cleaving through the fog came the lean bows of a grey destroyer, then another.

Kelly, leading, had arrived, accompanied by five more sisters.

She had steamed nearly eighty miles along the treacherous rock-bound coast through fog, sometimes missing jagged uprearing spears of rock by 100 yards or so until almost by a miracle they had found the entrance to the fiord and had steamed up it.

If the soldiers were grateful, so too were the German bombers.

They warmed to their task. They had shadowed the destroyers up the fiord because, although the ships were concealed, their masts had showed above the fog. Bombs had been dropped, no hits were scored but more than twenty men were killed or wounded.

In the clear air off blazing Namsos the Germans laid on the lash. For the destroyers to go alongside would have been suicide.

Reluctantly, the destroyers turned and raced back into the concealing fog down the fiord while the hapless soldiers continued with their dispersal. In the steep-sided hills behind the town the British rearguard held out against increasing German weight, fighting for precious time; time enough for the ships to return once more to take off the men on the quays. For them, the thin hopeless line, there could be only surrender.

Kelly's risky dash came at the end of another full-speed rush from the Thames. The extensive repairs had been reviewed and anything not absolutely essential was crossed off to be done another day. The paramount problem was 'Get *Kelly* to sea'. She sailed on schedule and arrived at Scapa in time to take part in the evacuation.

Another attempt was made under fog the next day. *Kelly* and her five destroyers, with the cruiser *York* and three transports, set out once more for Namsos, *Kelly* leading.

The fog had dispersed and soft twilight coloured the fiord a delicate grey as they raced up to Namsos, not certain whether the town was by now in the hands of the Germans.

From the decks of the ships it seemed, looking at the shore, that war was a million miles away. Dark houses framed lighted windows; from some smoke rose.

Then the fleet rounded the last bend and saw Namsos.

War was but an arm's length away. From end to end the town blazed. Houses, warehouses, mountains of stores on the quays were burning with a fiery red glow which lit up the whole fiord.

Still nobody knew whether the Germans had penetrated Namsos and sited guns to bear on any ships approaching.

The only way to find out was to go in.

Under cover of the destroyers' and cruiser's guns the transports weaved their way alongside. Almost directly in their path lay the burning Asdic trawler *Aston Villa*. She had fought a good fight against aircraft with her puny armament and was now dying.

Nearly 7,000 troops, British and French, waited on the quays for evacuation. Time was precious. As some of the men filed on board the transporters, the destroyers closed in and ferried others off to the *York*.

The troops were lifted off in four hours of precious darkness, a darkness which saved them from bombing. Night work was not the métier of the German bombers. That came later for bombing towns in Britain.

The destroyer *Afridi* lifted the last batch, making certain that no wounded stragglers were left. Then she turned her lean bows towards the sea and raced down the fiord in *Kelly*'s wake.

Ashore, the occasional thud of a gun and a rattle of small-arms fire told that the forlorn rearguard was still buying time.

The fleet, the cruiser, destroyers and transports suffered from no illusions. They knew that as soon as the first tinge of grey dawn crept into the sky the German bombers would descend on them like hawks.

And it was so.

First a scouting plane high in the sky, picked out by the sun which was yet to light up the fleet. Then the bombers. From just before five o'clock in the morning until well into the afternoon the rescue fleet was almost continuously bombed. The Germans threw into the fight not only their medium bombers but the Stuka dive bombers.

For *Kelly*'s men these steep-diving, screaming horrors were something new, but they soon learned that once a dive bomber was committed to a dive it had to more or less come straight down with no weaving. The pom-pom waited for one such diving plane which seemed to be shrieking down straight for *Kelly*. Before it could release its load the pom-pom thumped a stream of glowing tracer into the belly of the plane. And it went on diving. Into the sea.

Suddenly *Bison*, the French destroyer, reeled out of line, mortally hit and burning. The other destroyers raced around her protectively then stopped to pick up the survivors, who were being machine-gunned by the German planes as they struggled in the water.

Afridi, engaged in this errand of mercy, was hit by several bombs, reared up and capsized. One hundred men went down with her.

After a long and soul-wearying trip the remaining ships limped into Scapa, handed over the soldiers they had rescued, had one night's rest then escorted the transports to the Clyde.

A few precious hours at anchor at Greenock came to an end when *Kelly* was ordered to the east coast to join up with the cruiser *Birmingham* and more destroyers seeking to find and fight a mixed force of German ships: a minelayer and escorting E-boats and possibly destroyers detected laying mines off Sylt.

One of Lord Mountbatten's own flotilla, *Kandahar*, was one of the force and in the evening she made contact with a submarine. *Kelly* joined in the hunt without conspicuous success beyond driving the submarine below where it could not signal. Then it was decided to rejoin the main force at speed, as in the gathering darkness they could see gun-flashes in the sky.

The destroyer *Bulldog*, which had become detached from her own flotilla, joined up with *Kelly* and *Kandahar* and the three steamed hard for the fight they believed was taking place to the north.

That hard steaming was causing concern on *Kelly*. Her oil

fuel was getting low. Her captain was informed that by midnight, at the present rate of consumption, she would have to turn for home.

Just before midnight—the latest *Kelly* could steam at high speed, absolutely the latest—it was decided to turn her in a few minutes.

The night was dark, cold and clear.

Suddenly an alert look-out saw a luminous line threading through the water towards *Kelly*.

His high-pitched yell reached the bridge.

'Torpedo to port.'

There was no time to turn. Everybody on the bridge held their breaths. The cream track ended abeam of *Kelly*'s bridge.

For five seconds everybody froze. Then somebody breathed.

'A dud.'

A second later *Kelly* reared up, half rolled over, there was a deafening explosion and a sheet of flame raged skywards. The torpedo had crashed into the forward boiler room. A great hole reached from her keel almost to upper-deck level.

She lay over to starboard. From the hole came the scream of escaping steam, a deafening shriek which gradually died away. Then above it came the thinner voices of wounded men, barked orders, the sullen wash of water tearing through the hole which had riven *Kelly* down to her keel.

A ship was dying.

Training began to tell. Damage-control parties swung into action. Reports filtered up to the bridge. Both boiler rooms were full of water. The starboard boiler had been blown aft and to starboard. But the Tyne men had built well. The bulkheads either side of the boiler rooms were holding.

Kelly might be dying, but she was going to die hard. The first shock gave way to feverish activity. To counteract the weight of water inside *Kelly*, and to try to counter the bad list, all top hamper had to go. Depth-charges were set to safe and were dumped. Ready ammunition on the upper deck was thrown overboard, as were torpedoes. All the boats except one whaler were lowered away.

Through this welter of shock, wounds, dying scream of escaping steam, came a crisp, collected voice:

'. . . The ship is *not* sinking, so do not panic.'

It was the focal point.

If the 'Old Man' says everything is going to be all right, then everything *will* be all right.

The work of rescue went ahead with feverish speed. Not only the work of saving the ship, but the merciful work of helping the wounded.

The sick bay had been smashed by the explosion, so wounded were taken aft. There was only emergency lighting and hand torches available. As men were released from the tortured metal which trapped them, they were tenderly carried to the surgeon who worked by the light of the torches.

A slim young telegraphist named O'Neill wriggled through a terrifyingly narrow gap into the radio office where five of his mates lay groaning. As he twisted and squirmed through the slit the doctor gave him a hypodermic syringe full of morphia so that he could ease their pain until they could be rescued.

In the meantime, *Bulldog*, having sent a signal to Admiralty that *Kelly* had been torpedoed, raced towards her and took her in tow. Visibility closed down as *Kelly* laboured along drunkenly behind *Bulldog* and in a high sea, legacy from a half-gale farther north, which made the task of towing infinitely harder. But the tragic procession got under way, circled protectively by *Kandahar*.

In the early hours of the morning those on *Kelly*'s bridge heard the snarl of a motor boat coming out of the darkness. They knew that, crippled as she was, *Kelly* was a sitting duck for another torpedo attack.

It was a German E-boat. It came racing out of the fog, a double plume of white water flung high from its bow. It tried to streak between *Bulldog* and *Kelly*, misjudged, hit *Bulldog* on the quarter, bounced off and slammed into *Kelly*'s bow, crashed all along her boat deck, clearing stanchions and davits and leaving most of her bottom added to the wreckage caused by the torpedo. The last *Kelly*'s crew saw of her was rolling away into the darkness obviously sinking, with her crew shrieking for help. Then there was silence.

The long night wore on, with the stricken *Kelly* wallowing astern of *Bulldog*. The only help she could offer was through a chain of men passing orders from the bridge to the emergency steering flat aft.

At last daylight came and *Kandahar* ranged herself alongside the cripple and took off the wounded. That operation, carried out in a rising, sullen sea, was a small epic on its own. But as the wounded were being transferred the German bombers arrived. They were driven off by a vicious anti-aircraft fire from the escorting destroyers and no hits were registered. Scarcely had they disappeared when three more planes droned across the sky. They were lined up in the destroyers' gun-sights and narrowly escaped an angry barrage. They were three Hudsons sent out as aerial escort. Two more destroyers arrived and later in the day two cruisers were added to the little fleet around *Kelly*.

A sad little service remained to be carried out. The dead, at least those who had been recovered from the chaos of twisted, riven metal, were laid out on the quarter-deck. As Captain Louis Mountbatten conducted the simple but solemn service it was punctuated by the harsh, sharp steering orders coming down the chain of men.

'. . . We commit their bodies to the deep . . . starboard thirty . . . ashes to ashes . . . dust to dust . . . midships . . .'

The silent figures in weighted hammocks slipped one after the other over the side. For them all pain and tribulation were finished.

Three thin whip-lash cracks of the volleys ended the service, then the alive concentrated on the task of staying alive, and keeping their ship alive.

The weather worsened in the afternoon and twice the tow broke. *Kelly*'s captain decided to send most of his crew to other destroyers. She was listing badly and there was a possibility that at the end of each of the crazy, surging rushes she would plunge under. The other destroyers sent boats to take off all but eighteen men, six officers and twelve ratings.

At that moment the Germans struck with a heavier force of bombers and met a terrific anti-aircraft fire from the destroyers and cruisers. Even *Kelly*, with her minute crew, struggling from gun to gun to help with the barrage.

Just before nightfall, as an angry sea clawed at *Kelly*, submarines were reported to be lying in the track along which *Kelly* was laboriously crawling.

She would be a sitting duck for a submarine, so the volunteers were taken off and spent a long, anxious night on *Bulldog*. The tow had parted in the night and *Kelly* lay alone, stationary, with the destroyers circling her solicitously until the morning, when the eighteen men returned and by superhuman efforts once more got a tow aboard. The slow procession got under way once more.

Two tugs appeared and as the tow-lines were passed yet another German bomber attack was launched, again without success.

The tugs began to take the strain and as they did they asked:

'Where to, sir?'

For the first time since his ship had been torpedoed Captain 'D' permitted a thin smile to cross his face.

'The Tyne. Where else?'

There was no water, practically no food, except what an expert little party of scroungers found; they were filthy from handling the greasy tows when they parted, they were tired beyond exhaustion point, but still drew deeply on an apparently bottomless well of courage.

After ninety hours they were in the mouth of the Tyne and her slow procession up that historic river was almost one of triumph. Shipyard workers sent a stentorian cheer skywards and hammered the still gaunt ribs of ships half built in a clanging chorus.

Hawthorne, Leslie's men at Hebburn were not so vociferous. This was the *Kelly* they had built—and patched—and she had come home to them grievously wounded with some of her dead still on her. But through it ran a thread of pride. Their work, and the work of the designer, had been proved in the fire and had shown a true temper.

The remaining dead were buried in Hebburn cemetery and the whole town went to the funeral and a tablet was placed at the head of the common grave.

It reads today for all to see, a tribute to those who gave all without the asking, a tribute also to a gallant crew and resolute men who had built and built well.

'HMS *Kelly*. In memory of the twenty-seven men killed in action with E-boats off the German minefields on the night of May 9th, 1940. This memorial was erected by officers and men of the ship and workmen of Hebburn Shipbuilding Yard.'

When *Kelly* was placed in dry dock and the water was drained out all who saw her were appalled at the ferocity of the damage and marvelled that she had survived.

Repairs this time were a massive job and took seven long months, but finally they were completed in time for *Kelly* to steam to Scapa where her working-up trials included several dashes out on submarine alarms.

One comment alleged to have been made by a workman at the Hebburn yard is worthy of being recorded.

'Look, mates,' he is credited with saying, 'since we built her and handed her over to you she's had both ends and the middle built again. You've got a new ship. Now be a bit careful with her. We can't go on building *Kellys* like this for you to bust up.'

Escorting, patrolling, depth-charging suspected submarines, trips to the edge of the Arctic, filled in most of her time, as did a journey south through the Irish Sea, during which *Kelly*, aided by one of Captain Mountbatten's party pieces, a full helm turn at speed, cleared off yet another set of guard rails, davits and boats.

Then Plymouth for repairs again and more hard work and eventually her bow was turned southwards to the sun, to

Gibraltar, into Mussolini's 'Mare Nostrum', to Malta where she met some more of the 'J's' and 'K's': and at the same time tasted the severity of the raids on the George Cross island.

There she had the usual tasks of a destroyer, which meant roughly ninety per cent sea-time escorting, patrolling and making nightly sweeps in search of Rommel's convoys.

One satisfying chore fell to *Kelly* and her sisters which must have brought a smile of recollection to Lord Louis. During the time *Kelly* was being virtually rebuilt on the Tyne Lord Mountbatten, taking eight destroyers of the 'K's' and 'J's', together with a cruiser and *Revenge*, had sailed from Plymouth with the intention of slamming invasion craft in Cherbourg. The destroyers and larger craft had poured shells into the outer harbour at the French port from a range of two miles while the bewildered Germans had hosepiped every fragment of cloud within reach. The damage done to the invasion barges was catastrophic from the Germans' point of view, and was eminently satisfactory from the destroyers' aspect.

Now he was to repeat the performance on Benghazi, where dock installations and ships in harbour were proving far too useful to Rommel's pressure against our forces.

Star-shell illuminated the harbour and each of the destroyers poured in 200 rounds at almost point-blank range, then streaked for Malta, leaving a chaos of smoking wrecks and shattered quays behind them.

But in the main it was hard work at sea, escorting, patrolling and trying to catch the elusive and coy Italian warships at sea.

On May 31st *Kelly* sailed with others to prevent a German seaborne landing on Crete to join up with the airborne troops which had landed the previous day.

The first casualty was *Juno*. She was sunk in one minute by heavy bombing.

Very soon most of the 'K's' and 'J's' were there—*Kelly, Kashmir, Kipling, Kelvin, Jackal, Kandahar, Kingston* and

Kimberley—and were hard at it sinking German surface craft and invasion convoys and were being dive bombed by Stukas for their pains.

During the hours of darkness *Kelly* and *Kashmir* discovered and sank some caiques heavily loaded with German soldiers and bombarded Maleme airfield, which was in German hands.

Most of the British ships were by now getting low on ammunition and were ordered to withdraw to Alexandria to stock up again.

Kelly and *Kashmir* turned on their best speed, but it was not enough. A swarm of vengeful bombers were streaking in low after them.

Oerlikon, pom-poms and 4.7-inch guns hammered at them, blowing some of them out of the sky. Then there was a heavy, dull explosion.

Kashmir, broken in two and a smoking, sinking wreck, was still defiantly fighting back until the waters closed over her.

The bombers concentrated on *Kelly*. She swung over hard to port to avoid a stick of bombs and while she was still turning at thirty knots a bomb got her at the after end of the engine room. She went on turning hard to port and turning over. So swiftly had she turned over that even when she was on the surface keel uppermost she still moved through the water.

Kelly was dying hard.

But die she did. Soon there was only wreckage of a damaged carley float, spare rafts and other debris on the surface, with men clinging to them, hanging on to life.

As she slowly slid under the water, the survivors, some of whom had served on her from the day she commissioned, raised a ragged cheer from caked lips as she went. Choking and coughing they also managed a few bars of:

'Roll out the barrel, we've got the blues on the run. . . .'

Around them the empty waste of water. Above them the blue sky, from which screamed Stukas machine-gunning the men in the water.

It seemed the end.

Then they heard gun-fire rolling over the sea and saw the white plumes of a bow wave. *Kipling* had arrived.

As her guns tore savagely at the dive bombers, her boats were lowered and rafts were tossed overboard to *Kelly*'s men and a few minutes later to *Kashmir*'s survivors.

Each time *Kipling* slowed or stopped to pick up survivors she was a sitting target for the dive bombers.

Mountbatten, blackened by oil and stunned by the noise and strain, still took over from *Kipling*'s bridge to supervise the rescue.

Then came a little tragedy which stands out from the larger picture. *Kipling*'s motor boat was being lowered to collect survivors when dive bombers attacked.

Kipling went full ahead, the motor boat dragging alongside. Somebody cut the forward boat falls, but not the after falls. *Kelly*'s first lieutenant, Lieutenant-Commander Lord Hugh Beresford, and Lieutenant Bush, of *Kipling*, clambered up a davit to cut the after falls, but the speed of *Kipling* tore it out of the deck. Both men were killed in the smash.

All *Kelly*'s survivors had been rescued and about half of *Kashmir*'s remained to be rescued. But the bomb attacks were increasing in severity all the time.

A desperate problem had to be decided by one man, and one man alone. Captain 'D 5', Lord Louis Mountbatten.

Leave *Kashmir*'s remaining men in the water and retire? Or risk losing them all in continuing rescue operations?

Kipling stayed.

She played cat-and-mouse with the bombers. Raced in at top speed, picked up a few, then raced away, until all were rescued. In doing so she hit what was believed to be *Kelly*, submerged just below the surface.

Then she finally turned for home, Alexandria, 400 miles away, leaking oil and at her best speed, twenty knots.

All that morning Lieutenant-Commander St Clair Ford wriggled his ship through more than forty air attacks, at times almost disappearing under the columns of water surrounding her until at last he took her beyond aircraft range.

As *Kipling* limped into Alexandria the oil-blackened, scarred and wounded survivors of *Kelly* and *Kashmir* were assembled on the upper deck to be greeted with a deafening roar of cheers.

Then for them rest at the Fleet Air Arm station, Dhekeila.

It was there Lord Louis Mountbatten, Captain 'D', said good-bye to his crew.

'. . . I have come to say good-bye. . . . The *Kelly* has been in one scrap after another, but even when we have had men killed the majority brought back the old ship. . . . Now she lies in 1,500 fathoms with more than half our shipmates. . . . Now they all lie together with the ship we love. . . . There isn't one of you I wouldn't be proud and honoured to serve with again. . . .'

Men cried and were not ashamed of their tears.

In Hebburn another tablet was placed on the grave of the men who had died fighting E-boats in the cold North Sea, a tablet to the men who had died under the hot Crete sunshine.

It reads:

'Also nine officers and 121 men who lost their lives when HMS *Kelly* was sunk in the Battle of Crete, May 23rd, 1941.'

It was just over twenty months that *Kelly* lived, a year and a half from the time the Hebburn men proudly handed over the ship they had built; and cheered her—and sorrowed over her when she had limped back after being torpedoed—had rebuilt her and sent her forth again.

Twenty months in which she had lived up to the finest traditions of the destroyer: 'Turn to the enemy.'

14

September 3rd, 1939.

And so to war.

At the outbreak of hostilities there were approximately 200

destroyers in commission. Of them, 100 were fleet destroyers and the remainder were designated escort destroyers; quite a lot of them were rather elderly ladies, but nevertheless quite capable of doing the job for which they were intended.

Within the first few weeks, once ships already sailing independently had arrived, the convoy system was adopted on roughly the plans of those which existed when the 1914–18 War ended.

The Germans had in commission fifty-six submarines, twenty-six of them between 500 tons and 700 tons capable of quite extended ocean passages, and twenty-six were of the coastal type which were intended to pick up the burden where their fathers and older brothers had relinquished it in 1918; i.e. the Western Approaches.

Of the twenty-six ocean-going submarines twenty-one of them were already on station at least a week before the formal declaration of war.

We have seen that in the closing weeks of the 1914–18 War the destroyer strength in home waters was 300 plus. And that was barely sufficient to cope with the patrols and convoy demands.

The number available at the outbreak of war in 1939 was a firm indication that until the emergency building programme gained momentum the way ahead was going to be hard.

Upwards of 200 destroyers may sound as if the odds of four to one were against the U-boats, but there were incessant demands on their services other than for convoy or patrol.

Once we see what those demands were the destroyer force available for convoy and U-boat-hunting groups shrinks alarmingly.

Two flotillas were on screening duties at Scapa Flow—seventeen destroyers. In the Humber nine more were required to screen a cruiser squadron based there. At Portland nine more were dancing attendance on two aircraft-carriers and two battleships. That is thirty-five destroyers earmarked for specific duties.

Gibraltar, Freetown, West Africa and the Mediterranean had thirty-nine, all for screening larger ships, and eight more were on the China station. Upwards of eighty-odd destroyers allocated to doing their intended job; i.e. screening large ships and protecting them from torpedo attacks.

That leaves eighteen ships either undergoing refit or not immediately in commission. A low percentage, all things considered.

Even some of the destroyers earmarked for that task of screening were not in the first flush of youth and of the others forty-two of them were 'V's' and 'W's' of 1918–19 vintage.

At the bases where the emphasis would be on convoy escort and submarine hunting, round about sixty destroyers were allocated. Portsmouth had twelve, Nore nine, Plymouth, upon which fell the main burden of Western Approaches, had thirty-two and Rosyth, which shared with Nore the task of escorting in the North Sea, had eight.

By no means a destroyer strength likely to engender a feeling of complacency. The 200 destroyers were spread rather thinly.

But theirs was not to reason why.

Theirs was to get on with the job.

The Germans struck first by torpedoing the liner *Athenia* within hours of the outbreak of war.

Revenge for this attack was not long in coming. On October 14th, little more than a month later, the aircraft-carrier *Ark Royal* was operating west of the Hebrides with the destroyers *Faulknor*, *Foxhound* and *Firedrake* screening her. They were hunting reported U-boats, and the destroyers found one. She tried a long shot with a torpedo at *Ark Royal*, missed, and the three destroyers leapt on her, sank her and took the crew prisoner.

That submarine was U-39 and the only regret the destroyer crews had was that it was not U-30, the submarine which had smitten the *Athenia*.

A week later, in the same waters, two more of the 'F's', *Fortune* and *Forester*, flushed U-27 and sank her. In fact, the destroyers showed quite a dividend in the next three months. *Imogen* and *Ilex* added U-42 to the bag off the south-west coast of Ireland on October 13th and in the same area a day later *Inglefield*, *Ivanhoe*, *Intrepid* and *Icarus* sent to the bottom U-45.

Before the month was out *Kingston*, *Kashmir* and *Icarus*, on screening duties in the North Sea east of Shetlands, fastened on to U-35 and she, too, was sunk.

By the end of December destroyers had built up quite a credit account in submarines sunk, apart from others damaged and forced away from convoys. The Germans lost, in that period, nine submarines. Three of them were foolhardy enough to try to penetrate the Dover mine barrage en route for the Western Channel and paid for their temerity. Five were collected by destroyers and the submarine *Salmon* sank the ninth.

Oddly enough, although some of the convoys running were only lightly escorted, they were not heavily attacked by the submarines. In the first four months of the war we lost 114 merchant ships, half of them in September when there were still a number of ships on passage independently.

Of that number only twelve were sunk in convoy and they were members *ex-officio* of the stragglers' club and to achieve that the Germans had lost roughly a sixth of their submarine force.

The grim days were yet to come.

The War Emergency Building Programme was getting under way, but the need for destroyers was ships actually in the water, not on paper, or as half-built red-rusted skeletons in dockyards.

The 'Havants', the 'Onslows', the continuation of the 'Hunts', the 'Saumarez' class, *Troubridge*, *Ulster*, *Valentine*, *Zambesi* and others were yet to come, and did in due course arrive and add to destroyer lustre. By June 1941, to anticipate things a little, the destroyer strength had risen to approximately 250 with another 160 building.

And they would not be enough in view of world-wide demands.

Those which were in service were hard-worked in the opening months of the war.

One of their tasks was to ensure the safe arrival of the British Expeditionary Force to France.

The war was but a few hours old when the advance parties were sailed from Portsmouth to Cherbourg in destroyers. Four days later the troopships carrying the main force sailed from Southampton and the Bristol Channel ports of Swansea, Barry, Newport and Avonmouth.

From that date onwards the troop and supply ships sailed regularly from those ports for Cherbourg, Nantes and Brest and St Nazaire.

The task of escorting them fell mainly on the destroyers of Plymouth and Portsmouth commands and it is a tribute to the destroyers that, despite the fact that the Germans had nearly twenty submarines ringing Western Approaches when war was declared (some of them had been on station for ten days before the outbreak), not one ship was lost. By the first week in October the destroyers had escorted in safety more than 160,000 men, 25,000 vehicles and nearly 150,000 tons of equipment. Moreover, regular convoys of reinforcements and supplies were delivered almost with the monotony of the daily delivery of milk to a doorstep.

It meant destroyers working flat out with practically no time between convoys, and the average sea-time of the destroyers of Portsmouth and Plymouth in those first two or three months of the war has been estimated as more than ninety per cent.

In addition, they had the task of sailing to meet Atlantic convoys approaching south-west Ireland at a rendezvous about twenty degrees west and escorting outward-bound convoys to the same area, where merchant ships dispersed.

Farther east, destroyers had the task of escorting four convoys a week down Channel from Southend while the responsibility for the safe keeping of the North Sea convoys was laid on the escort destroyers of Rosyth Command.

That was the pattern of life for the destroyers for the first winter of the war. Monotony, escort, the occasional submarine hunt and a night or two in harbour before resuming the mixture as before.

Until the first confused events now known as the Norwegian campaign.

The broader and more complicated diplomatic canvas is not for this story. We and the Germans had long recognised that taking and holding Norway was a valuable and intricate part of the domination of the northern waters.

The fact that the Germans moved first and resolutely has nothing to do with the story of destroyers except that on them fell the main burden of hot action.

Our diffident approach in the first instance was the decision to lay a minefield in Vestfiord. This was to be done by four destroyers with another four as escort. The covering force were *Hardy*, *Hotspur*, *Havock* and *Hunter*. In the background, lending weight, was *Renown* with a screen of four destroyers, *Greyhound*, *Glow-worm*, *Hyperion* and *Hero*.

The weather was bad, rather more than half a gale with visibility not more than 1,000 yards.

On *Glow-worm* came the startling yell: 'Man overboard.' *Glow-worm* turned hard over to start a search for the unfortunate rating and continued the search for some time. She never rejoined the force to which she was attached.

Some time later *Renown* received a signal from *Glow-worm* that she was in contact with two German destroyers and a few minutes later that she was in action with them.

The German destroyers were part of a screen for the German heavy cruiser *Hipper*. The German destroyers were hit by *Glow-worm* and turned away. *Glow-worm* pursued them, although her commanding officer, Lieutenant-Commander Gerard Roope, guessed that what the German destroyers were doing was to lead him into contact with heavier forces.

He took the risk, feeling that if and when he made contact with a heavier force and could signal the position to *Renown* it could lead to something decisive.

Glow-worm sighted *Hipper*, started a sighting signal, but a brutal twist of fate saw it never completed. *Hipper* opened fire on *Glow-worm* and the first salvoes wrecked her radio office.

Glow-worm fired one salvo of torpedoes, which missed.

Again *Glow-worm*, pitching and tossing her way over a turbulent sea, fired another salvo of torpedoes. They too missed. *Hipper* was hitting *Glow-worm* and nobody could have quarrelled with Roope had he decided to withdraw in the hope of repairing his radio office or meeting another British ship which could transmit his sighting signal.

Instead, with one or two of his guns out of action, he turned towards *Hipper* on a ramming course.

Time and again as she pitched and tossed she was hit by *Hipper*'s guns, but she bored in and rammed *Hipper*, damaging her severely.

Still under a drenching fire from *Hipper*, *Glow-worm* withdrew, turned her bow once more for the German cruiser and, although slowed down by her wounds, tore in once more to ram with her one remaining gun blazing away.

Hipper practically blew her out of the water.

Thirty-one survivors were picked up, her commanding officer was not one of them, and they spent the rest of the war in a prison camp. The whole story of *Glow-worm*'s fight was not told until after the end of hostilities. Then Lieutenant-Commander Roope was awarded a posthumous Victoria Cross. Another destroyer man was to earn one, again posthumously, within a short time, both men who had grown up in the tradition of the small ships.

In the meantime destroyers on escort farther west and south-west; off the Orkneys and Shetlands, in the lower reaches of the North Sea, the Channel and Western Approaches were rather puzzled at the almost total absence of U-boats.

Convoys passed in and out with scarcely a threat.

The reason was not far away.

The submarines had been recalled to lend their strength to the opposition the Germans expected to their invasion plans in Norway.

Strangely enough they played a conspicuously minor role in that campaign.

15

In the confused operations which followed the invasion of Norway destroyers played a large and gallant part. The first destroyer casualty was *Gurkha,* sunk on April 9th by dive bombers while screening *Rodney*. That was the Navy's first experience of that form of attack of which so much had been heard when the Germans had overrun Poland.

Captain Warburton-Lee, in the destroyer *Hardy*, was ordered to go into Narvik, where it was believed German transports were unloading troops and supplies, and was to sink the transports.

Hardy sailed in with *Hotspur*, *Havock*, *Hunter* and *Hostile.* From information gained from a pilot station Captain Warburton-Lee had every reason to believe that not only would he find transports off-loading at the head of the fiord, but would also find six large German destroyers there.

In actual fact there were ten German destroyers there. Captain Warburton-Lee signalled his intention of attacking at dawn. He was working under direct orders from the Admiralty, thus creating for Admiral Whitworth a somewhat invidious position. As Captain Warburton-Lee had signalled his intention of attacking, Admiral Whitworth had to decide whether to allow Warburton-Lee to go in alone or to delay him long enough to reinforce him.

It was not to be the last occasion when direct intervention by the Admiralty over the Commander-in-Chief's head was to lead to confusion.

Hardy sailed in at dawn through heavy snowstorms and

arrived off Narvik at 4 am. With her as she steamed into the harbour were *Hunter* and *Havock*, and they sank the German commodore's ship, the *Wilhelm Heidkamp*, the *Anton Schmidt* and heavily damaged three destroyers which were more or less taken by complete surprise by the audacity of the dawn attack. *Hotspur* and *Hostile*, following shortly afterwards, helped to sink three more merchant ships.

Somewhere lurking in the fiord were at least three more German destroyers.

The fiord at which Narvik is the head is really one of three spreading out like fingers. Narvik lies on Beistfiord, then there is Rombaksfiord, and finally Herjangsfiord. At anchor in Herjangsfiord were three more German destroyers: *Zenker*, *Gliese* and *Koellner*. At the sound of firing they weighed and steamed into the main fiord, Ofotfiord, the wrist of the wide spread hand, and opened fire on the British destroyers. At the same time, from another fiord nearer the sea two more heavy German destroyers sailed and engaged the five raiding destroyers, catching them between two fires.

Hardy was soon disabled and Captain Warburton-Lee was killed in the first few minutes of the fight. *Hunter* was deluged with shells and sank in the middle of the fiord and *Hotspur*, badly damaged and unable to steer, drifted on to the sinking *Hunter*.

Hostile and *Havock* had escaped the concentrated fire from the five German destroyers and the way was open for them to the sea, but they turned and raced back to the assistance of *Hotspur*.

It was almost a suicide turn, two destroyers turning to face five. But the Germans had been so badly mauled by *Hardy*, *Hunter* and *Hotspur* that they declined to press home an attack and *Hotspur* was brought clear.

On the way out *Havock* surprised an ammunition ship, the *Rauenfels*, and literally blew her out of the water.

By half past six the fight was virtually over.

Hunter was sunk in the middle of the fiord, *Hardy* had drifted ashore.

For the loss of two destroyers and one disabled the Germans had paid with two destroyers sunk, five more damaged and seven supply and transport ships sunk.

Captain Warburton-Lee was awarded a posthumous Victoria Cross.

The direct hit on *Hardy*'s bridge killed or wounded all on it as Captain Warburton-Lee made her last signal: 'Keep on engaging the enemy.' *Hardy*, on fire and out of control, was driving ashore when Captain Warburton-Lee's secretary, Paymaster Lieutenant G. H. Stanning, despite a severe wound which had smashed one of his feet, struggled to the wheelhouse and took over until he was relieved.

Lieutenant Stanning was awarded the D.S.O.

It was characteristic of destroyers that even as *Hardy* went ashore on the south side of the fiord the one gun which could be brought to bear went on firing at the German destroyers which were hitting at crippled *Hunter* and *Hotspur*.

Owing to some confusion in signals, it was not known at the time exactly how many German ships were still in the region of Narvik. There were the five which had hammered Warburton-Lee's destroyers and it was suspected that at least two or three more, and possibly a cruiser, had stolen into the fiord under cover of the snowstorm-blasted darkness.

The destruction of these enemy ships was made a priority. Admiral Whitworth transferred his flag from *Renown* to the battleship *Warspite* and arranged screening and support from nine destroyers, four 'Tribals' *Bedouin*, *Cossack*, *Eskimo*, and *Punjabi*, *Hero*, *Icarus*, *Kimberley*, *Forester* and *Foxhound*. Some of them have occurred in this narrative already. From the outbreak of war they had been driving full out, escorting, screening, submarine hunting, minelaying. Now they were to be led into a real destroyer battle for which Warburton-Lee had given them the blue print three days previously.

Shortly after midday on the 12th, *Warspite* and her nine destroyers entered the fiord. *Warspite* launched a reconnaissance plane which paid an immediate dividend despite the heavy snow-squalls. It reported one German destroyer hiding in a bay near Djupvik on the south side of Ofotfiord, ideally placed for a torpedo attack on the British ships as they steamed in.

Bedouin and *Eskimo*, leading the line, surged ahead and before the German destroyer *Koellner* could fire more than one wild salvo, torpedoes from *Bedouin* and *Eskimo* hit her. The British ships steamed on, leaving the German burning furiously. One salvo from *Warspite* finished her off.

In the meantime *Warspite*'s aircraft had spotted a submarine, U-64, at the head of Herjangsfiord, bombed her and sank her.

Warned by the firing, six German destroyers steamed out to meet the British force. Then followed a truly destroyer action, destroyer against destroyer. At times they were tearing across one another's bows so rapidly that had *Warspite* fired there was a chance that she would have hit a friend as well as a foe.

The German destroyers, all modern, were more heavily armed than the British, but at the range the fight took place it counted for little.

But as a matter of interest they were armed with five 5.5-inch guns as opposed to the British destroyers' 4.7-inch, and their torpedo armament was eight tubes.

The action abeam of Narvik was fast and hard-pounding until the Germans withdrew, four of them to the head of Rombaksfiord, two into Narvik and the seventh into Herjangsfiord.

Through the afternoon the battle raged, with the British destroyers slamming away at the Germans. The destroyer *Diether von Roeder*, close inshore at Narvik, had the temerity to fire at *Warspite* as the battleship stood off in support of her raging destroyer force.

Cossack, *Foxhound* and *Kimberley* tore into the harbour, wrapped *Roeder* in flame and in a few minutes she blew up with a mighty roar.

In turning to come out, *Cossack* ran on to a wreck of one

of the destroyers sunk by Captain Warburton-Lee's destroyers three days previously. And there she stuck for a while, but not out of the fight.

Cossack's gunners had an engaging duel with a German shore battery, which soon learned that firing from a stationary ship at a static target was a piece of fruit cake for destroyer men. Commander R. St V. Sherbrooke, commanding *Cossack*, just let his gunners get on with it while he and his pilot worked out the problem of freeing *Cossack*.

Through the afternoon and into twilight the destroyer fight raged. The British destroyers, their guns hot from the almost continual firing, tore around like terriers in a stack yard. Despite men wounded and killed, despite damage, this was something for which they had been built. They were, to use an American phrase, collecting the pay-off for long hours, even long weeks, of monotony, for a hard winter, now behind them, of incredibly hard work with little tangible to show for it.

They drove the four remaining German destroyers up Rombaksfiord where they had them trapped, but trapped in a position that to get at them would mean hard fighting.

Behind them they had left the German destroyers *Koellner*, *Gliese* and *Roeder* sunk, *Kuenne* ashore and a wreck in Herjangsfiord.

Four remained.

At the head of Rombaksfiord were the powerful destroyers *Wolfgang Zenker*, *Berndt von Arnim*, *Hans Ludemann* and *Georg Thiele*. Trapped without a doubt, but still a fighting force and still capable of inflicting mortal damage on the British destroyers.

Against these four raced *Eskimo*, *Forester*, *Hero*, *Icarus* and *Bedouin*. The Germans had retreated behind a smoke-screen which filled the fiord.

Eskimo, leading through the smoke-filled bottle-neck of the fiord, was attacked by *Georg Thiele* lying in ambush with another destroyer lying close to her.

Georg Thiele fired a torpedo which blew *Eskimo*'s bow into a tattered shambles of twisted metal.

Bedouin, *Forester*, *Hero* and *Icarus*, following close behind, smote *Georg Thiele* with savage salvoes so that she could only drift ashore to become a total wreck.

The other destroyer laid a smoke-screen and retreated behind it to join her sisters trapped at the head of the fiord.

Through it, in hot pursuit, raced *Hero*, commanded by Commander H. W. Biggs, *Forester*, commanded by Lieutenant-Commander E. B. Tannock, *Icarus*, commanded by Lieutenant-Commander C. D. Maud, and *Bedouin*, commanded by Commander J. A. McCoy.

They, with Captain Warburton-Lee three days previously, were to be the first destroyer captains to have an opportunity to fight German destroyers in a destroyer versus destroyer mêlée since the Jutland battle twenty-five years back.

They were to suffer nothing in comparison, in fact they were to show that the breed still ran true.

They had to tear through a smoke-filled fiord to find and fight an enemy, at least three destroyers more heavily armed than they were.

And into the smoke they tore . . . to an anticlimax.

They were prepared to face gun-fire and torpedo attack from the trapped Germans.

They sliced through the thinning smoke expecting to be met by a blasting fire. As they emerged they saw three destroyers facing them almost at point-blank range.

Almost as one ship the British destroyers opened fire. There was no reply.

Suspecting a trap, the British destroyers raced on, guns blazing, into the rock-bound fiord narrower than the lower reaches of the River Dart.

Still no reply from the three German destroyers.

The Germans had abandoned them. One of them had apparently been damaged in the earlier fight and had been scuttled.

The British destroyers turned to retrace their way out of

the fiord, leaving behind them the three virtually wrecked German destroyers *Wolfgang Zenker, Berndt von Arnim* and *Hans Ludemann.*

Admiral Whitworth's signal: 'Enemy must be destroyed without delay . . .' had been carried out.

Whatever the outcome of the Norwegian campaign, and however dismal the final reading, the two battles of Narvik must go on in glowing threads of gold on the destroyer escutcheon.

In the first battle one British destroyer was sunk, another went ashore a total loss and a third was severely damaged.

And the price they extracted? Three destroyers sunk, half a dozen supply ships destroyed, an ammunition ship blown up and harbour installations severely damaged.

In the second battle, three days later, eight German destroyers were smashed, a U-boat sunk, for the price of two destroyers—*Eskimo* and *Cossack*—damaged.

During the mid-afternoon *Cossack* succeeded in freeing herself from the wreck under her bow, and it was found that although damaged under water she could proceed, which she did with a sister in close escort.

The wounded from the destroyers were transferred to *Warspite* and the British force, battered but triumphant, withdrew to the open sea. As they passed the entrance to the fiord, a small Norwegian ship steamed out and with the gaping guns of the destroyers swinging menacingly on her proudly announced that she had *Hardy*'s survivors on board.

On a more saddening note two other British destroyers added to the lustre which adorns the history of the small ships.

It was the pattern of *Glow-worm*.

The aircraft-carrier *Glorious*, having embarked RAF Hurricane fighters and their personnel as part of the final withdrawal from Norway, was steaming homewards with two destroyers to screen her, the *Acasta*, commanded by Commander C. G. Glasfurd, and *Ardent*, commanded by Lieutenant-Commander J. F. Barker.

Scharnhorst and *Gneisenau*, raiding northwards to hit at

our convoys taking troops back to Britain, sighted the smoke from *Glorious*. *Scharnhorst* opened fire at 28,000 yards range, well beyond anything the carrier or destroyers had. Almost the first salvoes started hitting *Glorious*. The two destroyers, in classic tradition, turned to meet the enemy and at top speed, laying a smoke-screen between the German heavy ships and *Glorious* as they raced, wriggled and twisted between columns of water which climbed up around them as they endeavoured to get within striking range.

Behind them, *Glorious*, overwhelmed by the fires which had broken out, was abandoning ship. *Ardent* fired her torpedoes at long range in the hope of hitting *Scharnhorst* and was almost immediately overwhelmed by a salvo which rolled her over and she sank.

The lone *Acasta*, in a forlorn and doomed dash, raced onwards, firing guns and torpedoes as she sped.

And she hit *Scharnhorst* almost amidships, damaging her. Then *Acasta* was hit time and again, slowed down, rolled over and sank, getting away one last shot before the waters covered her guns.

In less than two hours the fight was over and all that remained, as the Germans turned away, making no attempt to pick up survivors, was wreckage to show that three gallant ships had fought there.

Three days later a small Norwegian ship picked up thirty-eight survivors from *Glorious* and one man from *Acasta* and landed them in the Faeroes.

Two men from *Ardent* were rescued by a German seaplane and were made prisoners of war.

In the few brief weeks the Norwegian campaign raged, destroyers did an enormous amount of work. They landed troops, they re-embarked them under heavy bombing, they escorted, they screened, they fought.

Whatever glory that did come out of that dismal portion of the war, destroyer men can hold up their heads with pride, remembering *Glow-worm*, *Hardy*, *Hunter*, *Warspite*'s nine raging destroyers at Narvik, *Acasta, Ardent, Afridi,* sunk during the evacuation.

Before the month of June was to run its course destroyers were to add to that glory.

16

On the morning of May 10th the Germans launched their mighty military machine out from the Ardennes and at the same time invaded Holland and Belgium.

Resistance in the Lowlands soon crumbled.

Plans already laid for demolition in the large ports of Antwerp, Amsterdam and Flushing had been prepared for what was accepted as the inevitable. The task of conveying the demolition parties fell to destroyers.

When the Dutch resistance faded and died the Netherlands Royal Family and Government had to be rescued and brought to Britain and the mixed force of Marines and Guards, which had been rushed over to help the Dutch in their fighting, also had to be extricated.

The Royal Family embarked on the destroyer *Hereward* and the Government on *Windsor*.

Neither destroyer could move until two humble little trawler minesweepers, *Arctic Hunter* and *Melante*, had hurried over from minesweeping in the Thames, and under constant air attack all day finally blasted a path through the mines laid by aircraft.

The tension mounted through the day as news filtered in that the Germans were racing towards the Hook.

No doubt had they been on a normal destroyer operation, which could mean anything, the commanding officers of *Hereward* and *Windsor* would have taken a chance, thanked the minesweepers nicely and would have raced across the partly swept waters.

But with their precious passengers risks had to be cut down

to the minimum. On the other hand it would have been catastrophic for them to be trapped in the Hook.

Six other destroyers, risking fog and mines, moved in and lifted the Marines and Guards with no time to spare and conveyed them safely to Dover.

While their bigger and later-type sisters had been driven almost to their limits in Norway, the older destroyers, largely 'V's' and 'W's', had been doing their task of convoying and patrolling farther south.

Now the heat and burden of the day was to fall on them. The first destroyer lost in those multifarious jobs being done by the small ships was *Valentine*, bombed while operating in the Scheldt, and *Winchester* was damaged. Every ship in the Nore and Dover commands which could move at all went to sea, and, except for brief intervals to re-ammunition and oil up, stayed at sea for the next three or four weeks.

Westminster was damaged and *Whitley* was sunk by savage bombing. True, there was some air cover provided at intervals by Blenheims and Hurricanes, but the former were too few and too slow to drive off the thrusting German bombers and the Hurricanes' endurance was too short to allow them more than half an hour over the area.

The activity swiftly moved down from the Dutch coast to the Belgian ports and destroyers evacuated large numbers of Belgian refugees, the inevitable small babies among them, and many were the improvisations achieved by the destroyer ratings to see that the babies were adequately fed.

Under pressure from the German armies which had engulfed Holland and Belgium, and from the divisions which had swept aside French resistance, the British Expeditionary Force and their retreating allies were becoming impacted in that perimeter which included Dunkirk, Calais, Boulogne.

Within a fortnight of the first German break-out through the Ardennes the greater part of the British Army in France and part of the French Northern Army were trapped.

In an attempt to hold the western flank of the perimeter at Boulogne, two battalions of Guards were hurried across, supported by destroyers of Dover and Nore commands. Their names began to become familiar, and will become even more so as the story of Dunkirk unfolds itself, their names will recur again and again, until for some of them the end comes with the waters closing over them.

Vimy, Venomous, Wild Swan, Whitshed, Vimiera, Venetia, Wessex, Wolfhound and some others laboured mightily to help the Army hold Boulogne and Calais. Some of them came under mortar- and rifle-fire while delivering troops and ammunition to the puny force trying to hold Boulogne and Calais, and while lifting wounded for transport back to Dover.

Boulogne inevitably fell and the troops placed ashore there had to be rescued. Under heavy air attack *Vimiera, Venomous, Venetia, Whitshed* and *Wild Swan* moved in to the quays and while the Welsh Guards boarded the destroyers in perfect order, the destroyers engaged enemy batteries and tanks at only a few hundred yards range. Each ship lifted approximately a thousand men, one covering another with gun-fire.

Admiral Bertram Ramsay, Vice-Admiral Dover, was convinced that there must be a number of British soldiers still engaged in holding the Boulogne section of the perimeter, or at least a part of it.

He dispatched *Windsor* under cover of darkness to try one more attempt at rescue, following her with *Vimiera. Windsor* found 600 of them and embarked them.

In the early hours of the next morning, May 24th, *Vimiera* crept cautiously into Boulogne. The silence was uncanny. For all they knew, the Germans had completely overrun the port and by now had sited batteries of powerful guns on the very quays.

Every shadow was a menace.

The best part of two battalions of Guards was still holding out some distance from the port. A messenger was sent to collect them and by 3 am nearly 1,500 of them were packed, jammed shoulder to shoulder, on the dangerously overloaded destroyer. Had one bomb hit her, or a shell, the slaughter would have been terrible.

Wessex was supposed to have followed *Vimiera* into the harbour, but she had run into trouble on the way over. Three hundred Welsh Guards, whom *Vimiera* could not take aboard, waited on the quay until daylight.

And waited in vain.

Boulogne fell into enemy hands completely on the morning of 25th and the perimeter was constricted to Calais–Dunkirk, Calais to be a supply port.

Before many hours passed it was realised that not only could we not hold Calais against the blitzkrieg armoured divisions of Germany, but we could not hold Dunkirk for any length of time. In that ever-constricting perimeter was almost the entire British Expeditionary Force.

Ashore in Calais was a mixed force of troops from the Rifle Brigade and a few tanks under command of Brigadier Nicholson. At midnight on May 24th–25th Brigadier Nicholson was tersely informed that his hard-pressed troops could not be evacuated and they would have to fight to the last.

Admiral Ramsay did not agree. He had placed destroyers offshore off Calais where, under almost constant bombing attacks, they had aided the Army with supporting bombardments until their gun crews were noise-stunned and their magazines were low.

And there were losses. *Vimiera* and the Polish destroyer *Burza* were damaged and *Wessex* was sunk.

Wolfhound and *Verity* managed to get into the bomb-and-shell-blasted harbour to land ammunition for the hard-pressed troops, a feat in itself.

Admiral Ramsay was furnished—somewhat belatedly—with a copy of the signal which had virtually doomed the Rifle Brigade, precariously holding parts of Calais, to virtual extinction.

Although I was not present when Admiral Ramsay received that signal I subsequently saw him, in the two years I served under him at Dover, receive equally vital signals.

I can imagine what happened. He would be sitting at his rather untidy desk—untidy, that is, to the casual observer because he knew where everything was on it, even down to the bunker state of the smallest minesweeper.

He would stare at the signal for what seemed a long, even an overlong, interval. Then, with a delicate touch, he would nudge it a few inches farther on to his desk, lean back, hands on the edge of his desk—and a full-scale operation was complete in his mind, leaving only details to be attended to by his staff.

His attitude towards the problem was this:

'The Navy put them ashore. All things being equal, the Navy will take them off.'

His harassed staff rounded up every armed yacht, trawler, drifter and liberty boat in the Dover Command, plus a number of lifeboats, small yachts and even sailing dinghies, and sent them over to Calais under cover of darkness with the trawlers as escort for what was a small-scale blue print of the subsequent 'Dynamo' operation which rescued so many from the port and beaches of Dunkirk.

Most of the holding force at Calais, and some of the Marines who had been landed for demolition work, were lifted and brought back to Dover.

Calais was abandoned to the triumphant Germans, and its loss constricted the perimeter until it contained just Dunkirk and a few-miles-long strip of sand.

A hard lesson learned in Norway—for that matter still being learned up there because the evacuation of troops was still going on—was that adequate air cover *all the time* was an essential.

The destroyers had proved beyond any doubt that they were quite capable of duelling with shore batteries. Several salutary lessons had been taught to German army gunners when they tried exchanging broadsides with destroyers.

The lesson was emphasised in the attempts to hold first Boulogne then Calais. And a greater emphasis was to be laid on the lesson in the next week or so.

In the light of various post-war inquests and revelations it has to be accepted that RAF bombers were undoubtedly blasting the Germans a long way inland, and undoubtedly relieving the strain on the ever-decreasing perimeter, but even today members of the crews of the ubiquitous destroyers and other small ships which gave of their best off that Belgian-Franco coast will take some convincing that adequate air cover was provided.

Personally, during the whole of one long, long hot day during which Stuka dive bombers provided an almost non-stop macabre orchestra over troops on the beaches, I saw but two RAF aircraft—and one yas a Boulton and Paul Defiant. It was going down, leaving behind a trail of thick smoke with three German fighters in close attendance until it crashed into the brassy sea.

By Sunday, May 26th, it was obvious that the British Expeditionary Force and part of the French Northern Army were trapped without any hope of breaking out, or getting away other than by evacuation by sea.

The task of getting off as many as possible fell on the already well-loaded shoulders of Admiral Ramsay.

While the preliminary details were being thrashed out, a tiny act of courage was happening in Calais. The Germans had taken the whole town, including the quays and the docks. Through the velvet darkness there crept into Calais, risking being blown out of the water, a yacht, the *Gulzar*, part of Dover's auxiliary force.

From inland the small crew of this erstwhile pleasure craft could hear the roar of German motor vehicles as they took over Calais. Some of *Gulzar*'s crew stole ashore to search for any wounded which the destroyers had missed. They found none. *Gulzar* started to steal away from Calais as stealthily as she had entered.

As they crept past the very end of the breakwater, known to thousands of holiday-makers in peace-time, there came a cautious hail.

Gulzar equally cautiously answered.

The hail came from a party of soldiers which had resolutely fought a small retreating action through the town, to the docks and to the end of the breakwater in darkness, feeling assured that when the time came the Navy would lift them off.

Gulzar embarked them—between forty-five and fifty soldiers—as a German armoured car came lumbering down the breakwater.

It was a miniature of the larger picture to be painted in fire and blood and smoke at Dunkirk and the beaches beyond in the next week or so.

At approximately 7 pm on Sunday, May 26th, a signal was made by the Admiralty to begin operation 'Dynamo'; to begin a naval operation which was then, and still remains now, unique in naval history.

The first intention of the operation was to lift about 45,000 troops from Dunkirk and the beaches close to the town.

The immediate necessity was for small cargo ships, many of them Dutch coasting ships which had fled before the invasion of their country, and fast cross-Channel ships.

To cover them destroyers were to patrol and escort them.

But after two days the destroyers started embarking men, and the tempo grew as did the number of men saved.

Within a couple of days of the beginning of 'Dynamo' the inner harbour of Dunkirk was virtually wrecked, but there still remained the breakwaters to the east and west of the harbour, and although not designed to take ships there was a fair depth of water alongside them.

It is as well at this point to view the problem facing Admiral Ramsay and his staff, both officers at Dover and those at Dunkirk.

The Germans were as close as Gravelines on the west and the Belgian town of Nieuport on the east. There were three main beaches: Malo, nearest to Dunkirk, Bray and La Panne just over the frontier into Belgium.

The overall plan was to lift most of the troops from the

harbour of Dunkirk and the remainder of them from the beaches.

Three routes were established: Route Z from Dover to a point closely abeam of Calais and thence along the coast to Dunkirk; Route X from Dover, round the Goodwins and thence to Dunkirk; and a longer Route Y from Dover, around the North Goodwins, proceeding well up to abeam of the Belgian coast off Ostend.

The evacuation on the first two days showed that given the ships a great many more troops could be saved than the original estimate of 43,000 to 50,000.

Admiral Ramsay called for more destroyers from Portsmouth, Plymouth and even as far as the fleet.

They were provided; at top speed.

One example will suffice. *Codrington*, secure to a buoy at Scapa, was ordered south. She sailed at 7.30 pm from Scapa and was tied up alongside an oiler at Dover twenty-three hours later.

Cautious but growing optimism pointed to the possibility that a far greater number of trapped troops could be saved.

To do it destroyers were recalled from patrols and escort and were ordered alongside the breakwaters at Dunkirk and to the beaches.

'Dynamo', as the world now knows it, began to gain impetus.

And in the operation a growing scroll of destroyer names began to appear.

In the first two days *Windsor* was damaged by bombing; *Wakeful*, loaded with nearly 700 troops, was torpedoed by an E-boat, the latest German menace on the north flank of the evacuation; *Grafton* was torpedoed by a U-boat; *Grenade*, after fighting off two heavy bombing attacks, was sunk by a third attack; *Jaguar* was bombed and disabled and had to be rescued by *Express*; *Greyhound* and *Intrepid*, rescuing troops from Malo beach, were repeatedly bombed but succeeded in taking off 500 troops each; *Saladin*, bombed a dozen times, should have been sunk by all the laws of

Moorsom. Paid a handsome dividend in the Jutland battle

Laertes, one of the Harwich destroyers

A little 'Hunt' class slams through it. Note anti-E-boat pom-pom

Chelsea, 1940. Ex-USS 'mothball' of destroyers-for-bases exchange

Two first-war veterans. *Whitshed*, which was at the Dunkirk evacuation from beginning to end . . .

. . . and *Walpole*, which fought against the *Scharnhorst* and *Gneisenau* in the Channel dash

Kelly. Safely in the Tyne after being torpedoed, 1940

Kelly. Had both ends and the middle rebuilt. Sunk at Crete

Javelin, from the same stable as Kelly

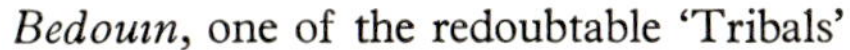

Bedouin, one of the redoubtable 'Tribals'

Daring, 1952

London, 1963

Bristol, 1972

averages but limped into Dover, to emerge a few days later like a giant refreshed.

So 'Dynamo' increased in tempo. Destroyers came from other bases, Rosyth, Harwich, Portsmouth and Plymouth, bases which virtually denuded themselves of destroyers, although the demands on them at their home bases were by no means diminished. Even fleet destroyers were spared from Scapa.

17

'Dynamo' began to hum on the morning of the 29th and rapidly reached a high and sustained note.

On the previous day and night, the darkness ripped apart by the glare of fires ashore, the destroyers worked away at the almost endless stream of weary soldiers.

Gallant, *Wakeful*, *Grafton*, *Greyhound*, *Impulsive*, *Wolfhound*, *Wolsey*, *Montrose*, *Sabre*, *Worcester*, *Anthony*, *Javelin* and *Vivacious*, besides others, shuttled either into the breakwaters or closed in to the beaches, each to load up and to return to Dover.

As they loaded up so they gave way to other destroyers: *Verity*, *Harvester*, *Esk*, *Montcalm*, *Shikari* and *Scimitar*.

By the end of the first full day of 'Dynamo' nearly 12,000 men had been taken from Dunkirk, either from the beaches or from the harbour.

Optimism grew. It seemed that if the pace lasted there was more than a chance that at least half the force trapped, roughly 150,000 men, could be saved.

In the meantime the destroyer losses were formidable, and the Admiralty, painfully conscious of other and heavy commitments, withdrew seven of the larger destroyers, *Icarus*, *Impulsive*, *Intrepid*, *Ivanhoe*, *Havant*, *Harvester* and *Javelin*—hard-bitten veterans of the Norwegian campaign—leaving fifteen, *Anthony*, *Codrington*, *Esk*, *Express*, *Keith*, *Malcolm*, *Sabre*, *Scimitar*, *Shikari*, and the faithful 'V's' and 'W's',

Whitehall, Winchelsea, Worcester, Windsor, Vanquisher, Verity, to take over the task.

Admiral Ramsay found that it was overloading them to expect them to keep up the shuttle service the destroyers had maintained up to then, and demanded that the 'H's', 'I's' and 'J's' be returned to him. They were.

The most northerly route of the three established, roughly the course taken by pleasure steamers to Ostend, had by the third day come under gun-fire from German shore batteries and for daylight operations was not used.

That left only the central route, X, almost a straight line from Ramsgate and the North Goodwins to Dunkirk Roads. This shortened the trip for the overladen destroyers and made attacks by U-boats and E-boats a lot more hazardous than was the case on the 'Y' route.

The total of rescued men began to grow and, accordingly, the number still ashore at Dunkirk shrunk. The 45,000 which the Government had hoped to lift from Dunkirk was soon passed; so, too, was the more optimistic figure of 150,000.

With the return of the larger destroyers an almost unbroken shuttle service from the harbour was maintained by destroyers, while smaller boats of every description worked at ferrying from the beaches.

Thursday the 30th showed the best day's figures.

More than 50,000 men were brought home, 29,000 taken off the beaches of Bray and Malo and the remainder from the breakwaters.

Through that day and the night the Germans bombed and shelled savagely without being able to do more than slow up the work slightly and so intensify the efforts of the crews of the ships, now almost at their last gasp from sheer exhaustion.

The following day was the peak of men taken from Dunkirk. Nearly 23,000 were taken off the beaches and more than 45,000 from the harbour.

La Panne was becoming too hazardous for ships to close it and the men waiting there were sent to Bray, where evacuation in small ships was going on apace.

Still the destroyers worked hard, lifting 1,000 men at a time, tearing across to Dover, landing their soldiers and racing back.

It was magnificent work, rewarding work, but demanding a price.

As the first grey tinge of the midsummer day touched the sky, the enemy intensified shelling and bombing. *Keith, Basilisk, Havant* and the French destroyer *Foudroyant* were sunk.

But still the figures rose, 64,500 taken off on the last day of May; the fourth day of the evacuation. On June 1st, despite bomber attacks and heavy shelling, another 64,000 were taken out of Dunkirk or off the beaches.

Of them, nearly 20,000 were rescued by destroyers.

Destroyer losses and damage were enormous and on June 2nd, with an estimated 6,000 British soldiers and 65,000 French soldiers still ashore in the ever-shrinking perimeter, Admiral Ramsay decided that daylight operations would be suspended. The beaches were now unusable and only a few stragglers trying to reach Dunkirk harbour remained on the sands.

The crews of the destroyers were beyond exhaustion point. They were drawing deeply from the well of fortitude. A brief spell was allowed them, then they streamed into Dunkirk once the evening shadows gave way to starlit night.

The sullen, deep red of the flames of burning oil installations lit up the harbour, punctuated occasionally as some store blew up.

Before the all-too-rapid dawn came 6,000 British, virtually all that remained, and nearly 30,000 French soldiers were brought to safety. To lift them, eleven destroyers, minesweepers and drifters entered Dunkirk.

Still it was not the end. The figures dropped by comparison for two reasons. The rescue work was now only nightfall work, and the French soldiers were having difficulty in disengaging themselves from the enemy. So long as they held the shrunken perimeter, now including part of the town and the harbour, with not more than a mile of Malo beach, then so much more time was being bought for the rescue ships.

On June 3rd about 35,000 French soldiers were left there. One last haul and all would be rescued. Those of us who served in the small ships at Dunkirk, particularly destroyer men, have no clear recollection of the last day and night. It seemed to be endless steaming, with snarling bombers probing overhead and bombing the head of wakes, flames and a pall of smoke, and seemingly an endless stream of men shuffling slowly down the breakwaters. Then somehow the ship was clear into open water again, more bombing, then tired but kindly hands in Dover, all those impressions impacted into one kaleidoscope without any feeling of passing time.

The night of June 3rd–4th was to be the last night, and there was more than a possibility that the ships engaged might find themselves fighting German tanks and batteries over open sights as they had at Boulogne and Calais.

Between forty and fifty ships were given this last task: *Express*, *Malcolm*, *Sabre*, *Venomous*, *Vanquisher* and *Whitshed*, with famous peace-time holiday passenger ships now impressed as personnel carriers, *Canterbury, Côte d'Argent, Lady of Mann, Royal Sovereign* and *Tynwald*. Behind them a swarm of smaller auxiliary ships.

Whitshed entered Dunkirk harbour, as she had done many times in the past few days, followed rapidly by the others, then the personnel carriers. There was reason for speed. In the centre of the town, and Dunkirk's docks ran far towards that centre, they could hear heavy rifle-, mortar- and gunfire.

The Germans were increasing the pressure.

The destroyers and other ships worked from the east and west breakwaters, frequently coming under probing artillery fire. At three o'clock the last of the troops, all French, were lifted from the moles and were on their way to safety.

Those still holding the Germans inland in the town had to be left behind.

The final accountancy was heart-warming. 'Dynamo' had been started with the hope of rescuing about 45,000 men. It had grown into an operation which the world is never likely to see again.

In fact 338,000 men were rescued and lived to fight another day to exact retribution four years later.

But the price paid in destroyers was heavy; heavy not only in destroyers sunk and damaged but because of the strain thrown on destroyer resources in the next couple of months.

One sad task was left to destroyers. *Express* took off the naval party which had been superintending embarkation on the moles and yet some more French stragglers. Then followed the grim task, as *Express* and *Shikari* escorted some blockships laden with concrete.

One was sunk by a mine, the others drove in between the piers to partially block the harbour.

As her tragic little convoy settled in the water, *Shikari* saw a group of men right at the end of the west breakwater.

Some were lying down, exhausted, some were wounded, as roughly applied bandages showed.

Shikari slipped expertly alongside and took them aboard. They were General Barthelemy, and more than 350 French soldiers who had fought their way right across France from the centre of the Maginot Line to Dunkirk, only to find they were too late.

So they thought until *Shikari* pulled alongside.

So 'Dynamo' ended.

More than forty destroyers were engaged in that operation, of which six British destroyers, *Basilisk*, *Grafton*, *Grenade*, *Havant*, *Keith* and *Wakeful*, were sunk, as were three French destroyers, and nineteen were damaged.

When the number of destroyers sunk or damaged in the Norwegian, Netherlands and Dunkirk operations is considered it will be appreciated that until the building programme could even begin to catch up, the weight thrown on destroyers in the immediate future would stretch that thin grey line to hair-thickness dimensions.

With the Germans in control of the coastline of Europe from Narvik to Brest, escorting coastal convoys down the North Sea and in the Channel was going to be arduous.

With U-boats thrusting out into the Atlantic from western and north-western French ports Atlantic convoys would feel the steel of the German attack.

In the Mediterranean, there the puffed-up Bull Frog of the Pontine Marshes—anxious to batten on a prostrate France—was to cause our convoys and fleet some anxious weeks, even more so when the Germans added their weight to his.

Truly, had the destroyer men stopped for any mental assessment of what lay before them they would have quailed and might have been forgiven had they faltered.

Their story in the succeeding year shows that they neither quailed, nor faltered.

In the meantime their tasks were by no means over. The triumphant drive by the Germans through northern France to Calais and Dunkirk had split the Franco-British forces. Any hope of re-equipping and landing the army taken off Dunkirk vanished like smoke in an autumn breeze.

Those Allied forces west of the German drive were concentrating on Le Havre and Cherbourg.

They had to be taken off, and the task was given to Admiral Sir William James, Commander-in-Chief, Portsmouth. Many of his destroyers had taken part in the Dunkirk operation.

They were to be committed to another, almost as large, and more complicated evacuation. Instead of the narrow straits they would be faced with the wide Channel between Le Havre and the Isle of Wight.

The work began. Operation 'Cycle' began to move.

Admiral James ordered the operation to begin on June 9th—five days after the last troops had been taken from Dunkirk—and in three days so far as Le Havre was concerned the evacuation was completed. There was heavy bombing and a cross-Channel steamer was sunk.

In this operation at the beginning, and in it to the end, were *Codrington*, six more British destroyers and two Canadian.

As the pace increased, so more destroyers from Portsmouth Command provided patrols and escorts and lifted men.

But farther east along the coast was developing a tragedy which the Royal Navy still profoundly regrets to this day.

The 51st Highland Division, attached to that part of the French Army which had failed to cross the Seine in time to get to Le Havre, was being forced into a tight perimeter around St Valery, about twenty miles west of Dieppe, a large port they had tried to reach but had failed.

Admiral James sent destroyers along the coast to reconnoitre and they came under fire from German batteries on the cliff-tops near St Valery, and *Ambuscade* was hit and damaged.

Preparations were made to take off the 51st Division and the French soldiers, and a number of small ships, with a strong destroyer escort under *Codrington*, assembled off the coast in readiness. The Scots withdrew from the perimeter on the night of the 9th and assembled on the beach and in the small harbour under fire from German tanks and mobile guns on the frowning cliffs overlooking the town.

Through the night they waited. No ships came.

The weather which had been miraculously well disposed at Dunkirk turned against the small armada waiting off St Valery. Fog closed in with visibility down to a few yards.

At daylight the divisional commander had to move his men back from the town. That day they even tried to drive the well-emplaced Germans back from their vantage points on the cliffs.

The operation was planned for the night to come.

But it was too late.

The French general, under whose command was the 51st Division, ordered his troops to lay down their arms.

For a while the Scots fought on, but it was useless expenditure of men and they, too, surrendered.

Ironically, the night they marched into captivity was ideal for an evacuation. With nearly 170 ships assembled the entire force could have been lifted had the French general decided to fight for just eighteen hours more.

Even so, from a small place at the eastern fringe of the perimeter a couple of thousand men were rescued under concentrated fire from the Germans.

And to the long list of destroyer casualties, although none was sunk, were added *Bulldog*, *Ambuscade* and *Boadicea*.

Once the French had asked for and been granted an Armistice, and had surrendered the whole French coastline from Belgium to the Spanish border, it became obvious that any hope of placing a British army once more in France had vanished.

The main task now was to extricate the troops left there.

The larger operation 'Aerial' was planned and under it troops were to be taken off at ports from Cherbourg, Brest and St Nazaire. So Plymouth Command came into the picture.

Admiral Dunbar-Nasmith, Commander-in Chief, Plymouth, shuttled every possible ship he could raise to the Bay of Biscay ports while his colleague east did the same to Cherbourg and St Malo.

The pattern by now was familiar, but on a broader canvas. Whereas Dover Command's 'Dynamo' had been impacted in the narrow Dover Straits, Operation 'Aerial', shared by Portsmouth and Plymouth, ranged along roughly 500 miles of open coast from Cherbourg to La Pallice.

Plymouth was able to use liners, one of which, *Lancastria*, was bombed and sunk with heavy loss of life.

To detail all the operations would be merely to say 'mixture as before and shake well'.

Losses, all things considered, including the wide scope of the joint operation, were astonishingly small.

Nearly 192,000 men were taken aboard and brought back to England. Between 'Dynamo', 'Cycle' and 'Aerial' nearly

560,000 men were saved, men who had fought, always on the retreat, but men with almost complete confidence that when they saw the glint of the sea at their backs the Navy would be there to take them off.

As it did.

And the backbone of the naval forces was provided by destroyers, the long lean ships manned by men who had no knowledge of their limitations.

18

Now we stood alone. France, vanquished and prostrate, the whole of her coastline in German hands, presented us with a problem frightening to contemplate.

To keep the wheels of the war machine moving, ships had to sail in convoy and convoys had to be escorted.

And in the main the weight of escorting had to fall on destroyers.

From the beginning of the Norwegian campaign to the final hours of the Bay of Biscay evacuations a tremendous call had been made on destroyers. And they answered it.

But there was to be no respite. Those which remained still had to face up to ever-increasing commitments. Coastal convoys had to be escorted from the Firth of Forth, down the North Sea, through Dover Straits and down the Channel.

The Germans wasted no time in hammering the coastal convoys by mining the routes taken by them, by E-boat attacks at night and by incessant bombing by day.

Much of the load of escorting these coastal convoys fell on the indomitable 'V's' and 'W's'.

A typical Channel convoy, for instance, of twenty-five to thirty ships, some coastwise vessels, some bound on an ocean voyage, would have as escort one or two destroyers, three or four Asdic trawlers and a couple of M.L.s.

Even while they had been at anchor at Southend the ships would probably have felt the doubtful benefit of a raid or two by high-level bombers. Once they sailed from the Thames, through the Dover Straits, they would be hammered again by high-level and dive bombers until the hours of darkness during which E-boats would attack.

Convoy CW8, code letters for a west-bound convoy, comprising twenty-one ships with two destroyers and auxiliary craft as escort, was severely mauled when it sailed on July 25th. In the first afternoon five merchant ships were sunk before the convoy reached the North Goodwins, and both destroyers were damaged but managed to keep steaming.

That night, in the few hours of darkness, E-boats hit the convoy and damaged four more ships. As soon as the red sun showed a thin sliver above the horizon, the bombers came back and sank three more, damaging two and again hitting one of the destroyers. Eleven weary ships crept past Dungeness where additional escorts from Portsmouth joined them.

When the losses were counted up from the first few 'C' convoys the Admiralty decided to discontinue them until more adequate protection could be devised, including a more constant air cover.

Two weeks later CW9 sailed the same route, this time with the new 'Hunt' class destroyers as escorts. These new, small destroyers were better equipped with anti-aircraft armament. Furthermore, as a result of pleas to the RAF, an umbrella of Hurricanes was arranged. As the convoy was approaching Beachy Head in darkness, E-boats attacked, sank three ships and badly scattered the remainder, so that when daylight came the convoy was straggling over ten miles of sea. But no dive bombers got at them.

Shortly afterwards sailing times for CW and CE convoys were altered so that they passed through the Straits in darkness (where as often as not they were ineffectually shelled by the big guns the Germans had set up on Cap Gris Nez).

While the coastal fight was going on, the thin grey line of destroyers based on Western Approaches, again some of them rather elderly ladies, were escorting ocean-going convoys a few hundred miles out into the Atlantic, leaving them with a slim through escort, and were picking up a homeward-bound convoy.

U-boats, now with bases on the north-west coast of France, began to exact their toll.

The convoys across the Atlantic, mainly from Halifax, would have a local escort of Canadian destroyers for 300 or 400 miles. The escort would be a long-range sloop, or an armed merchant cruiser, like the *Jervis Bay*; then, somewhere about seventeen degrees west, the Western Approaches destroyers would meet them.

On paper that was ideal. In fact it had complications. Bad weather would delay, even scatter, an east-bound convoy, and the destroyers, limited for fuel, would have to use up precious time, and oil, rounding up the scattered ships before starting the main job of escorting them in.

The rendezvous had to be extended to roughly twenty degrees west to meet the growing menace of the U-boats, which now, of course, had a much longer endurance in Western Approaches than they had had when they had to journey from their German bases.

The Germans lost no time in establishing air bases in north-western France and from it flew four-engined Focke-Wulf Condor long-distance planes well out into the Atlantic to locate convoys and ships sailing independently.

This time we had no valuable naval base in Southern Ireland, which would have been of tremendous advantage. There was no Queenstown force to harry the submarines in the area either with hunting groups or with additional escorts. Eventually the convoys had to be re-routed around the north of Ireland.

The sorry tale of losses began to assume serious proportions towards the end of June and into July 1940.

In June, while the revised convoy system was still fluid and escorts were sailing to seventeen degrees west, U-boats sank fifty-eight ships before the new routes came into operation. The submarines soon discovered the amendment to routes and in July sank thirty-eight ships.

For the four months, up to October, U-boats had a total bag of 217 ships, of which 144 were sunk in convoy.

In those few months half a dozen names began to appear as U-boat aces. It was before the wolf-pack system, and submarines hunted individually, although they could be heard chattering to one another over the radio at night-time.

The names to be remembered by the overworked destroyers were Kretschmer, Endras, Prien, who had courageously penetrated into Scapa Flow and had sunk the *Royal Oak*, Fraucheim, Jenish and Schepke. They were the aces, with the rest of the high cards falling right for them.

Convoy after convoy was attacked by these men and the tonnage credited to them became astronomical.

In August fifty-six ships were sunk, in September fifty-nine, and in October sixty-three ships were sent to the bottom.

That period for the U-boat commanders was known as 'the happy time'. For the thin drawn escorts they were heart-break months.

The submarines were attacking at night on the surface, where their superior speed was of immense advantage against the slow corvettes making up the escort.

A typical escort of that period for a convoy of forty ships or more would be one destroyer and three corvettes. The destroyer would be ahead of the convoy, a corvette disposed to each wing of the convoy and the third corvette bringing up the rear.

A convoy of this size would be spread over six or seven square miles and there would be wide and inevitable gaps on each side open for submarines to penetrate and attack.

What was described as a strong (!) escort for a convoy of sixty ships was made up of three destroyers and seven corvettes. An escort of that size could afford, but only just afford, to send a destroyer tearing off to force down and possibly attack a submarine, and that left gaps in the defence.

In the main the escorts had to grin and bear it until a submarine audaciously came in close.

But before the end of the year, although only eight submarines were sunk between July and November, one of them was Jenish in U-32. On October 30th he tried to torpedo a ship, missed and the destroyers *Highlander* and *Harvester*, unencumbered by any merchant ships, raced in and fastened on to U-32 with their Asdic.

While *Harvester* stood off to keep the ring, Commander W. A. Dallmeyer, in *Highlander*, dropped an accurate pattern of depth-charges over the submarine, blew her to the surface and riddled her with salvoes of 4.7 gun-fire.

U-32 lasted only a few minutes, sufficient for twenty-nine of her crew to jump into the water from whence they were rescued by the grimly triumphant destroyers.

Among the survivors was Hans Jenish.

The urgent, crying need for destroyers was being gradually met as new ships came off the stocks, and those which had been extensively damaged in the prolonged campaigns of Norway, the Netherlands and France once more came back into commission.

Unfortunately for Western Approaches, the situation in the Mediterranean called also for destroyers, and many of the later types, including the fleet destroyers, were dispatched to that war zone.

In those summer months of 1940 the threat of invasion was real. Should it occur, the spearhead of the attack on the invasion craft would be destroyers and to meet that threat demands were made on the Home Fleet and Western Approaches. The destroyers 'commandeered' from the Home Fleet greatly reduced the operational scope of the large ships, and those taken from Western Approaches reduced the escorts, already pitifully thin, to almost vanishing point.

Although the number of U-boats operating during those late summer and early autumn months was by no means large, they included the half-dozen ace submarine commanders who between them sank almost two-thirds of the shipping sent to the bottom.

Admiral Raeder, in a report to Hitler, was fully aware of this, pointing out that the obvious weakness of the British defence and escort forces was of great advantage to the submarines.

Winston Churchill's observations to the First Lord and the First Sea Lord were markedly similar.

He wrote: '. . . The repeated severe losses in the north-west approaches are most grievous. . . . There seems to have been a great falling off in the control of these approaches. No doubt this is due to the shortage of destroyers through invasion precautions. . . . We cannot go on like this.'

In the meantime the destroyers, backed up by corvettes and anti-submarine trawlers, were doing their desperate best. Along the east coast thirty-odd destroyers, some of them of the latest type, were held poised to smash at the invasion where and when it was launched.

In Nore Command, for instance, there were the best part of five flotillas of destroyers. How invaluable they would have been in Western Approaches!

Secret negotiations were going on with America to obtain the release to us of fifty of their mothball fleet of average destroyers. Finally, in return for bases in the West Indies, America agreed.

The destroyers started to arrive. They were old, designed and built to take part in the First World War, and were the American counterparts of our own faithful, and almost indestructible, 'V's' and 'W's'.

Younger sisters, in fact, to those destroyers which had crossed the Atlantic to help tilt the scales in our favour in the submarine campaign of 1917–18.

The urgent need, particularly in Western Approaches, was for any type of craft with enough speed and armament to enable them to escort a convoy and attack submarines threatening that convoy.

The 'four-stackers' went a long way to fill that bill.

They had not been modernised as our 'V's' and 'W's' had been, their submarine-detection devices were out of date and they had to be adapted in our already overworked yards, but they were welcome.

In anticipation of the completion of the bargain, British crews had already been sent to Halifax, where they were to take over, and the American Navy had already started bringing the destroyers forward from reserve ready to hand over.

Early in the autumn they started arriving in groups, sailing the same waters their elder sisters had sailed under the Queenstown Command nearly twenty-five years before.

Many a middle-aged merchant captain, with memories of the First World War when he was a junior officer, must have blinked twice or three times when he found that his western-ocean escort was formed partly of the same, rather odd-looking, slim four-funnelled destroyers which had escorted him then.

With one difference. These were flying the White Ensign.

As they arrived, they were named after towns, of which the name *Campbeltown* is probably the most famous for her glorious end in the St Nazaire raid.

As the threat of invasion died away, Western Approaches found themselves in the luxurious position of being able to afford two, even three, destroyers to certain convoys.

And the submarines began to suffer. In that succeeding winter they exacted a greater toll from the U-boats, and, what was more, wiped out the German submarine aces.

Jenish, in U-32, had already fallen to *Highlander* and *Harvester*.

Prien, who had *Royal Oak*'s scalp at his belt, was the next.

The hard North Atlantic punished convoys, escorts and submarines alike and the rate of sinkings began to fall.

Only one serious attack was made on a convoy from Halifax by four submarines, but of that four, two were commanded by Kretschmer and Schepke. They sank eleven ships, including an armed merchant cruiser, the *Forfar*.

But with the threat of invasion receding, additional destroyers became available and in the first three months of the year 1941 the toll of U-boats sunk began to climb.

On March 7th, while escorting an outward-bound convoy, two corvettes, *Camellia* and *Arbutus*, flushed U-70 to the surface and destroyed her. The submarine attack was continued by another, U-47, commanded by Prien. The destroyer *Wolverine* detected the sub on the surface, raced in and forced her to dive. *Wolverine* showered the spot with depth-charges, checked the thundering blasts from each, waited for the submarine's next move, or for her to burst to the surface. *Wolverine*'s Asdic operators and depth-charge crews knew that there had been the perfect attack.

There came a dull, rolling explosion under water and, slowly, wreckage came to the surface amid extensive patches of oil. It was a kill. Complete, without survivors.

Ten days later a group of submarines attacked a convoy homeward bound from Halifax. It was the beginning of the wolf-pack system of attack by submarines. A submarine, sighting a convoy, signalled to others, who thereupon closed in until a pack was formed and a concentrated night attack was launched on the convoy.

The escort with the Halifax–Liverpool convoy knew from the wireless chatter—and from Western Approaches signals—that they had been detected and shadowed for a couple of days.

The attack came during the hours of darkness on March 16th–17th.

The destroyers, darting about like tireless sheepdogs around a wolf-worried flock of sheep, were forcing the submarines to submerge. *Vanoc*, commanded by Lieutenant-Commander J. G. Deneys, picked up a strong echo on her Asdic, held it and raced over the twisting submarine.

She dropped a pattern of depth-charges, fired star-shell and waited.

A rolling, pitching bulk came to the surface. It was U-100. Although disabled, the submarine still wriggled and twisted, but *Vanoc*, building up full speed, rammed the submarine abeam of the conning tower.

It was the finish for U-100 and for Schepke.

Still the attack continued and *Walker*, commanded by Commander D. G. Macintyre, forced another submarine, U-

99, to dive, plastered her with depth-charges and sank her.

From this one emerged as a survivor Otto Kretschmer, to spend the rest of the war as a prisoner of war in Canada.

To round off the picture, less than a week later a comparatively humble Asdic trawler, *Visenda*, sank U-551.

In three weeks Western Approaches escorts had destroyed five submarines, one-fifth of the Germans' operational number, but, far more valuable, they had also disposed of three of the Germans' much-lauded 'aces': Prien, Kretschmer and Schepke.

It was virtually the end of the individual attacker. From thence onwards attacks were made by the wolf-packs.

Three weeks later *Wolverine* was to add another U-boat to her bag. With the sloop *Scarborough* she sailed to meet a convoy from Halifax and made contact with it after it had been rather badly mauled by submarines.

Wolverine promptly sank U-76, which rather foolhardily underestimated the ability of a destroyer as compared with a lumbering merchant ship.

The halcyon days for the submarines were over. Slowly but inexorably Western Approaches escort forces were strengthened. Savage attacks were made on convoys, it is true, and the price paid in ships sunk was heavy. But only once again, off the American coast in 1942, before the Americans, barely recovering from the shock of Pearl Harbour, had time to organise anti-sub units.

From the grim days of the autumn of 1940 until the end of December 1941, thirty-eight submarines were sent to the bottom, mainly by escort forces. From that period emerges one aspect which was to grow as the Battle of the Atlantic continued its terrifying progress.

Nearly all attacks by submarine packs were made at nighttime by submarines on the surface. This nullified our Asdic and gave the Germans an added speed. Apart from the destroyers, few of the escort ships were capable of catching a submarine in a surface chase. A night attack on the surface had been tried and proved by the Germans in 1917–18, yet that writing on the wall—or on the waves if you prefer it—had been more or less ignored in pre-war training.

But several factors began to give escorts a slight edge. These were the introduction of radar, or RDF; an intense form of flare—the 'snowflake'—which turned night into day; the building and training of an escort group as a group, to remain as a group; light aircraft-carriers and oilers in the convoy from which escort ships could refuel and cross the Atlantic and the ever-increasing number of destroyers coming from the yards. Some of them were classified as sloops or frigates.

To all intents and purposes they were built to destroy submarines and the men in them bore all the characteristics of destroyer men.

The closing days of December 1941 brought a heartening confirmation that given the ships—destroyers, sloops, frigates—still in desperate demand—the submarine toll could be held down to reasonable proportions.

A convoy homeward bound from Gibraltar had as escort twelve destroyers, sloops, corvettes and a light carrier, *Audacity*. This escort was commanded by Commander F. J. Walker, undoubtedly the outstanding anti-submarine officer of the Navy. Before war-weariness overtook him and led to his death in 1944, he had set the pattern in his 'Bird' ships: *Starling*, *Magpie*, *Kite*, *Wild Goose*, *Wren* and *Woodpecker* and become the scourge of the submarines.

He was awarded the CB, four DSOs and the undying worship of the more than 1,000 men under his command.

In the 1941 convoy he was in *Stork* and the convoy was only a couple of days out before it was realised that it was being shadowed by a submarine and by the inevitable circling Condor. The wolf-pack started to gather around the convoy. *Audacity*'s Martlet aircraft detected a shadowing submarine and *Stork*, with a couple of 'Hunt' class destroyers, attacked it and eventually sank it.

That was U-131.

U-434 followed the next day, sunk by two 'Hunts', *Stanley* and *Blankney*.

Audacity's aircraft fought the German reconnaissance planes out of the sky and the convoy steamed on with its tail in the air.

Around it, either in actual contact and attacking, or somewhere not far away ready to launch another attack, were upwards of twelve to fourteen submarines.

To one of them fell the next victim, *Stanley*. She had turned to investigate a contact and was sunk by another submarine, U-574. That submarine's triumph was short-lived.

Stork blew her to the surface and by the light of 'snowflake' rockets rammed her.

In the two succeeding nights it looked as if the wolf-pack was getting the upper hand despite the size of the escort.

Audacity, whose aircraft had played such an important part in the early part of the fight, was torpedoed in the hours of darkness as was a merchant ship.

Deptford, searching around after *Audacity* had been hit, gained a firm contact, attacked and sank U-567. One other ship was sunk in the convoy before the U-boats called off the five-day battle, claiming two merchant ships, one light carrier and a destroyer for the cost of four submarines sunk and several more damaged.

Of the convoy of thirty-two ships, thirty arrived safely in this country.

That was to be the pattern for the next two years or so when the Germans flooded the Atlantic with subs. At one time, during the acute period of 1942 and early 1943, it was estimated that between ninety and 100 subs were working in the Atlantic, mainly in Western Approaches from Iceland south and far out into the western ocean, down as far as Gibraltar and Freetown.

Still the cry went up for escort ships and more escort ships.

But the demand was equally incessant from other theatres of war.

In the Mediterranean, after an heroic fight against Mussolini's cardboard army, Greece had now come up against the steel of the German forces.

Farther north, Russia, loudly demanding help, was getting it.

In each instance the weight of the effort rested to a great extent on destroyers. There were not enough, not nearly enough, but those that were went on to add to the laurels already bestowed on the small lean ships over the years.

19

After France fell and Italy entered the war it was recognised that the Mediterranean would become one of the principal theatres of war.

No matter how hard the way would become, to relinquish it to the Axis powers would amount to virtual suicide and would make a present of the Middle East oil supplies.

Destroyers whose names have appeared before in this narrative, in Norway, at Dunkirk and Western Approaches, began to appear in Admiral Cunningham's dispatches.

Although the cards were heavily stacked in favour of the Italian Navy, attempts to bring it to a full-scale fleet action never quite succeeded.

There were actions, it is true.

Off Calabria, in July 1940, while Admiral Sir Andrew Cunningham was covering a convoy from Alexandria to Malta, a portion of the Italian fleet was at sea for the same purpose, covering a convoy to North Africa.

The Italians had the superior speed—and used it to get away from anything more than a long-range gun battle.

A better opportunity presented itself in March 1941 when the Germans prodded the reluctant Italian fleet into staging an operation against the troop convoys running from Egypt to Greece.

Vice-Admiral Pridham-Wippell, in the cruiser *Orion*, with *Ajax*, *Perth*, *Gloucester* and nine destroyers, was already at sea, and Admiral Cunningham sailed in *Warspite*, with *Barham*, *Valiant* and the carrier *Formidable*.

The Italian force consisted of the battleship *Vittorio Veneto*, four cruisers and fifteen destroyers.

Once again, immediately they found themselves faced by a fighting force the Italian fleet turned for home.

Vittorio Veneto was hit by a torpedo from an aircraft and was slowed down. She wrapped around herself a tight force of cruisers and destroyers to present a terrifying barrage against aircraft.

Eight torpedo bombers from *Formidable* tore through it and hit a ship which they reported was *Vittorio Veneto*. Actually it was the heavy cruiser *Pola*. She slowed down and stopped.

It was now darkness and the moment came for which the destroyers were waiting. Captain P. J. Mack, in *Nubian*, raced off, followed by *Mohawk*, *Juno*, *Janus*, *Hero*, *Hereward*, *Hostile*, *Hasty* and two or three more.

Unfortunately, Captain Mack, through no fault of his, passed astern of *Vittorio Veneto* and her screen in the darkness and missed the jackpot.

The crippled cruiser *Pola*, and her two nurses *Zara* and *Fiume*, were right in the path of the pursuing British battleships. The destroyer *Greyhound* flooded the Italian ships with light from her searchlights, the battleships reduced them to shambles in a few minutes and continued the chase, leaving the destroyers *Stuart*, *Griffin*, *Havock* and *Greyhound* to finish the job.

Although there was a screen of Italian destroyers around the smoking wrecks, they showed no fight but raced around like a few sheep detached from the comfort of the main flock.

Havock started the ball going by slamming a few salvoes into a destroyer and finished her with a torpedo. Another blundered into *Stuart* and was torpedoed for her error. Then the destroyers, with guns blazing and torpedoes at the 'ready', set about the three smoking cruisers.

Stuart torpedoed *Fiume*, *Jervis* sent the *Zara* to the bottom, then joined with *Nubian* to destroy *Pola*. A satisfying night's work by the destroyers with the unhappy thought that but for an alteration of course by the Italian admiral in *Vittorio Veneto* the whole enemy force would have been brought to battle, with the destroyers doing just what they were evolved and built to do—to race into the enemy fleet in a torpedo attack.

But, despite these highlights, grim sombre days were descending on the Mediterranean. Malta was to be besieged; Greece, having smartly rapped Mussolini, was to crumble against the iron-hard German veteran forces.

And a tragedy as big as Dunkirk was to be played out in Crete.

Once again a tremendous task was to be thrown on destroyers. They were to ferry troops and stores, and shortly afterwards were to be called upon for the sad task of lifting soldiers from the shores of Crete.

Before the evacuation was complete destroyers whose names had become almost household words were to sink beneath the waters of the eastern Mediterranean.

The background to the evacuation of Crete, so far as this story is concerned, can be told in a few words. While the British and Greek armies were fighting grimly against the Axis powers on the mainland, a forward base was established on Crete. Suda Bay became a base for the Navy. As events moved inexorably on the mainland, more troops and Marines were ferried across to Crete. There was no adequate air protection, apart from a few Fleet Air Arm aircraft.

The German-Italian war machine rolled over the forces on the mainland and large numbers of troops were evacuated from Greece.

All available cruisers and destroyers were placed to the north of the island for the purpose of fighting off any attempt by the Germans to land troops.

Instead, the Germans first bombarded the airfield at Maleme, then started landing paratroops and gliders. No time was lost by them in attacking the naval forces with relays of bombers.

The Navy had already had a foretaste of what was to come in the evacuation of troops from the mainland. For that task —code-named 'Demon', a name which brought bitter recollections of 'Dynamo' at Dunkirk—six cruisers, nineteen destroyers, some corvettes and trawlers and three transports were used.

The number of troops to be rescued was less than a fifth of those on the Dunkirk beaches and docks, but the task was, if possible, a more difficult one. The bases at Suda Bay and Alexandria had no comparison with Dover, Ramsgate, Margate and Chatham.

But in five nights the Navy rescued nearly 51,000 troops from places on the mainland nearly 200 miles apart. In the operation four transports were sunk and two destroyers, *Diamond* and *Wryneck*, attempting to take men off the sinking transport *Slamat*, were heavily bombed and went down with heavy loss of life.

Unlike at Dunkirk, the evacuation was not the completion of the task. In fact, it was the beginning of another.

The Germans were determined to take and hold Crete. After a brief period for ammunitioning, storing and oiling, the Navy buckled down to its task.

To the west of Crete were *Warspite* and *Valiant* with ten destroyers. At the eastern end were the cruisers *Naiad* and *Perth* with four destroyers and not far away were the cruisers *Dido*, *Orion*, *Ajax* and four destroyers. In theory all nicely placed for a swoop on any seaborne troop transports trying to reach Crete from the mainland. In fact, all well within range of the German bombers and vulnerable through lack of air cover.

The destroyer *Juno* was sunk in the early afternoon of May 21st, the first naval casualty in the defence and evacuation of Crete.

There were to be others.

Later that night it was reported to Rear-Admiral Glennie, in *Dido*, that troop-carrying vessels had been sighted off Canea, near Suda Bay on the north-west tip of Crete. *Dido*, with her consort cruisers and the destroyers *Janus*, *Kimberley*, *Hasty* and *Hereward*, intercepted the convoy of troop-carrying vessels and decimated it. No accurate figure of losses of enemy troops can ever be arrived at, but conservative estimate put it at between 4,000 and 5,000.

A fair night's work.

But at daylight on the 22nd the German Air Force began to lay on the lash.

The cruiser *Naiad* and her destroyers caught out a convoy of troop-carrying Greek caiques, but at the same time came under heavy air attack.

The destroyer *Greyhound*, detached to sink a caique full of German troops and on her way to rejoin the squadron, was hit by two bombs and sunk. *Kandahar* and *Kingston*, racing to pick up survivors, then came under heavy attack. *Kingston* was damaged but continued to steam.

Still the Germans poured aircraft into the sky. *Naiad* was damaged and slowed down, the cruiser *Gloucester*, steaming to support, was severely damaged and sank later. Then followed the cruiser *Fiji*. She was sunk trying to cover *Gloucester*. More than twenty air attacks were delivered at *Fiji* before she was mortally stricken and rolled over.

Meanwhile, the confused fighting to hold Crete was still going on ashore, although Suda Bay, continuously bombed, was ruled out as a base.

During daylight hours the naval forces withdrew to the south-west and south-east of the island of Crete, returning at nightfall to search for troop-carrying vessels.

Through an error in signalling, the heavy ships were recalled to Alexandria, leaving *Kelly*, *Kipling* and *Kashmir* to search in the night for survivors of *Fiji*, and *Kelvin* and *Jackal* to look for survivors of *Gloucester*.

Kelly, commanded by Captain Lord Louis Mountbatten, had arrived the evening before from Malta, bringing with her some redoubtable destroyers. With *Kelly* were *Kashmir*, *Kipling*, *Kelvin* and *Jackal*.

During the search for *Fiji*'s survivors, *Kipling* developed engine trouble and had to drop out of the search. At dawn *Kelly* and her accompanying destroyers withdrew to the south-west, but had left it too late. They were sighted by twenty-five dive bombers who flashed down out of the sky and almost immediately and repeatedly hit *Kashmir*. She went down in a minute or two. *Kelly* wriggled and twisted and avoided the first few bombs, but, while on a full-speed turn, she too was hit and capsized, to float keel upwards for twenty minutes or so.

Kipling, having repaired her engine defect, raced in, picked up 279 survivors from the two ships and despite air attacks reached Alexandria safely.

The hopeless fight ashore on the island continued on its weary way for a few more days, but the writing was on the wall. On May 27th the decision was made to give up the fight and the Navy was committed to taking 32,000 battle-weary bewildered soldiers from under the noses of the snarling bombers who were operating mainly from the small island of Scarpanto. An attempt to reduce the threat of that airfield had been made the day previous by aircraft from *Formidable*, and in doing so, while screening the aircraft-carrier, the destroyer *Nubian* had her stern blown off.

The incensed Germans drove off the Fleet Air Arm bombers, who were not strong enough in any case to do more than temporary damage, then flew south and caught *Formidable* and her screen of destroyers as they were withdrawing, about a hundred miles from Mersa Matruh.

Suda Bay, of course, was by then lost to us and the main evacuation was to be made from two small ports: Heraklion halfway along the north coast, and Sphakia on the south coast across the waist of the island from Heraklion.

The garrison at Heraklion was holding out stubbornly, despite a series of attacks on the ground and frequent visits from German bombers. To rescue the 4,000-odd men there, Admiral Rawlings took *Dido*, *Orion* and *Ajax* and six destroyers to the little port and lay off there while the destroyers ferried the soldiers out to the cruisers.

By 3.30 am on the morning of May 29th the Heraklion garrison were taken off. The squadron had been attacked while on its 400-mile run from Alexandria and while embarking troops, and the destroyer *Imperial*'s steering gear developed trouble and almost at the last moment of the evacuation it jammed hopelessly, requiring a major engineering feat to repair it.

Admiral Rawlings decided to sink her.

To have waited for *Imperial* to be repaired would have endangered all his squadron. *Hotspur*, a long way off in time and distance—and experience—from the Battle of Narvik, closed in to the disabled destroyer, took off the 500 soldiers on her and sadly destroyed *Imperial*.

By then it was daylight, and the raging bombers came again as the rescuing squadron raced for the Kaso Straits at the east end of Crete and for the open sea to Alexandria.

In the prolonged attacks both *Orion* and *Dido* were hit and damaged, with severe casualties among the soldiers on their decks.

And another valuable, veteran destroyer was lost.

Hereward, the destroyer which had carried the Dutch Queen to safety, had taken part in the Dunkirk evacuation, had convoyed ships, had hunted submarines—in short had been a typical destroyer—was hit, slowed down and eventually drifted ashore, where her crew were made prisoners of war.

Hereward was a complete wreck.

Decoy was hammered also, but managed to keep steaming and eventually reached Alexandria.

Three nights were taken to lift the troops from Sphakia, using three cruisers, *Phoebe, Perth* and *Calcutta*, with three destroyers on the first night and four destroyers on the succeeding nights. There were the inevitable air attacks through the night and into daylight and, as the force withdrew, *Kelvin* and *Napier*, their decks crowded with soldiers, were hit and damaged but were still able to move.

The cruiser *Calcutta*, an anti-aircraft cruiser, was sunk

when only fifty miles from Alexandria.

All it had been asked to do the Navy had done. It had destroyed any attempt at seaborne landings, it had escorted transports, it had rescued most of the troops from the island. It had learned yet again the bitter lesson of Norway and Dunkirk—that air cover was imperative.

Having to work from a base 400 miles away meant almost 1,000 miles of steaming before it could start to operate, and for the whole of that time, almost to the doorstep of Alexandria, it had come under savage bombing attacks.

The evacuation complete, there came the sad accountancy.

The Greek and Crete campaigns had cost us two battleships damaged, *Warspite* and *Barham*, six cruisers damaged, three cruisers sunk. The destroyer losses were even more formidable, showing how much of the load had fallen on them. Six destroyers were sunk, and seven were damaged, thirteen destroyers of the total force of thirty-two employed. Nearly a half of them.

After the last lifting of troops from Sphakia it was estimated that around 4,000 troops still remained on Crete and it was mooted that yet one more cruiser-destroyer dash be made to get them off. It would have been an impossible task.

Not more than five or six of the destroyers at Alexandria were fully operational and some of them were nursing wounds.

Furthermore, the soldiers ashore had scattered inland and there was no way of mustering them at any of the small ports.

Finally, with the Germans in complete command of the air, it would have been suicide.

So ended the evacuation of Crete; successor to the evacuation of Greece, and the sorry retreats of which we had had our fill: Norway, Dunkirk, the Bay of Biscay ports. So far as the Navy in general and destroyers in particular were concerned, it had been turned into yet another epic, another page blazoned in gold in the history of destroyers.

20

While the events in the previous chapter were drawing to their tragic close, many miles away in the North Atlantic some 'Tribals' of the 4th Flotilla were playing a short but spectacular part in another drama.

On May 21st the German battleship *Bismarck* and the heavy cruiser *Prinz Eugen* had broken out, sighted by cruisers in the Denmark Straits—that stretch of dismal water between Greenland and Iceland—and had been hunted across the Atlantic by battleships, cruisers and aircraft. *Prinz Eugen* had escaped to Brest, but *Bismarck*, crippled by torpedo aircraft, was being brought to bay by Admiral Tovey, C-in-C Home Fleet, in *King George V* and a widespread net of battle cruisers, cruisers and a few destroyers.

As the fleet closed the net, so some of the destroyers screening the flag-ship had to return to harbour to oil up. But the need for replacement destroyers was vital. They were forthcoming.

Thus, by a twist of fate, some of the 4th Flotilla, *Cossack*, carrying Captain Philip Vian as Captain 'D', *Sikh*, *Zulu*, *Maori* and the Polish destroyer *Piorun*, were escorting a troop convoy south bound and had in fact barely crossed the path *Bismarck* was taking in her desperate attempt to get under air cover from the French coast.

At 2 am on May 26th *Cossack* and the other 'Tribals' swung away from the convoy, leaving it with a slender escort, to obey a signal from Admiralty to replace the departed destroyer screen around *King George V* and *Rodney*. They hammered through a rising sea all day and towards evening. Captain Vian had picked up a sighting report from a Catalina earlier in the day and without hesitation had altered his course. Instead of following the letter of his instructions to join Admiral Tovey, he had steered for *Bismarck*'s estimated position.

Bismarck had, during the evening, been hit by a torpedo in an attack by Swordfish aircraft and her steering gear and rudders were jammed.

Sheffield, which had been shadowing *Bismarck*, guided *Cossack* and the other destroyers to *Bismarck*, which they then proceeded to worry all night.

Captain Vian, knowing his commanding officer, Admiral Tovey—an old destroyer man—knew that what he was doing would meet with complete approval. Admiral Tovey would gladly do without a screen so long as the destroyers kept in touch with *Bismarck* and harried her through the night until he could bring his racing capital ships to action with the German battleship.

Captain Vian spread his destroyers in a line of search and they pounded on into a heavy sea under a storm-lashed sky with surface visibility varying between 2,000 yards and 10,000 yards as rain-squalls slammed the ships.

Then, in the grey evening light, *Piorun* made contact. Looming in the late evening murk, she picked up the crippled *Bismarck*. Now, Polish destroyers, like Polish airmen, may have had their minor faults, but nobody could deny their one-track idea once they got *anything* German in their sights.

Piorun promptly reported her contact, turned towards *Bismarck* and opened fire at around 12,000 yards. It is doubtful if any of her shells—if they landed—did any material damage to *Bismarck* except to inform her that she was not alone in the spindrift-topped seas.

While Captain Vian thoroughly approved of *Piorun*'s audacious pugnacity, he was reluctant to see one of his destroyers damaged by gun-fire from *Bismarck*'s guns. He had different plans for the night which was closing in on them.

He was all in favour of torpedo attacks on *Bismarck* during the hours of darkness, but his primary idea was to cling like a limpet to *Bismarck*, whose reduced speed he had reported to Admiral Tovey.

If a torpedo attack *could* be delivered and *did* slow

Bismarck down by even a fraction, without serious damage to a destroyer, then it would be a considerable bonus. But shadow and hold was the first task.

Admiral Tovey, on *King George V*, probably permitted himself the luxury of a brief smile. He had hunted *Bismarck*, had lost a ship, *Hood*, in the hunt, had also lost *Bismarck* for two agonising days. Now destroyers, led by one of the most redoubtable destroyer men of the war, were harrying *Bismarck*. He knew that even if eventualities led to an all-out attack by the destroyers in an attempt to keep *Bismarck* from the safety of her much-wanted air cover, and only one destroyer was left, then *Bismarck* would be attacked, would be held and would be reported.

Through the night the destroyers held on grimly to *Bismarck*. Captain Vian worked his destroyers round until they were in a fan formation to south-east of *Bismarck*—astride her course to safety.

Then they started their harrying attacks.

Commander Henry Graham, in *Zulu*, delivered the first torpedo attack. He had manœuvred *Zulu* until she was on *Bismarck*'s quarter, turned to an attacking course and *Bismarck* broke into a ring of venomous fire as her secondary and main armament blazed away at *Zulu*. Her torpedoes fired, *Zulu*, framed in climbing columns of water, turned away and listened for the explosions. There were none.

But while *Bismarck* was busily trying to blow *Zulu* out of the water she was suddenly bathed in the brilliant orange-tinted white of a star-shell.

Commander Harold Armstrong, in *Maori*, profiting by *Zulu*'s audacious attack, had raced in to less than 4,000 yards, fired a star-shell which illuminated *Bismarck* clearly and turned in to deliver two torpedoes, turned away, and as the star-shell was still hanging in the air turned back to her target and released yet another.

Even as *Maori* turned away to pitch and roll through the white columns of water thrown up around her by *Bismarck*'s guns, a deep-throated booming thud travelled through the water. A brief, vivid green-white explosion was framed against the dark bulk of *Bismarck*'s hull. One torpedo had struck home.

Bismarck's guns reached frenzy point as they belched possible destruction at *Maori*, salvoes falling so close that they threw more water over *Maori* than was achieved by the steep and punishing sea.

Maori, her task well and truly performed, took her place in the shadowing half-ring.

As with *Zulu* and *Maori*, one closing in while the other poised for attack, so it was with *Cossack*.

Captain Vian took *Cossack* to within a little more than 5,000 yards, but this time *Bismarck* was ready. She had detected the 'you-hit-her-and-run—then-I'll-belt-her' tactics of the destroyers. *Bismarck*'s side was ringed with fire. *Cossack* reeled through the gleaming white columns of water, fired three torpedoes, then raced away.

Cossack waited. THUD. Another torpedo had struck home. *Cossack* resumed her place in the half-circle.

Admiral Tovey's smile undoubtedly widened. The fates which had been against him in the earlier parts of the chase were now for him.

Although *Bismarck*, hidden from him by distance and the night, was not more than half a dozen hours' steaming time from comparative safety, she was having the heart and soul harried out of her by destroyers.

Admiral Tovey might even have sent his thoughts backwards to little more than twenty-five years when some British destroyers had turned their plunging bows towards German battleships and had forced them to turn away.

The breed was still true.

Sikh, commanded by Commander Graham Stokes, closed in to *Bismarck* and hit her yet again with another torpedo. *Bismarck* could now only crawl.

A grey wild dawn, with the sea but a few shades darker than the colour of the sky, showed *Bismarck* that ringed around her, barring her creeping progress to the east, were the five destroyers.

They had virtually completed their task. Interpreting Admiral Tovey's unspoken guidance, they had found *Bismarck*, had harried her through the night, had attacked her, had slowed her down and now, when the dawn had come, they were still there, shadowing her, reporting her every move to the capital ships devouring distance astern.

They came, they saw, they sank her.

Conjecture is idle.

No one can tell what might have happened had Captain Vian taken his destroyers onwards to fulfil the letter of his instructions; to replace the departed screen.

As it was, the 'Tribals' wrote boldly in the destroyer history. Wrote boldly for all to see.

They were to write more in the ensuing days, some of it deeply tinged with tragedy, but all of it true to the tradition of destroyers.

21

The Mediterranean never ceased to boil in the closing months of 1941 and the earlier part of 1942. The Navy strove hard to pass through convoys to Malta and at the same time struggled to prevent supplies reaching the Afrika Korps.

The position in Malta had not become really critical, but escorting supply ships, fast merchantmen of the Clan line, and the irrepressible *Breconshire*, which must have intimately known every wave from Gibraltar to Alexandria, threw an enormous amount of work on the depleted destroyer strength.

But they had their moments of highlights.

Cossack's famous captain had now been promoted to rear-admiral and was flying his flag in the light cruiser *Naiad*, with *Dido*, *Euryalus* and half a dozen destroyers, and was busy from one end of the Mediterranean to the other.

These cruisers were light, only 5,500 tons or so, and their

main strength was in their anti-aircraft weapons.

In one of the operations, escorting four supply ships to Malta from Gibraltar in January 1942, the destroyer *Gurkha* was sunk. This destroyer was laid down and was originally intended to be christened *Larne*, but the almost immortal name in destroyer history passed to a third ship. The previous destroyer of that name had been sunk off Norway in 1940.

The ebb and flow of the tide in North Africa had turned against us early in 1942 and the Army was driven back east of Derna, losing, of course, advanced airfields from which aircraft could lend valuable aid to convoys at sea.

While searching for enemy convoys off the African coast between Mersa Matruh and Sollum, *Naiad* was torpedoed by a submarine. Most of her crew were picked up by destroyers and Admiral Vian transferred his flag to *Dido*.

On March 20th six destroyers and the cruiser *Carlisle* set out as escort for *Breconshire*, *Clan Campbell*, *Pampas* and *Talabut* from Alexandria to supply Malta.

Admiral Vian sailed shortly afterwards with *Cleopatra*, *Euryalus*, *Dido* and four more destroyers, collected six 'Hunt' class destroyers and later the cruiser *Penelope* and the destroyer *Legion*.

Inevitably the gathering of ships was reported and the Italians sailed a battleship, the *Littorio*, and half a dozen destroyers from Taranto, and three cruisers, the *Trento*, *Goriza* and *Giovanni Della Bande Nere*, and four destroyers from Messina shortly after midnight.

So the force to defend the convoy of four ships was five light cruisers, eleven fleet destroyers and half a dozen of the light 'Hunt' class, which could scarcely be expected to join in any fleet action.

Bent on finding the convoy and destroying it, and possibly eliminating some of the covering force, were one battleship, two eight-inch cruisers, one six-inch cruiser and ten destroyers.

On paper the initiative was with the Italian ships. They had no convoy to restrict their movements.

Admiral Vian had worked out precisely what he would do in the event of an attack on a convoy he was escorting, and had gone over it point by point with the captains of the ships under his command. Only *Penelope*, which had sailed from Malta, had not had the benefit of the conferences.

The destroyers with Admiral Vian were *Jervis*, *Kipling*, *Kelvin*, *Kingston*, *Legion*, *Zulu*, *Hasty*, *Sikh*, *Lively*, *Hero* and *Havock*.

A redoubtable array of destroyers, nearly all of which had seen service from Norway, Western Approaches and in the Mediterranean.

Admiral Vian had arranged that the cruiser *Carlisle* and 'Hunt' destroyer *Avon Vale* would cover the escape of the convoy with a smoke screen.

The other ships, disposed in five divisions, would also make smoke 'and would carry out diversionary tactics', which the destroyers tersely and rightly translated as 'attack through the smoke'. Which they did.

The Italian force was sighted about 2.30 pm and Admiral Vian's 'Standing Orders' slipped into smooth operation. Although the orders for any action—sent by air from Alexandria to Malta—to *Penelope* had not reached her, *Penelope*, commanded by Captain A. D. Nicholl, had no doubt about what was required of her.

The Italian force first sighted was made up of three cruisers and four destroyers and there was no sign of the battleship *Littorio*.

Admiral Vian's ships turned north-west to get between the convoy and the Italians, while the convoy itself swung south, with the five remaining 'Hunt' class destroyers in close escort. While the British cruisers and destroyers were making dense smoke-screens, an air attack on the convoy developed but was resolutely defended by the close escort and no ships were seriously damaged in that phase.

The Italians turned away and after a brief long-range gun duel, with no damage to either side, Admiral Vian steered to overtake the convoy.

In less than half an hour the Italian force was sighted to the north-east again, this time *Littorio* and four destroyers had joined up. In effect they were following almost in the wake of the original convoy course.

From Admiral Vian's point of view the wind was coming from an ideal quarter. It was about thirty miles an hour and blowing from the south-east. The sea was rougher than the destroyers liked it, but they plunged into it, throwing solid masses of water away from their sharp bows, which contrasted acutely with the dark smoke streaming from their funnels and sterns.

It was punishing work for the destroyers and light cruisers, but there could be no thoughts of easing down. There was a possibility that the Italian force would try to work to the east of the clouds of dense smoke, then strike south-west after the convoy.

Sikh, leading *Lively*, *Hero* and *Havock*, were alone when they sighted the Italian ships as Admiral Vian was striving to hold the weather gauge, and at the same time not to be foxed into going too far to the east, leaving a gap through which the Italian battleship and cruisers could stream southwards after the convoy.

Almost at once, *Havock* was hit by a fifteen-inch shell, was disabled and was detached to join the convoy.

Rolling and pitching, at times blinded by the showers of heavy spray thrown bridge high, the destroyers laid a smoke-screen and tore into the Italian force.

Admiral Vian returned west as fast as he could steam to stop this new threat by the enemy of working round ahead of him to get at the convoy.

Cleopatra and *Euryalus* burst through the smoke laid by *Sikh* and the other destroyers to find themselves confronted by *Littorio*.

Sikh, *Lively* and *Hero* had held off the heavier force and had averted what might have become a tragic situation.

They had fought with guns and torpedoes and, with the added threat of torpedoes from the cruisers, the battleship and her screen of destroyers turned away north-west.

Admiral Vian was worrying about the Italian cruisers, but meanwhile *Jervis*, *Kipling*, *Kelvin* and *Kingston* had hammered their way through heavy sea, darted out of the smoke-screen and engaged *Littorio* at about six miles range. With their guns blazing, they rolled, pitched and twisted in to 3,000 yards and fired torpedoes. *Littorio* was forced to turn away once more. Her gun-fire was erratic, to say the least. At the distance the destroyers were engaging her she should have blown them out of the water. *Kingston* was hit once by a heavy shell, as she slammed into range, but continued on long enough to get her torpedoes away.

Once more *Sikh*, *Lively* and *Hero* came plunging out of the smoke to hammer away at the battleship with their puny guns as they closed in to torpedo range. Supporting fire came from Admiral Vian's light cruisers, which had now detected the missing Italian cruisers. They had joined up with *Littorio*.

One big shell hit *Lively* as she burst out of the smoke-screen, but she too, although on fire, got her torpedoes away.

By seven o'clock the Italian force had decided that it had had enough. No ship in the force had been damaged, not once had any ship, or the force as a whole, shown any degree of resolution and not once had any of the Italian destroyers shown any inclination to attack the light cruisers and destroyers which were harassing—and decisively defeating—the larger ships in their force.

The convoy, despite heavy air attacks, was saved, but tragically it did not reach Malta as a whole.

The Germans launched a savage air attack on it, hit and disabled *Breconshire* and sank the *Clan Campbell*.

Havock and *Kingston*, damaged in the Second Battle of Sirte—as it was named, there had been a brief skirmish in the same area a few months previous—could not return to Alexandria and had to go to Malta.

But the darker side of the picture emerges here. The destroyer position in the Mediterranean was acute. Nine fleet destroyers were out of commission in Alexandria, damaged in action. Five more lay at Malta. The 'Hunt' class *Southwold* was sunk off Grand Harbour by a mine while helping the crippled *Breconshire*; *Legion* was sunk by a bomb in harbour; *Jaguar* was torpedoed while escorting a tanker.

Seventeen destroyers either sunk or not available was a formidable load to carry.

Admiral Cunningham, after hauling down his flag as C-in-C Mediterranean, journeyed to London before going on to Washington. And there he told the powers-that-be that to run any more convoys to besieged Malta there would have to be a lot more destroyers available, many many more.

Even as he was laying down this fundamental dictum, some of the precious destroyers from this compact, deadly theatre of war were being sent to the Far East. No help of material size could be borrowed from Western Approaches. The Battle of the Atlantic was at its height and destroyers were as precious as gold.

Farther north, convoys were being forced through the Barents Sea to the aid of Russia, and the incessant demand for that work was 'more destroyers'.

So, then, to those which were in the Mediterranean fell the brunt of the work, a task which would have been heavy for three times the number of destroyers.

After the convoy which Admiral Vian had fought so hard to get through, the Germans and Italians increased the pressure of bombing on Malta.

The island was starting the intense siege which was ultimately to earn it the admiration of the free world and resulted in the King bestowing on it the George Cross.

The intense raids were concentrated to begin with on the dockyards, where ships crippled in action were being repaired as quickly as the dockyard staff could perform the task.

In a prolonged raid early in April the destroyer *Lance* was sunk in dock, and *Kingston*, a cripple, was again damaged. *Gallant*, which had played an epic part in the Dunkirk evacuation, was so badly hit that she had to be beached.

In an attempt to get *Havock* away to Alexandria after she had been repaired following the hit in the Sirte battle, she went helplessly ashore on the Tunisian coast. Raid followed raid and at last the battered *Kingston* was sunk. The 5th Destroyer Flotilla which had so bravely sailed to war in the early months was shrinking.

Havock, which had fought in the First Battle of Narvik with Captain Warburton-Lee, was to leave her bones red-rusting on that hostile Tunisian beach.

Somehow Malta had to be supplied and maintained. And somehow the Axis convoys to North Africa had to be slowed down if not stopped.

Work for destroyers.

22

Heroic attempts were being made from Gibraltar to deliver aircraft to Malta using the U.S. aircraft-carrier *Wasp* and the aged *Eagle*, but these moves were for defence.

Enemy convoys had to be attacked.

Early in May the Axis powers started a convoy for Benghazi. Captain A. L. Poland led some of the victors of the Second Battle of Sirte to intercept. He sailed in *Jervis*, with *Jackal*, *Lively* and *Kipling*. It was almost a suicidal mission. They were sailing into waters above which the enemy had complete control. Inevitably they were sighted by patrolling aircraft, which signalled back their whereabouts to an enemy airfield on Crete.

The Germans dispatched thirty crack bombers—the dreaded Ju 88's.

In the first attack *Lively* was hit and sunk. Shortly afterwards *Kipling* and *Jackal* were bombed. *Kipling* went down and *Jackal* was set on fire. Captain Poland ranged *Jervis* alongside her and, as the crew fought the guns and the fire, tried to take her in tow. They struggled through the short night, but it was a losing battle. At dawn the bombers would return. Reluctantly it was decided to sink *Jackal*, yet another veteran, and *Jervis* alone sailed on to reach Alexandria with more than 600 survivors of the sunken destroyers crowding her decks.

The price was mounting, the destroyer strength was shrinking.

Reinforcements began to arrive in the first weeks of June. The cruiser *Birmingham* arrived at Alexandria with four destroyers and the cruisers *Newcastle*, *Hermione* and *Arethusa*, with six destroyers, followed a few days later.

It was decided to send two convoys in an attempt to supply Malta. One from Britain through the Gibraltar Straits, under the code-word 'Harpoon', a convoy of six ships, and eleven from Alexandria under the code-word 'Vigorous'.

'Harpoon's' escort in terms of ships was formidable. There was the battleship *Malaya*, the cruisers *Kenya*, flying the flag of Admiral A. T. B. Curteis, *Liverpool* and *Charybdis*, the anti-aircraft cruiser *Cairo*, two aircraft-carriers, *Eagle* and *Argus*, and seventeen destroyers, besides some fleet mine-sweepers.

The *Malaya* and the other heavy ships escorted the convoy until it reached the narrows between Cape Bon and the toe of Sicily, at which point the main escort turned back. But before that, on the morning of the 14th, aircraft from Sardinia—dive bombers, torpedo bombers and high-level bombers—slammed home a severe series of attacks. One of the merchant ships, the Dutch tanker *Tanimbar*, was sunk and *Liverpool* received a crippling hit in the engine room. She was turned round and sent back to Gibraltar with a destroyer escort *Antelope*, which for most of the trip towed *Liverpool*.

On the laborious way back to 'The Rock' *Liverpool* and *Antelope* had to fight off repeated air attacks by small numbers of aircraft and it is rather surprising that the Italians did not concentrate more aircraft on what was virtually a sitting duck for them.

But *Antelope*, with her lamed tow, did arrive safely at Gibraltar.

During the afternoon the convoy, with heavy ships and close escort, passed out of the range of the Sardinian airfields and came under the hammer blows of German bombers based on Sicily, mainly the extremely efficient Ju 88.

There was damage, but no losses.

That night the heavy ships turned back while the convoy slipped between Pantellaria and Cape Bon, carefully shepherded by the anti-aircraft cruiser *Cairo*, nine destroyers and the mixed bag of minesweepers.

Captain C. Hardy, in *Cairo*, might have longed for some air cover, but when he surveyed the calibre of the nine-strong destroyer escort he undoubtedly found some cause for satisfaction.

Bedouin, commanded by Commander B. G. Scurfield, was leader, with *Marne*, *Matchless*, *Ithuriel*, *Partridge*, the Polish destroyer *Kujawiak*, a 'Hunt' class ship, and the 'Hunts' *Badsworth*, *Blankney*, *Middleton*. Many a western-ocean convoy would have been pardoned jubilation at such an escort.

At dawn on the 15th a patrolling Beaufighter from Malta detected and reported an enemy squadron sailing south of Pantellaria. There were two cruisers and five destroyers. That same force had been shadowed and reported by submarines on the 13th as sailing from Cagliari, north of the convoy. They had arrived at Palermo and covered by darkness had evaded the submarine *Unbroken* by slipping between the mainland and the small island of Marittimo.

Now it was racing to attack the convoy.

By the time the aircraft's report had been digested the Italian force was about fifteen miles north of the convoy and at 6 am was sighted.

The drill was well rehearsed. *Bedouin*, in absolute conformity with destroyer tradition, took the fleet destroyers north to meet the immensely superior enemy force while *Cairo* and the 'Hunt' class destroyers wrapped a smoke-screen around the convoy.

Bedouin, Matchless, Marne, Ithuriel and *Partridge* worked up to more than thirty-two knots and almost immediately came under savage fire from the cruisers, which outranged them.

They were to take part in an action which had been duplicated time and time again in the story of destroyers. There was an enemy in sight. Steam towards him. Truly could the hackneyed lines of the poem of the 'Charge of the Light Brigade' be applied to them.

'Theirs not to reason why
Theirs but to do—or die. . . .'

While the convoy steamed on, shrouded in smoke from the close escort, the fleet destroyers raced to get to grips with the Italian cruisers.

But before they could do so *Bedouin* and *Partridge* were hit. At 18,000 yards range the destroyers could make no reply except to continue racing towards the Italian force. *Bedouin* was hit amidships and *Partridge* on her stern. They lost way and came to a rolling stop, while *Ithuriel, Marne* and *Matchless* tore past them.

At 8,000 yards *Ithuriel* opened fire on the leading cruiser, *Raimondo Montecuccoli*, and almost immediately registered two hits which turned her away. *Matchless* and *Marne* engaged the Italian destroyers, hitting one and driving the others off. Although they had turned away, the Italian cruisers and destroyers, because of their superior speed, were almost ideally placed to insert themselves between the convoy and Malta. They turned in again as, at that moment, *Cairo* and the 'Hunt' class destroyers came racing out of the wind-driven smoke-screen and were almost immediately engaged. The Italian cruisers divided their fire between *Cairo* and *Blankney, Middleton, Badsworth* and *Kujawiak*, and shortly after seven o'clock *Cairo* was hit, but fortunately not seriously.

While only the minesweepers remained as escort for the convoy, the merchant ships were attacked by German bombers of the dreaded Fliegerskorps X, bombers specially trained for attacks on shipping. The first wave sank the American ship *Chant* and disabled *Kentucky*.

Captain Hardy recalled *Ithuriel*, *Marne* and *Matchless* to assist in the defence of the convoy, meanwhile laying another thick smoke screen between the merchant ships and the Italian cruisers.

They hovered about beyond it, but decided against steaming through it with the possibility of meeting three or four destroyers waiting there to launch torpedoes.

By 11 am the convoy, with *Kentucky* in tow, was making a steady course once more for Malta when another air attack was delivered in which the merchant ship *Burdwan* was disabled.

A long way astern lay the crippled *Bedouin* and *Partridge*. Between them and the convoy was the *Kentucky*, being towed by the fleet minesweeper *Hebe*.

Early in the afternoon the Italian cruisers and destroyers returned to the attack. They came across the little *Hebe*, struggling manfully to keep *Kentucky* moving at about five knots, and started to hammer her.

Cairo, *Matchless*, *Marne* and *Ithuriel* tore back to discourage that effort and the Italians were driven off. It was decided to abandon *Kentucky*, and she was torpedoed.

Much as Captain Hardy would have liked to go back westward even farther to cover *Bedouin* and *Partridge*, his primary task was to deliver the convoy to Malta.

Bedouin and *Partridge* would have to work out their own salvation—if there was one.

Partridge had managed to repair her steering gear which had been damaged in the hits registered on her by the cruisers, but *Bedouin* still lay helpless. Although his ship was still partly crippled, Lieutenant-Commander W. A. F. Hawkins passed a tow to *Bedouin* and started the heartbreaking task of towing her.

It was then the frustrated Italian cruisers and destroyers found them. *Partridge* immediately slipped her tow, laid a smoke-screen around *Bedouin* and steamed away in the hope of drawing the Italians after her. She was repeatedly straddled and once again was brought to a stop with jammed steering gear.

Her effort went for naught.

Although the Italian cruisers and destroyers were a little diffident about penetrating the smoke-screen in search of *Bedouin*, a torpedo bomber lifted over it, dropped down towards *Bedouin* and delivered the *coup de grâce*. With her last shot the destroyer shot it down.

Partridge managed a hasty repair and steamed away alone, a sad end to a gallant effort.

Commander B. G. Scurfield, captain of *Bedouin*, was rescued with many of his crew and was made a prisoner of war in Italy.

In a letter to his wife, which was later published in *Blackwood's Magazine* in 1945, he crystallised the outlook of the true destroyer man in half a dozen crisp sentences.

'This was what I had been training for for twenty-two years' (he wrote) 'and I led my five destroyers up towards the enemy. I was in a fortunate position in many ways, and I knew what we had to do. The cost was not to be counted. The ship was as ready for the test as we had been able to make her. I could do no more about it.'

No better epitaph could ever be worded for destroyer men.

Commander Scurfield must have known that his ship was doomed, yet he fought her to the last against repeated air attacks.

Partridge, limping along with steering gear disabled, waited for the attack to shift from *Bedouin* to her. The cruisers had shelled her at long range but had made no attempt to get to close quarters, neither had their accompanying destroyers.

In fact, they had been warned that a striking force of Malta's Albacores were out on the rampage and they turned away north at their best speed.

Finally *Partridge* limped into Gibraltar two days later.

The troubles of the convoy were not yet over. *Tanimbar*,

Chant, *Burdwan* and *Kentucky* had been lost, but the two remaining ships, *Troilus* and *Orari*, reached Malta under air cover, but *Orari*, the Polish destroyer *Kujawiak*, *Matchless* and the battered *Hebe* ran into a minefield. *Kujawiak* was sunk and the others damaged.

So ended Operation 'Harpoon'. Valuable stores were driven through to Malta but the cost to the attenuated destroyer force was heavy.

Bedouin and *Kujawiak* were gone, *Matchless* and *Partridge* were badly damaged.

At this time, of the total force of destroyers in the Mediterranean nineteen were laid up in dockyards, all seriously damaged in attempting to force through convoys to Malta.

Now to follow the fortunes of convoy 'Vigorous' which sailed from Alexandria on June 12th.

A feint convoy of four merchantmen, escorted by the cruiser *Coventry* and eight destroyers, had sailed the evening before in the hope that it would draw the Italian fleet to sea committing it to a line of advance. It was ordered to steam through the night then reverse course on the 12th to join up with the main convoy of seven merchant ships. On the morning of the 12th the German aircraft found them and attacked, badly damaging one of the merchant ships, the *City of Calcutta*, and she had to drop out.

When finally the two convoys merged into one it covered an immense area of water.

Admiral Vian's escort for the eleven merchant ships consisted of seven cruisers, an anti-aircraft cruiser, twenty-six destroyers, in addition to corvettes and minesweepers.

And inevitably the convoy was spotted. The first victim soon fell to the bombers. The *Aagterkirk* straggled, unable to keep up, and was ordered to return to Alexandria. A squadron of Stukas found her, screamed down out of the morning sky and *Aagterkirk* disappeared in a gout of flame and smoke.

Another straggler, the *Elizabeth Bakke*, was also ordered to return and did arrive back safely. So the convoy had been at sea little more than twenty hours and already had lost three ships.

There was no hope of hiding this convoy or sending it on any considerable diversion, and in any case through the night German and Italian aircraft almost continuously dropped flares above it.

Hanging on the fringe of the convoy through the night were Italian E-boats, and Admiral Vian tightened up his convoy of merchant ships and disposed his destroyers around them. Just before midnight he was told that the Italian fleet had sailed from Taranto, consisting of two battleships, the *Vittorio* and *Littorio*, four cruisers and around a dozen destroyers.

In the Second Battle of Sirte, although the odds had been heavily against him, Admiral Vian had at least two important factors on his side, apart from his own audacity. The weather had favoured him and that cunning old fox Admiral Cunningham had given him a more or less free hand to run his battle as immediate events had dictated.

But Admiral Cunningham was now Washington bound, and Admiral Harwood, while being a brilliant officer, had imposed on 'Vigorous' the cramping hand of remote control. It had happened before, in fact, while 'Vigorous' was being battled towards Malta; it was to happen again much farther north within a week or two when, because of that remote control, the initiative was removed from the admiral on the spot and Arctic convoy PQ17 was massacred.*

Air Marshal Sir Arthur Tedder and Admiral Harwood agreed that the RAF would heavily attack the Italian fleet if it showed up, while Admiral Harwood would control the movements of the convoy.

There is no scope in this book for analysis of the delay and confusion in signals which led to the convoy being turned back on its tracks, turned again and yet again in its final and inglorious return to Alexandria.

Two days out and the convoy was already in trouble. Two

*See *Gates of Hell*: Ewart Brookes

corvettes, the *Erica* and *Primula*, veterans of the Western Approaches Atlantic battle, had developed engine trouble and had been forced to limp back. The convoy had progressed so far west that the desert-based Hurricanes and Kittyhawks could spend only minutes over the ships.

While they were available the bomber attacks on the convoy were broken up, but in the evening hours the weight of bombing increased. In fact, it never stopped. Wave after wave of bombers assaulted the convoy and sank yet another merchant ship, the *Bhutan*.

Equally serious was the expenditure of ammunition. In twelve hours or so of constant action most of the escorting ships had used up fifty per cent of their ammunition.

Through the night the destroyer screen, specially disposed by Admiral Vian, fought off the E-boats and the convoy made progress.

Then at 2 am came one of those disastrous remote-control signals. Confused and untimed signals from aircraft had misled Admiral Harwood into thinking that the Italian fleet was ominously close and he signalled Admiral Vian to turn back along the hard-won and painful course he had battled over.

Destroyers were busily engaged in a complicated fight with E-boats when the order came.

They had to break off their fight to take part in the 180 degrees emergency turn in darkness. The E-boats made the most of their chance. While the forty-odd ships were reversing course, they struck, torpedoed *Newcastle* and sank the destroyer *Hasty*.

This signal which misled Admiral Harwood was twelve hours old when he received it.

In an attempt to slow up or turn the Italian fleet, four obsolete Wellingtons, armed with two torpedoes apiece, made contact with the enemy fleet about 3.30 am, delivered an abortive attack and returned to Malta.

This attack was followed by Beauforts, which hit and partly disabled the cruiser *Trento*, which was later located and sunk by one of our submarines, the *Umbra*.

At dawn, or shortly after it, the convoy was again turned west in the hope that the Italian fleet would be attacked and turned away by the RAF. Liberators based on Egypt tried, and failed. Only one hit on *Littorio* was registered and it did little material damage.

After study of the contemporary reports it is easy to see how the remote control was misled.

Liberators, synchronising their attack on the Italian fleet with that of Beauforts from Libya, claimed twenty-three hits. In fact, they made but one inconsequential hit on a battleship.

Because it was assumed from these reports, which were received some hours late, that the Italian fleet was heavily engaged with aircraft, it was considered a reasonable risk to commit the convoy to a westerly course once more. So Admiral Vian turned the convoy round to steam straight towards the advancing Italian fleet.

Yet again came another signal from a scouting aircraft that the virtually intact enemy ships were not more than 100 miles from the convoy and were still steaming fast on a south-easterly course.

Through the afternoon the convoy fought off repeated air attacks and during them arrived a signal to Admiral Vian leaving it to his discretion whether to retire or not.

His ships were almost denuded of ammunition, the cruiser *Birmingham* had been damaged and the destroyer *Airedale* sunk. Furthermore, another merchant ship had fallen out for lack of speed.

Vian pushed on for a while but realised that the hardest part of his journey was yet to come and there was a strong possibility that many of his ships would be caught out without ammunition.

On receiving this report, Admiral Harwood signalled to the convoy to once more turn about.

This it did in the evening while under heavy air attack.

On the sad and wearisome journey back to Alexandria the cruiser *Hermione* was torpedoed by a submarine and the

Australian destroyer *Nestor*, which had been damaged earlier, had to be sunk.

'Vigorous' had cost a cruiser and three destroyers sunk, with other ships damaged.

The attempts by 'Harpoon' and 'Vigorous' to supply Malta had demanded the collective effort of seventy-six war vessels to try to get seventeen merchant ships through.

Two arrived.

In cold figures the destroyer losses for both convoys were five sunk: *Bedouin, Kujawiak, Hasty, Airedale* and *Nestor*.

More were to be lost in the succeeding months before the advance into North Africa altered the situation and Malta was relieved.

Meanwhile, far to the north destroyers were carrying a tremendous burden in thrusting through convoys to Murmansk.

Although the scene was different, the ingredients were the same.

23

The first half of 1942 was a hard time for destroyers. The Battle of the Atlantic had increased its tempo, with escorts drawn thin upon the water and the submarines ranging far and wide even to the American coast.

While the battle for Malta steadily grew hotter, and shortly before Admiral Vian outbluffed and outfought an Italian squadron in the Sirte battle, destroyers were paying the price much farther east.

Electra, which had convoyed across the roof of the world from Iceland to Murmansk, found herself part of a composite fleet of Dutch, American and British forces facing a much superior enemy off Java. Her end was typical of destroyers. She sighted the Japanese cruisers, wrapped a smoke-screen around the cruiser *Exeter*, which had been hit in the first few minutes of the action, raced through the screen to attack and received the full weight of fire from three cruisers. Her end was inevitable, but until the water closed over her, her last gun kept firing.

Electra's name is most certainly deserving of being inscribed in the ever-expanding history and tradition of destroyers.

Within a few hours *Encounter* and *Jupiter* were also sunk. *Encounter* found herself the lone destroyer to screen four cruisers under command of a Dutch admiral.

Once again it was a destroyer who first sighted the enemy —*Encounter*. In the first minutes of the action the Dutch cruisers *De Ruyter* and *Java* were sunk. The remains of the Allied squadron, the cruisers *Perth*, *Houston* and the damaged *Exeter*, managed to escape to Soerabaya, where *Exeter* was repaired and sailed once more with *Encounter* and the American destroyer *Pope* as escort.

Shortly after dawn on February 29th they ran slap into a Japanese squadron of four cruisers and nine destroyers.

Encounter and *Pope* started the classic defence—a smoke-screen around the limping *Exeter*—and for a time fought off the Japanese ships. But eventually *Exeter* was hit repeatedly and came to a stop. The enemy hammered away at this sitting duck until she was sunk. Then they turned the full heat on to *Encounter* and *Pope*.

Bombers struck and sank *Pope*, leaving only the little *Encounter* alone to fight them. Which she did until she was a smoking shambles, then they turned away, leaving her to sink.

Thousands of miles away, the destroyers with which *Electra* had sailed to Murmansk were resolutely pushing through convoy after convoy to meet the incessant demands from our most recent ally.

At a price.

Admiral Tovey, Commander-in-Chief in his grim bastion Scapa Flow, was compelled to stretch his destroyer force until it was thread-thin. Demands from Western Approaches for more destroyers could be met only by taking them from the destroyers he so badly wanted to cover his convoys through the Barents Sea.

In turn, incessant demands from the Mediterranean found destroyers playing a humourless sort of maritime musical chairs, with but brief stops in the smoke- and flame-ridden music.

Bedouin, *Matchless*, *Marne*, are names which appear in the Malta convoys, as do *Badsworth*, *Blankney* and other 'Hunt' class destroyers. They appear again in the Battle of the Atlantic with other ships which also fought the convoys through to Russia, destroyers like *Achates*, *Venomous*, *Virago*, *Whitehall*, *Worcester* and others.

They would battle their way against U-boats and bombers to Russia, fight their way back again to find that Admiral Tovey had reluctantly agreed to lend them to Western Approaches and thence to the Mediterranean. Or even, as was the case with *Electra* and *Encounter*, to the Far East.

The first of the famous 'P' convoys to Russia were tentative affairs until the Germans realised that the supply route was no brief, spasmodic, purely symbolic effort.

The pattern of escort followed familiar lines. Destroyers and smaller ships formed the close escort with a covering force of heavier ships waiting in the offing for their cue should any German battle cruisers decide to take part. But in the main the fight was against U-boats and the seemingly endless supply of German bombers which were based on the tip of Norway, minutes' flying time from that bottle-neck between North Cape and Bear Island through which the convoys had to pass no matter what previous diversions they might have made.

Like the Fliegerskorps X in the Mediterranean, the German bombers in the far north were highly trained for attacking merchant ships.

Even as destroyer history had been written in Norway, at Dunkirk, in the Atlantic, in the Mediterranean and the Far East, so it was added to with every convoy that was thrust through.

And soon the price was demanded—and paid.

Escorting convoy PQ7's nine ships in January 1942 was

one of the surviving 'Tribals' *Matabele*. She was sunk and went down in a few minutes, south of Bear Island. A rescue ship not far away raced in to pick up survivors. There were men bobbing about in the water supported by their lifebelts. But they were dead—frozen in little more time than it takes to soft-boil an egg.

To attempt to describe every convoy to Russia, each one an epic story in courage—and tragedy—would take volumes. The pattern was all too familiar, as in the Malta convoys and those across the western ocean. The initiative lay with the enemy. He had U-boats which could hang around the fringe of the convoy almost throughout the duration of the convoy; he had bombers which could range far and wide across the bleak waters through which the ships were sailing and he had heavy surface ships which could race out, raid a convoy and be back in harbour by the time avenging ships could arrive.

Occasionally there would be a sortie of German destroyers, armed with five-inch guns, fast and big enough to engage in a stand-up fight to draw away escorting destroyers while a couple more slammed into the lumbering merchant ships.

On all too rare occasions the destroyers on the frozen run were able to meet the enemy with odds not overwhelmingly against them.

One such occasion was convoy PQ13, which sailed from Iceland on March 21st, 1942. It was nineteen ships strong and three days out when a screaming, demoniacal gale scattered it far and wide. The gale blew for four days in unabated fury, then the escorts had the heartbreaking task of rounding up the ships.

Covering this convoy was the cruiser *Trinidad* and a screen of two destroyers, *Fury* and *Eclipse*, to act as detached escort.

While the close escort of destroyers, minesweepers and corvettes were rounding up the scattered ships, German bombers chanced on a sight to gladden their eyes. Scattered over the wide sea were a number of merchant ships slowly recovering from the battering given them by the gale. And not a warship in sight.

The bombers sent off a joyful call to their comrades and buckled down to the task of sinking as many ships as they could.

Also in answer to this call sailed three German destroyers to join in the slaughter. Before they were able to start on their part in the massacre a snowstorm obliterated the ships except for one, a Panamanian ship which they sank after extracting information from the crew of the details of the convoy's proposed route.

Back along that line raced the German destroyers, intent on finding the convoy.

They ran slap into *Trinidad*, *Fury* and *Eclipse*.

In the twinkling of an eye the three German destroyers found themselves embroiled in a fight. Through the snowstorm sped *Fury* and *Eclipse* at thirty knots, at times appearing to steam through a waterfall.

Fury and *Eclipse*, throwing solid water over their bridges and blinded by driving snow, hurtled into momentarily clear space. It was to last not more than a minute or two, but in those fleeting seconds the German destroyer Z26 came slicing across their bows.

Fury and *Eclipse* gave her everything they had, and the German destroyer was soon wrapped in flame as repeated salvoes hit her and sent her to join so many other ships fathoms below.

The two remaining destroyers, although big enough and powerful enough to have fought the *Fury* and *Eclipse*, and even big enough to have been a threat to *Trinidad*, took advantage of a blinding snow-squall to escape.

There was an unfortunate end to this fight. A 'wildie' torpedo fired by *Trinidad* circled madly, turned and slammed into *Trinidad* and eventually she limped into Kola.

There was to be another occasion when British destroyers were to demonstrate that the last thing they would do would be to count the odds against them.

Convoy PQ15 sailed from Iceland at the end of April 1942 while convoy QP11 sailed from Russia, both convoys being timed to pass each other off Bear Island where a large force of heavy ships could give them cover against a foray by German capital ships.

Covering convoy QP11 was the cruiser *Edinburgh* and six destroyers.

The U-boats gathered in force to smite PQ15 and QP11. U-boat 456, shadowing QP11, gained an unexpected bonus. She came across the cruiser *Edinburgh* as she turned on a leg of a zig-zag course and promptly torpedoed her.

Edinburgh turned slowly and with an escort of two destroyers, *Forester* and *Foresight,* started the long limp back to Murmansk.

U-boats promptly radioed that there was a cruiser crawling eastward and three German destroyers raced seawards to reap what harvest they could.

They elected to hammer convoy QP11 first as an appetiser. In the fight which followed, *Amazon* was damaged, but with the other destroyers succeeded in driving off the Germans, leaving Commander M. Richmond in *Bulldog* with three effective ships with which to protect his charge.

Through the long first day of May he maintained a running fight in which he taught the Germans a lesson. Try as they might, they could not penetrate the three ships' screen.

Time and again the three German destroyers, with miles of room in which to work, thrust again and again, but each time they found *Bulldog* and two others waiting with flaming guns.

Eventually the German destroyers called 'best', to Commander Drummond and turned eastward in search of *Edinburgh*. And found her.

Around her they also found two alert destroyers, *Forester* and *Foresight*, by no means modern destroyers and in weight of armament quite outclassed.

For a while the German destroyers, having been given a salutary lesson by *Bulldog*, elected to stay and fight at long range. Finally they hit *Forester* repeatedly and she staggered away, finally to a stop, rolling on the uneasy glassy sea. Even then she managed to force a German destroyer away as it raced in to fire torpedoes at *Edinburgh*. The torpedoes hit *Edinburgh*, almost cutting her in half, and in steaming around to cover her, *Foresight* was severely punished and she, too, came to a stop.

The three tragic ships, stopped, rolling, immobile, seemed an easy dish and the emboldened German destroyers closed in for the kill.

And learned that so long as a British destroyer's gun is above water it will shoot. *Edinburgh* and *Foresight* between them deluged the German ship *Hermann Schoemann* until she, too, was a smoking shambles.

Then, with the three ships at their mercy, the Germans, after picking up survivors from the *Hermann Schoemann*, tore off to the west.

The explanation is comically simple. Four fleet sweepers sent out to assist *Edinburgh* came steaming through the haze and were mistaken for British destroyers.

And of them the Germans had had enough.

Foresight and *Forester* repaired their damage and set course for Murmansk. Before they turned away they had one sad task. A last office for the ship they had escorted.

They had to sink *Edinburgh* by torpedoes.

Constant political pressure was being applied to Admiral Tovey to run repeated convoys in order to keep Russia supplied, and the escorting of them threw a tremendous load on escort ships, mainly destroyers. They had the days of endless daylight and almost within hours of leaving Iceland on the outward run, and Kola on the homeward voyage, they were spotted, reported and attacked by U-boats and bombers.

The unnecessary massacre of convoy PQ17 has been told in detail elsewhere. It was yet another example of an attempt to run a convoy from a desk a couple of thousand miles away, just as an attempt had been made to convoy 'Vigorous' from Alexandria to Malta, virtually disregarding the senior officer on the spot.

And it was doomed to the same fate.

PQ18 was sailed in desperation and was heavily punished. The long days of sunlight, the weather, the bombers and the U-boats rendered it almost impossible to push through a convoy without catastrophic losses in both merchant ships and invaluable escorts. So no convoys of any strength attempted the Murmansk run until winter set in. To convoy QP15, a homeward-bound convoy, fell the dubious honour of being the first one to attempt the run with the added protection of bad weather. And it had that.

Admiral Tovey had been fighting to have convoys restricted to twelve or fourteen ships, convinced as he was that a more compact convoy with a strong escort stood a better chance than a large array of ships. But, somewhat wearily by now, he had to sail QP15 twenty-eight ships strong. They were all in ballast, high out of the water and when a real Arctic gale hit them they were scattered over hundreds of square miles.

There was small comfort. The gales which smashed the convoy also hampered the U-boats and frustrated the long-range reconnaissance planes.

More by luck than judgment, two merchant ships were located by submarines and were sunk. In this convoy destroyers had to show that there was scarcely a limit to what they would not attempt.

An American Liberty ship broke in two parts and by some miracle both parts survived. Destroyers, working like blacks to gather together the remnants of the convoy, found both halves. In the foulest of weather they battled to get tows aboard, an epic feat in itself, and reached Iceland after a heartbreaking tow, at times going as fast sideways as they were going ahead.

Admiral Tovey was now relatively well off for cruisers and destroyers. Those ships which he had 'loaned' to Western Approaches and the Mediterranean were now returning to him at the conclusion of the invasion of North Africa.

They were soon to be employed, with nostalgic recollections of the 'Med' sunshine and the pleasures of Gibraltar, as they suffered in acute misery in the Arctic.

As the weather had proved an ally for QP15, it was

decided to send another strong convoy to Russia in December.

The designation 'P' had been abandoned for Arctic convoys and they now sailed under the prefix 'JW'.

JW51 sailed in two parts, the first part, JW51A, sailed from Loch Ewe on December 15th and arrived safely at Murmansk on Christmas Day.

JW51B sailed on December 22nd.

And around that convoy was fought what is now accepted as a classic destroyer fight against astronomically long odds.

24

Convoy JW51B was made up of fourteen ships: four British, nine American and one Panamanian. From Loch Ewe to Seidisford the convoy was escorted by the minesweeper *Bramble* as senior ship, three 'Hunt' class destroyers, *Blankney*, *Chiddingfold* and *Ledbury*, two 'Flower' class corvettes, *Hyderabad* and *Rhododendron*, and two trawlers, *Northern Gem* and *Vizalma*.

East of Iceland the fleet destroyers, which were to escort the convoy all the way, were waiting. There were *Onslow*, commanded by Captain R. St Vincent Sherbrooke, *Oribi*, *Obedient*, *Obdurate*, *Orwell* and *Achates*.

That veteran *Bulldog* should have been part of the escort, but she had been damaged by bad weather on her way to Iceland and did not come under starter's orders.

The 'Hunt' destroyers bade JW51B farewell, good luck and turned away.

The remainder closed up around the convoy.

The overall picture was briefly this. A return convoy RA52 was to sail from Russia and the two convoys, outward and homeward bound, were to pass each other through that bottle-neck between the tip of Norway and Bear Island.

Astern of RA52, to lend aid if heavy enemy surface craft decided to draw cards, were *Sheffield* and *Jamaica*, with Rear-Admiral Robert Burnett flying his flag in *Sheffield*.

Also at sea, but some distance from JW51B and RA52, were the battleship *Anson*, the cruiser *Cumberland* and the destroyers *Forester* and *Impulsive*.

Every ship, both the escort and the larger units, was a veteran. They had been tried in the balance and had been found not wanting.

Achates, whose job was to steam at the tip of the convoy and make a smoke-screen around it in the event of a surface attack, had lived almost a lifetime of fighting. She had sailed with other convoys to Russia, notably PQ16, and had fought off day-long attacks. She had fought through with a QP convoy, had had her bow blown off by a mine and had emerged from repairs to be in time to form part of the escort of PQ18.

She had been one of the ships loaned for the North African invasion, had sunk a submarine and had been destroyer escort to the troopship *Warwick Castle* when she had been torpedoed in a gale in the Bay of Biscay.

And the crew of *Achates* remembered sister ships, *Acasta* and *Ardent*.

The young crew of *Achates* had no illusions left.

JW51B plugged steadily onwards, each turn of the propellers carrying the ships nearer to Russia—and nearer to the German air and sea bases.

Lurking in those bases, the Germans had the pocket battleship *Lutzow*, the *Tirpitz*, the heavy cruiser *Admiral Hipper*, the cruisers *Köln* and *Nurnberg* and ten destroyers. On the day that JW51B sailed from Loch Ewe Admiral Raeder was able to report to Hitler that all those ships were ready for sea. The Germans were cock-a-hoop. They had slaughtered PQ17 and had taken heavy toll from PQ18. From then onwards convoys to Russia had been stopped except for a lone dash by a fast and audacious ship.

They, too, were aware of the vital necessity of getting supplies through to Russia and had no illusions about the stubborn British Admiralty. Sooner or later convoys would be resumed.

From September U-boats had maintained ceaseless patrols across the convoy routes and long-range planes had scouted far and wide. Through September and October and into the foul Arctic weather of November and December, the patrols had watched the routes like patient Indians watching for a wagon train lumbering across the Western plains.

Sooner or later a convoy *would* come and the Germans were determined to massacre that one. Raeder was anxious to show what his surface ships could do in order to soften Hitler's bitter and acrimonious comments on them.

Hipper and *Lutzow* and six destroyers were brought to immediate notice for steam immediately patrolling U-boat U-354 reported a convoy en route for Russia. Lieutenant Herschleb was rather generous in his estimated speed of the convoy. He gave it as twelve knots. Nine was nearer the mark.

There had been some confusion in the German naval headquarters for a few days, as a vague sighting report had come from another U-boat which had, in actual fact, sighted JW51A.

But Herschleb's report was firm and factual, giving course and estimated speed and number of ships and an accurate position. Armed with these facts, Admiral Kummetz's staff pored over charts on *Hipper* and arrived at a position where they thought they would smash into the convoy. And *Hipper*, *Lutzow* and the six destroyers sailed.

The plan was for *Hipper* to take three destroyers, *Friedrich Eckholdt*, *Richard Beitzen* and Z29, while *Lutzow* was to have as a screen Z30, Z31 and *Theodor Riedel*. The two forces were to split, *Lutzow* and her destroyers were to search along the estimated convoy route seventy miles south of *Hipper*. The destroyers of both forces were to spread into a searching screen fifteen miles apart ahead of the heavy ships. This meant a screen roughly seventy miles wide. Amplified by frequent reports from two submarines, U-354 and U-626, which were hanging on to the skirts of the convoy, meeting it was almost a certainty.

The weight of armament against the British forces was

overwhelming. *Hipper* had eight eight-inch guns and *Lutzow* had six eleven-inch guns and the German destroyers had either four or five five-inch guns.

An almost impassable barrier of flame and shell barred JW51B's path to north Russia. Either of the two German forces alone could wreak havoc, and with the two joined together even if *Sheffield* and *Jamaica* showed up the odds were on the Germans.

Even as the German staff had pored over charts and had evolved their plan for slaughtering JW51B so had an ice-cold brain assessed exactly what could be thrown against him. And what he could do.

Captain Sherbrooke was by no means the flamboyant, dashing destroyer captain of the tear-in-and-be-damned-to-the-odds type. He knew what the Germans had available and what might happen. Behind that almost chilly reserve was a man who had grown up in the destroyer tradition. He had proved it in other fights. He had commanded *Cossack* in the Narvik battles. Before he sailed from Loch Ewe he had decided exactly what he would do with his escort ships in the event of a surface attack, up to and including the loss of *all* his escort ships, provided he could buy time. Time for the heavier British ships to join issue, time in which the merchant ships could escape. Come what may, he had decided that nothing would draw him away from the convoy. Any ships that attacked him would have to fight him around, and for, the convoy.

He saw to it, also, that the other ships in the escort knew what was expected of them. To the ultimate.

The sky lightened in the forenoon of December 31st. A so-called dawn. To the north of JW51B, and closing in on it, were *Hipper* and her destroyers, to the south of it were *Lutzow* and her destroyers. Steering by guess and by God, after foul weather, also to the north of the convoy, were *Sheffield* and *Jamaica*.

Contact! *Obdurate*, living up to her name, sighted the vague outlines of ships, challenged, received no reply, challenged again and was answered by a ripple of flame.

The battle for JW51B had started.

To the north, *Hipper* and the destroyers were to draw off the escort, decimate it, while *Lutzow* and her destroyers were to smite the convoy—and also smite such fragments of the escort as escaped *Hipper*.

Each destroyer in the British escort knew down to the letter what part they had to play. From ahead and astern of the convoy *Onslow*, *Obedient*, *Orwell* and *Obdurate* tore through the rising sea to protect the port side of the convoy. *Achates* started making smoke to hide the convoy and the remainder of the smaller ships closed up.

Out of the snow-squalls loomed a larger ship and around her destroyers.

It was *Hipper*.

Hipper emerged from a flurry of snow to find four destroyers racing towards her, spitting fire, and a long smoke-screen from *Achates* behind which the convoy was escaping to the south—and possibly into the guns of *Lutzow*.

Hipper concentrated on *Achates* at 10,000 yards range and wrapped around her climbing columns of water. From them, hit and limping, emerged the little *Achates*, still making smoke and adding to it smoke from fires started onboard.

Onslow, Obedient, Orwell and *Obdurate* made repeated snarling attacks at *Hipper* and forced her and her destroyers to turn away northwards by threatening torpedo attacks—the one thing *Hipper* dreaded. To be crippled by torpedoes and subsequently caught by a superior force was the last thing Kummetz wanted.

Yet to fulfil his task he would have to dispose of the defiant British destroyers before closing in on the convoy to destroy it. And for the time being the destroyers were carrying the fight to him. With guns blazing, they raced to meet *Hipper* and forced her to turn north into the protection of a snow-squall. Then the destroyers resumed course parallel to that along which the convoy was expected to steam.

First round went to Captain Sherbrooke. A heavy surface

craft had made contact with his convoy and had been driven off.

But it was the end of round one only, not the end of the fight.

Somewhere to the north of Captain Sherbrooke's force was *Hipper* and three powerful destroyers, which, having discovered the convoy, could choose the time for another attack.

Briefly, *Hipper* showed up alone without her three destroyers, which added to the worries of Captain Sherbrooke. *Hipper* was doing the classic manœuvre, drawing the escort away from the convoy while other ships tore in to attack it. Where were her destroyers? Were they slipping between *Onslow* and the others while *Hipper* engaged them in a tip-and-run fight?

Nothing would have pleased Captain Sherbrooke more than to be able to thrust his destroyers hard at *Hipper* in an all-out torpedo attack. He might have lost one, possibly two ships, but in the fluctuating visibility, sometimes down to less than a mile as snow-squalls swept over them, he stood a reasonable chance of scoring hits on *Hipper*.

Instead, he confined himself to short pugnacious rushes implying a torpedo attack. Once again *Hipper* turned away to the north.

Captain Sherbrooke regretted the absence of the redoubtable *Bulldog*. Had she been there with *Achates* he might have been inclined to leave the immediate protection of the convoy to those two destroyers, both of which had had previous experience of fighting against superior destroyer odds. In fact, some months previously *Bulldog* had outfought and outmanœuvred a heavier German destroyer force attempting to attack convoy QP11 in almost the same way that Captain Sherbrooke was thwarting *Hipper*. But *Bulldog* was not there. Neither was *Oribi*. Her gyro compass had broken down. She had lost touch with the convoy, and the British force was two valuable destroyers short. To close-herd the fleeing convoy there was only *Achates*, already hit and fighting fires aboard, two corvettes and a trawler.

Somewhere either to south of him or north, he knew not

where, Captain Sherbrooke was aware that *Sheffield* and *Jamaica* were supposed to be in support of him. Like the convoy, they had been forced off their course by the bad weather and they could have been ten or 100 miles away.

Hipper was more or less content to continue her tactics, engaging the attention of the British destroyers, even trying to tempt them farther north while the convoy steamed south into the guns of the *Lutzow* and her destroyers.

Once *Lutzow* and her destroyers got amongst the merchant ships, *Hipper* would then be able to close in and do her share. No matter how much courage there was, four destroyers and a lame duck making smoke could not save it.

Once again *Hipper* turned south, slicing out of a snowstorm to find *Onslow* and *Orwell* barring her path. The two destroyers received the full brunt of the cruiser's broadsides. *Onslow* could reply with only two of her guns, the others were iced up. *Onslow* was hit again and again and Captain Sherbrooke was severely wounded in the face.

In little more than a minute *Onslow* was on fire in several places. More than fifty of her crew were dead or dying.

Orwell, racing astern of *Onslow,* saw the leader reel away, dark, ominous smoke-clouds, tinged deeply with the red of fires, rolling from her.

Orwell tore round *Onslow*, making a smoke-screen to protect her for the time being. This made *Orwell* the principal target for *Hipper*. Lieutenant-Commander N. H. G. Austen, commanding *Orwell*, was faced with an acute dilemma. Should he push on into a torpedo attack against *Hipper* in an attempt to save *Onslow*? To do so would probably mean destruction for him and still possibly leave *Hipper* free to also demolish *Onslow* and then the convoy.. *Obedient* came racing back to support, wriggling between spouting columns of water as the Germans fired at her.

Three destroyers, one of them a flaming shambles, were all that lay between *Hipper* and convoy JW51B. The stage was set for a massacre which would outdo even PQ17 for sheer destruction.

And *Hipper* turned away into the concealing curtain of a snow-squall.

The explanation is almost comically simple, although heavily tinged with tragedy.

Previously Captain Sherbrooke had detached the mine-sweeper *Bramble* to search for a laggard ship which had lost the convoy in the bad weather. *Bramble* appeared out of the snow to the north of *Hipper* and was reported as a destroyer.

A crippled destroyer and two desperate consorts in her gun-sights was one thing. Another destroyer to the north was a complication. It made *Hipper* the meat in the sandwich. Where there was one there might be more in those snow-flurries through which *Hipper* had been slipping.

Hipper turned the full weight of her broadside on the little *Bramble,* a minesweeper with one four-inch gun, seven officers and just over 100 men, and in a few minutes turned her into a floating charnel-house.

Leaving the virtually destroyed *Bramble, Hipper* once more turned south to deal with the stubborn destroyers, *Orwell* and *Obedient,* now senior ship commanded by Commander Kinloch, and the crippled *Onslow.*

Hipper had fulfilled almost to the letter her part of the plan for the destruction of the convoy. She had attacked the escort, had drawn it off while the convoy turned south into *Lutzow*'s gaping guns.

But *Lutzow,* steaming on a narrow converging course to that of the convoy, assumed that the gun-fire was *Hipper* dealing fire and death to the convoy and she waited patiently for the remnants of the fleeing convoy to drop into her lap. She actually steamed across the van of the convoy only a couple of miles ahead of it without firing a shot.

In her probe through the snowstorms *Hipper* once again came across the floating wreck *Bramble,* once more slammed into her and finally left one of her destroyers, which had belatedly joined up after a fruitless probe north, to finish off the little sweeper.

But this brief interlude for assassination had taken valuable time. And closing in from the north came Force R, *Sheffield* and *Jamaica*. Even with their arrival the odds still lay in favour of the Germans. They had a pocket battleship, a heavy cruiser and six destroyers intact. The British force was two cruisers, three effective destroyers and two lame ducks, one, the *Achates*, virtually sinking.

On *Sheffield* Admiral R. Burnett was unravelling a perplexing series of problems. Had the convoy been attacked from the south and was flying north? Or had it been smitten from the north and was retreating south? And where were the enemy ships? And what were they?

It was possible, from Intelligence reports and the intense radio activity on the part of the Germans, that he might run into a couple of heavy cruisers, a pocket battleship and any number of destroyers.

Finally. Where was the convoy? South of him? Or north of him?

The sound of gun-fire south of him answered some of his problems and following the classic tenet he steamed for the sound of it. What he had heard was *Hipper* smashing *Bramble*.

Soon *Sheffield* was threading her way through the thinning smoke-screen left by *Achates*. On her radar screen were two large contacts, one, *Hipper*, was seven miles distant, the other, *Lutzow*, was eleven miles off and the speed they were moving showed them to be fast surface craft.

Sheffield closed the range on the first contact to four miles, opened fire and in a couple of salvoes was hitting *Hipper* and starting a fire. *Jamaica* followed suit and also scored hits.

Hipper realised that the party was virtually over. No longer was it only a trio of destroyers left to defend the convoy.

Lutzow fired a few salvoes at the convoy without scoring a hit.

Then the German forces retreated, leaving the crippled *Onslow*, the sinking *Achates*, and *Obedient*, *Orwell* and *Obdurate* to shepherd JW51B safely to its destination.

It had been a copybook defence of a convoy in true destroyer tradition.

Through a long day they had fought off the heavy cruiser, risking everything.

Poor little *Achates* finally sank, but from the German naval records came her valediction, as indeed it was for all the destroyers commanded by Captain Sherbrooke, who was awarded the Victoria Cross.

Admiral Kummetz wrote:

'The British destroyers conducted themselves very skilfully. They placed themselves in such a position between *Hipper* and the convoy that it was impossible to get near the ships. They made very effective use of a smoke-screen with which to hide the merchant ships. They dodged *Hipper*'s fire by taking avoiding action and using smoke. They forced *Hipper* to run the risk of a torpedo attack when using her guns on the merchant ships.'

Praise indeed.

Apart from his intense interest in *Onslow*'s battle in the Barents Sea and its immediate outcome, Admiral Tovey must have felt a nostalgic note creeping into appreciation of the fight. A little more than twenty-five years previously he, commanding the destroyer *Onslow*, only half the size of Captain Sherbrooke's command, had thrown his crippled and lone ship at the van of the German capital ships in the Battle of Jutland and by his implied threat of a torpedo attack had forced them to turn away. This *Onslow* was living up to the example he had set.

25

By late 1943 enemy naval operations were being nicely contained. The Italian fleet had been liquidated by the Axis' junior partner's surrender. In the Atlantic, British, Canadian and American destroyers, together with the hunting groups of sloops and light aircraft-carriers, were making the lot of the U-boats a hard and bitter one.

Ships were being sunk, it is true, but not at the rate of sinking of even a year back.

Along the east coast and the south coast the gallant old 'V's' and 'W's' had earned the respect of the E-boats. In fact, the E-boat historian laid it down firmly that the E-boats considered the small escorting destroyers accompanying coastal convoys as being the worst of the hazards they had to face.

Destroyers which had fought to a point of extreme exhaustion in the Mediterranean were departing to new scenes. At least, some of them did. They sailed for the Far East, where they came under the command of a man who had handled them before, Admiral Sir James Somerville, and above him Admiral Lord Louis Mountbatten, now elevated to supreme command in South East Asia, but so recently a destroyer man.

With the heat dying down in the Mediterranean, *Queen Elizabeth, Valiant, Renown,* the French battleship *Richelieu* and the fleet carrier *Illustrious*, with attendant destroyers, sailed for Ceylon.

Others, one would hazard a guess, returned rather wearily to Scapa Flow with the winter prospect in front of them of yet more arduous convoys to Russia.

Immediately following the success of getting convoy JW51A through unscathed, and the humiliation of two large German craft in their attempt to ambush JW51B, two more convoys were sailed in quick succession. Convoy JW52 of fourteen ships sailed on January 17th from Loch Ewe and JW53, a convoy of twenty-eight ships, sailed on February 15th. The inevitable atrocious weather hammered the convoys, and six ships of JW53 were damaged and were forced to turn back, but none was sunk or damaged by the enemy, although the convoy was sighted by a U-boat which homed Ju 88's on to it.

Then it was decided to send no more convoys until the autumn. Churchill had promised Stalin thirty ships loaded with the usual supplies and deck cargoes of planes, tanks and trucks—even railway engines—by the end of February.

That promise had been fulfilled with six ships to spare.

So the destroyers which had returned to Scapa after somewhat enviously watching their sisters depart for the Far East were in time to make the Kola Run yet again.

They found a new chief as C-in-C Home Fleet, Admiral Bruce Fraser, whose ideas for pushing convoys through were markedly similar to Admiral Tovey's.

The convoys had to sail, therefore they had to be escorted mainly by destroyers; cruisers would be in the offing and at sea; following the pattern would be the 'heavies'.

There had been changes, too, in the German High Command. Raeder had given way to that ruthless exponent of submarine warfare, Dönitz. After the defeat of *Hipper* and *Lutzow*, Hitler had hurled himself into one of his celebrated rages and had threatened to reduce the German heavy ships to scrap and draft their crews into his hard-pressed armies.

Dönitz, no confirmed lover of big ships, least of all German big ships, nevertheless had some idea formulated for some extensive raids into the Atlantic and persuaded Hitler to let him have *Scharnhorst* to join his northern forces so that some time in the near future he could try smiting a convoy, without restrictive orders on the commanding officers.

Hitler agreed and *Scharnhorst* sailed north.

Scharnhorst was a name engraved deeply in British naval memories. She had destroyed the *Rawalpindi*, had smashed the *Glorious* and her attendant destroyers *Ardent* and *Acasta*; she had caused us endless trouble in an Atlantic foray and had humiliated us by an audacious dash through the Channel.

Scharnhorst's was a scalp about which to dream.

Towards the end of December 1943—almost a year since *Onslow* had beaten off *Hipper* from convoy JW51B—convoy JW54B sailed northwards. With Iceland only a few hours astern, it was inevitably spotted by a U-boat, one of several astride the convoy route.

On December 23rd Admiral Bruce Fraser sailed in support in *Duke of York*, with *Jamaica* and a screen of four of the latest fleet destroyers, *Savage*, *Saumarez*, *Scorpion* and the Norwegian destroyer *Stord*.

The cruiser screen for the convoy was *Belfast*, *Norfolk* and *Sheffield*, with Admiral Robert Burnett in command.

A day or two after JW54B had sailed for Russia, a large convoy, RA55, had sailed from Kola.

The respective senior officers were old hands at Arctic convoys. Captain James McCoy, in the redoubtable *Onslow*, was senior officer of JW54B's escort, with a mixed bag of British and Canadian destroyers, and Captain Ian Campbell was commanding the powerful escort for RA55 in *Milne*.

A turbulent, wind-lashed, snow-blanketed Christmas Eve wore its way into a dismal Christmas Day as the convoys approached and passed each other abeam of Bear Island, with the persistent submarines hanging to the fringe of JW54B.

As the morning wore on, the snow cleared and the inevitable snooper plane spotted the convoy and reported it. Miraculously it failed to locate either *Duke of York* or Burnett's cruisers.

Admiral Fraser, gifted with that extra sense that some Scots have—probably passed down through generations of men who had probed the glens for an ambush by Claverhouse and his troopers—decided that RA55 was safely away to the west and JW54B was nearing the flashpoint, which he felt was bound to come.

He ordered JW54B to turn 180 degrees and steam back on its course for three hours. A complicated move for heavily laden, labouring merchant ships to execute, but they did it.

Furthermore, he ordered Captain Campbell to send four of his destroyers from the fringe of RA55 to join with Captain McCoy around JW54B.

Musketeer, *Matchless*, *Opportune* and *Virago* turned away from RA55 and raced to join JW54B, a welcome addition in destroyer strength.

In the German stronghold of Altenfiord, Rear-Admiral Bey, flying his flag in *Scharnhorst*, was assessing the latest submarine and aircraft reports.

Bey was a different type of man to Ciliax on *Tirpitz* and Kummetz in *Lutzow*. He was a destroyer man, but recently promoted from Commodore Destroyers in Norway, and had survived the destroyer battle of Narvik three years before.

He sailed, planning to contact the convoy with his destroyers in the early morning, then at daylight he would strike, massacre the merchant ships and be racing homewards before any avenging heavy ships could intervene. If they were at sea.

Fraser's three-hour turn of the convoy had deceived Bey. He crossed in front of the convoy and was warned by a U-boat that he was too far north.

Scharnhorst turned about and steered south-west.

In the meantime the Admiralty had picked up signals which told them an important point.

At 3.40 am it was passed to Admiral Fraser.

Scharnhorst was at sea!

While *Scharnhorst* was probing south-west, Admiral Burnett was slamming through a rough sea north-west, closing to *Scharnhorst* every minute.

Belfast first picked up a radar contact shortly after 8.30 at seventeen miles. The morning was still dark, but clear. Then *Sheffield* sighted the dark bulk of the enemy ship. At that moment *Belfast* opened fire with star-shell and flooded *Scharnhorst* in a baleful white glare. Almost at once *Norfolk* scored a hit on *Scharnhorst*'s fore-top and another on her foredeck. The columns of water from other eight-inch shells climbed up alongside her.

Scharnhorst turned and fled to the south-east, heading into a heavy sea which made it impossible for the cruisers to hang on to her. *Scharnhorst* had also lost touch with her destroyers, which were still vainly searching south-west of the convoy.

South-west of the convoy also was Admiral Fraser and between his force and Burnett's they were rapidly closing the bolt-hole to Altenfiord.

Admiral Burnett, although he had lost *Scharnhorst*, shrewdly assessed that the German would turn from his easterly course to north-east and then to south-west and would endeavour to hit the van of the convoy.

He placed his cruisers there just in time. Out of the morning murk loomed *Scharnhorst* again. Like a division of destroyers, the cruisers turned ninety degrees and steaming abreast slammed into the German ship once more.

Meanwhile Commander Fisher was driving *Musketeer*, *Matchless*, *Opportune* and *Virago* into a vicious sea, endeavouring to join Admiral Burnett's cruisers, and made contact with the cruisers shortly before midday.

The convoy was the bait—the prize *Scharnhorst* wanted, not a fight with British cruisers. Admiral Burnett kept his force slicing across the convoy route in broad zig-zags with Commander Fisher's division of destroyers five miles east of him.

Duke of York's destroyers, too, were taking a beating as they strove to keep up to the twenty-four knots the big ship was maintaining. They were plunging their razor bows into rearing seas, from which the tops were being blown like smoke from a volcano, hovering for a few breathless seconds on the crests, then diving down into the green-black valleys, threatening every dive to broach to as they bored upwards again.

Scharnhorst by now had lost touch with her five destroyers, which were methodically sweeping on north-east, south-west reciprocal courses well south of the convoy.

So at midday this, then, was the position without dwelling too much on the weather factor.

Convoy JW54B was on a north-easterly course carrying it farther away all the time from its designated course. Well to the south-west of it were *Duke of York*, *Jamaica* and the four attendant destroyers.

To the east of the convoy, ten miles distant, were Admiral Burnett's cruisers, with *Musketeer*, *Matchless*, *Opportune* and *Virago* five miles east of the cruisers.

And somewhere was *Scharnhorst*.

Had Admiral Burnett called wrongly? Had *Scharnhorst* evaded him? Was she even now coming up from the south-east with her five destroyers to hit the convoy on its south flank?

It was all agonising guesswork, with the massacre of a convoy and possibly some escorts if the guess was wrong.

At midday Captain McCoy used the discretion given him and turned the convoy from a north-easterly course back to a south-easterly one. So even if *Scharnhorst* had battered the cruisers and destroyers, then forged west, she would have missed the convoy which was wriggling away sandwiched between *Scharnhorst* and her destroyers.

Even as Captain McCoy re-aligned his merchant ships, *Belfast* obtained a 'blip' on her radar. Admiral Burnett had called correctly.

Scharnhorst was about twenty miles distant. Fifteen minutes later she loomed up into view.

Belfast, *Norfolk* and *Sheffield* opened fire and *Musketeer*, *Matchless*, *Opportune* and *Virago* raced towards her, pitching, rolling, at times hammering into solid water in an effort to get in a torpedo attack. At the same time they gave tongue with their 4.7-inch guns.

The German ship once more turned away to the south. But *Scharnhorst* had exacted some payment. One of her shells smashed one of *Norfolk*'s turrets and another hit her behind the bridge, starting a fire and killing one officer and six ratings. But *Norfolk*'s speed was not reduced. She kept her place in the line.

Scharnhorst was still being driven away from the prize she wanted—the convoy—which she had not even sighted. Its position was signalled to *Scharnhorst* by one of the lurking U-boats, but the signal was delayed and was misleading. It gave the position of the convoy as it was about 10 am. On their present sweep the German destroyers would have cut into the van of the convoy which could have led to a nice destroyer fight. The five heavily armed German destroyers against seven lighter armed British destroyers spread around the convoy as were Captain Sherbrooke's ships when *Hipper* had appeared almost a year ago.

It must remain conjecture.

Scharnhorst turned the German destroyers west to search for the convoy. And they missed it.

Scharnhorst, thwarted of her prey—the convoy—decided that sufficient unto the day was enough. Her powerful bows turned south for home. Another force to her south-west had been reported by a scouting aircraft.

Captain Hintze and Admiral Bey wanted no part of any British destroyers racing at their ship out of the murk, risking all to score a shot or two with a torpedo, so slowing her down. It was doubtful if they could sink her, but damage could vitally affect her speed.

Safety lay south. So Bey thought.

But plunging through the heavy seas *Duke of York, Jamaica* and *Savage, Saumarez, Scorpion* and *Stord* were rapidly narrowing that bolt-hole. Admiral Fraser, by turning the convoy round in a three-hour switch, had deceived Bey, forcing him to probe north for the convoy, and had robbed him of time.

The cruisers and Fisher's destroyers could not keep up the high speed *Scharnhorst* was achieving, but the cruiser's radar showed her every move and they were passed to *Duke of York,* who accepted them in silence.

The short, grey Arctic day of three or four hours swiftly faded but still the cruisers shadowed the German giant.

Onboard *Duke of York,* Captain Guy Russell, her commanding officer, and Admiral Fraser kept an iron control over their impatience.

Their ship was pounding along west to east to meet a powerful enemy racing north to south. They would have to reach the point of intersection with *Scharnhorst* still north of it or she would escape, to sally forth another day, to threaten yet another convoy.

Shortly after four o'clock the radar gave a clear-cut 'blip'.

Scharnhorst! Nearly twenty-four miles away and too near that narrow gap. Escape was still possible. Nothing the Navy had there could catch *Scharnhorst* if she really ran and escaped to the south.

For half an hour more *Duke of York* kept up a punishing pace, even more punishing for the destroyers and for *Jamaica.*

Scharnhorst was in range.

In plain language *Duke of York* signalled to the faithful shadowing cruisers: 'Illuminate the target with star-shell.'

Duke of York had arrived and was opening business.

Her fourteen-inch guns bellowed out as *Belfast* lit *Scharnhorst* up with star-shell and in the first salvo smashed *Scharnhorst*'s foremost turret. The next reduced her quarter-deck to a shambles.

But those hits did not slow her down.

Scharnhorst swung away to the north, only to find the plunging cruisers and their four destroyers barring that escape route. Given time, *Scharnhorst* could have demolished most of that force, but time was something which, for her, was running out. Even if only one surviving destroyer got through and damaged her it would have enabled that thundering giant astern of her to catch her up.

And Bey had no illusions. The British would throw three cruisers and three destroyers flat in his path so long as *one* of them survived to hit his ship.

For him, safety lay only to the east and the hope that his superior speed would carry him far enough away for him to wriggle round his pursuers in the darkness and race to safety.

Admiral Fraser looked at his leaping, gyrating destroyers, *Savage*, *Saumarez*, *Scorpion* and *Stord.* Solid mountains of water were smashing on to them. They were rearing and pitching like wild horses.

Once a sea took hold of one of them and broached her to, it would be her end.

But there was a job for them. A job for which destroyers were built, a job for which the officers and men had trained, a job which was their heritage.

From somewhere—and it is a golden tribute to their builders—they found extra speed, extra strength to stand up to the incredible battering. *Savage* and *Saumarez* hammered their way ahead to range on the port side of *Scharnhorst*, *Scorpion* and *Stord* followed suit to the starboard side.

The classic torpedo attack. Turn as she might, *Scharnhorst* would be a target. *If* the destroyers could get there. To the north of this drama Commander Fisher's four destroyers were slugging their way, trying to get into a position to join in the torpedo attack.

But *Scharnhorst* was holding her own. *Duke of York* was dropping astern; the overtaking destroyers, burning oil at a fantastic rate, were only creeping up on her.

Then one of *Duke of York*'s plunging salvoes hit *Scharnhorst* again below the water-line.

Her speed dropped from thirty knots plus to less than twenty. The destroyers began to overhaul her. *Scharnhorst* engaged them fiercely with her secondary armament and white columns of water climbed around the closing destroyers. In return they arrogantly opened fire, hitting her again and again. The 4.7-inch shells were little more than are the darts driven into the shoulder of a bull in the arena. It was the death thrust of torpedoes she feared.

As yet, *Scorpion* and *Stord* were undetected as they laboured to reach *Scharnhorst*'s starboard quarter.

Scorpion and *Stord* were ready to fire when *Scharnhorst* turned to starboard very obligingly, spotted the two destroyers and continued the turn to comb a double salvo of torpedoes.

One struck home.

Scharnhorst continued her turn until she was steering south-west, presenting herself as a target to *Savage* and *Saumarez*.

Officers watching the radar screen on *Duke of York* held their breaths as long as they dare. The destroyers were moving in to suicide range. Three thousand yards . . . 2,500, 2,000. Even the wildest of gunners should be able to hit them at that range.

Scharnhorst was lit up almost constantly by star-shell as

Savage and *Saumarez* hurled themselves at her.

The inevitable happened.

Saumarez was hit again and again at less than 2,000 yards, her decks were swept in a killing shower of steel splinters. Twenty-two men were dead or wounded in one second. But *Saumarez* plunged on, fired four of her torpedoes as she turned away. *Savage* sent in her full salvo of eight.

As they circled away, the destroyers heard a dull explosion . . . then another . . . and yet another. Three hits.

They had delivered *Scharnhorst* to *Duke of York*.

The battleship, which had ceased firing when the destroyers were so close, opened up again. So did *Jamaica* and so did *Belfast*, racing south in the darkness.

Scharnhorst was almost constantly framed in lethal flame, was being scientifically smashed as she herself had smashed *Rawalpindi*.

Scharnhorst was by now merely creeping through the water at less than five knots.

Plunging out of the darkness to the north of her came *Opportune*, *Virago*, *Musketeer* and *Matchless* in two sub-divisions. *Musketeer* and *Matchless* attacked from the port side, *Opportune* and *Virago* from the starboard. Between them they fired salvoes of torpedoes deep into *Scharnhorst*'s already-stricken vitals. She was just a flaming wreck.

Admiral Fraser recognised that eight vengeful destroyers practically climbing aboard *Scharnhorst*, none of them fully aware of whether *Scharnhorst*'s destroyers were in the battle or not, was a situation which could lead to tragedy.

He ordered the triumphant destroyers away from their prey and ordered *Jamaica* and *Belfast* to finish her off with torpedoes.

There was a dull, heavy explosion, the glowing mass became dimmed.

All that remained was a merciful task.

Scorpion and *Matchless*, their roles drastically changed, searched for survivors. Of 1,903 officers and men of *Scharnhorst*, thirty-six ratings were rescued from the freezing sea.

Despite the punishment meted out by the sea, despite the punishment from *Scharnhorst*'s guns, the destroyers had gone almost to a point of certain destruction to fire torpedoes.

They had lived up to the destroyer tradition: 'Where there is an enemy close in and attack with torpedoes.'

Dogmatic. Flat. No saving clauses.

The Battle of North Cape was by no means the end of the Russian convoys. In fact, they continued carrying supplies to an ungracious and ungrateful ally up to the point where the advancing Russians were battling in the streets of Berlin.

There were losses, tragic losses, of ships which had made the arduous trips time and again. U-boats came at them with new weapons and were in time defeated.

The Battle of the Atlantic continued with somewhat abated ferocity, it is true, but winter and summer, destroyers formed the backbone of the convoy escorts.

Some of those which had battled across the roof of the world eventually found themselves part of the build-up to vanquish the arrogant Nippon who had bestrode the Far East.

Saumarez, which had dealt one of the first death blows to *Scharnhorst*, led another flotilla of five destroyers in a classic ambush which destroyed the Japanese heavy cruiser *Haguro* in May 1945. With her was *Virago*, which had also fought against *Scharnhorst*.

They gathered for D Day, escorted convoys, kept the ring against U-boats, fought off E-boats and some of them must have been weary when VE Day finally came.

Destroyers which were only lines on paper when *Scharnhorst* was sunk started to come off the stocks—in time for peace.

And what giants they were! Nearly three times the size, and twice the armament, of the slim, elegant destroyers which had fought in the First World War, which for that matter had fought through the Second Global War.

Now, even those comparative giants of 1945–6: the 'Battle' class, *Jutland* and her sisters, the 'Weapon' class, *Crossbow* and her sisters are outclassed. Compare a 'Dainty' with even a 'V' or 'W'. The 'Dainty', of 2,600 tons.

For me, I shall always treasure memories of the 'V's' and 'W's'.

I saw them at the end of the 1914–18 War. I saw them throughout the 1939–45 War. One more than any other I remember. The *Walpole*. I met her, a gallant old lady, around the time of the Dunkirk evacuation. I met her on east-coast convoys, I met her in Western Approaches, I met her once, thankfully, when she spared a few moments to elegantly discourage an E-boat which was showing predatory inclinations towards my very small ship.

I saw her last in Portsmouth. The war had ended. Near her lay a surrendered German destroyer, spick, span, shining like a yacht.

Walpole was a bit battered in places, rust showed here and there (but only outboard). In any one month of her past five years she had put in more sea-time than the German destroyer had all through the war.

Now her career was ending. Soon the breaker's white-hot flame would end it all for her. But no flame can ever quench the heritage she and her sisters helped to form over those long, long years.

HMS *Walpole*, a destroyer relegated finally to an escort frigate, *sans* torpedo tubes, *sans* one boiler room.

But a ship, a destroyer. A *real* destroyer.

A ship I would have loved to command.

At the time of writing a destroyer is being laid down of approximately 5,000 tons, HMS *Devonshire*.

Will her captain hurl her into action, regardless of the fact that he has a ship costing several million? As Evans hurled *Broke* into action, as Lieutenant-Commander Tovey turned his small craft to meet the might of the German fleet at his top speed of ten knots, as Roope threw *Glow-worm* at his mighty adversary, as Sherbrooke did against *Hipper*, as Vian in *Cossack* harried *Bismarck* through a long night, as *Ardent* and *Acasta* did in their effort to save *Glorious*, as *Savage* and

Saumarez, and *Scorpion* and *Stord*, and *Matchless* and *Musketeer*, and *Opportune* and *Virago*, threw themselves at *Scharnhorst*?

If he is a true destroyer man he will.

And he would not be on her bridge if he wasn't. Because men don't reach command in destroyers unless they have grown up to it, have that something which halllmarks a destroyer man, that State of Being.

26

(This additional chapter written by Douglas Reeman)

At the end of the Second World War in 1945, and with the grim echoes of Hiroshima and Nagasaki still reverberating around the globe to remind us of man's new skill at self-destruction, the Royal Navy was confronted with the vital necessity for change. Not since steam had ousted sail, and oil fuel had swept away the drudgery of coaling ship had such a challenge been envisaged.

Britain had entered the war prepared to accept new inventions and advanced tactics which are inevitable when two determined enemies confront each other. But basically the navy's strategy was firmly built around the strength of capital ships and the support made available by the aircraft carrier force. These in turn would be protected by the *maids of all work*, the destroyers, much as they had been in the First World War.

By the close of hostilities it was apparent even to the *old guard* that the era of the battleship and battlecruiser was finished, and the days of the vulnerable aircraft carrier numbered. The realities of guided missiles and nuclear-powered submarines were still on drawing-boards and in secret experimental stages, but the war's lessons were being studied with mounting concern.

The Germans had produced plenty of ideas, some of which, had they come earlier to the scene of battle, might indeed have turned the tables, or at best brought the war to a bloody stalemate.

The V.1 and V.2 rockets which fell on South-East England were serious enough, especially as a threat to civilian morale, but perhaps more significant was the German radio-controlled bomb. Due to the need for maximum security during the Allies' invasion of Sicily and then Italy in 1943, the bomb and its effectiveness were little publicised. And later, with greater military advances and then peace with all the confusion of demobilisation and the return to normality, it was overshadowed, ignored except by those directly involved in planning a post-war fleet.

The bomb could be launched by and directed from an aircraft, and homed on to a surface unit with a high degree of accuracy. When the Allies invaded the Italian mainland the radio-controlled bomb caused severe damage to several valuable naval units, including the battleship H.M.S. *Warspite*, a veteran of the Mediterranean campaign, the cruiser H.M.S. *Uganda*, and two American cruisers, *Philadelphia* and *Savannah*. They were, with other vessels, put out of action when they were desperately needed to support our forces ashore, and suffered heavy casualties.

The enemy's weapon must now be seen as the first truly effective guided missile. As in the old days of wooden ships, the design and construction of each vessel had to be based on the weapons then available and the propulsion to carry them where they could be most effectively used. So then, the radio-controlled bomb paved the way for new naval strategy, and new vessels to partake in it. The question which faced the designers was, where was the destroyer's role in this new navy?

As in two world wars, the tune was to be called by the destroyer's old enemy, the submarine. The immediate post-war pattern was shattered when the fast submarine became a reality. Previously, because of their low underwater speed, submarines were in constant danger from surface warships designed to locate and attack them. New hull design, better propulsion units and finally nuclear power made the well-tried methods of detection and destruction as useless as the sailing ship had been against armoured steel. It was then that the frigate really came into her own, taking over much of the destroyer's role, and many of the heavier destroyers still in service or building on the stocks at the end of the war were rebuilt and reclassed as frigates.

It was not until the early nineteen-fifties that the first new class of destroyers was put into service. There were eight of them in all, and in their day were the most powerful small warships afloat. They were called the 'Daring' class, and because they bore little resemblance to their predecessors and none at all to the frail turtle-backs of the nineteen-hundreds, they were often called 'Darings', rather than given their proper titles.

With a displacement of 2,800 tons and a complement of nearly 300 officers and ratings, they incorporated every modern device, including fully automatic radar-controlled guns, and later Seacat guided missiles. More like light cruisers than destroyers as we had known them, they had a top speed of thirty-four knots.

But even as the 'Darings' became fully operational it was obvious that they could never fill the gap left by the vanishing power of the heavier warships. The guided missile had become a force to be reckoned with. It was equally apparent that a small vessel with a large pay-load of missiles had gained ascendancy over larger orthodox warships.

The destroyer was no longer needed to screen and protect the majestic line of battle, for there was none. The great ships had departed in the smoke of Matapan and Midway, or maybe even earlier at Jutland. Even cruisers were fast becoming a dying breed, and those still in service were being rebuilt to perform varying roles as commando ships and helicopter cruisers. In the sixties, with the birth of the vertical take-off aircraft and its ability to back up the already successful anti-submarine helicopter, the giant carrier too was marked to be phased out.

For the first time in her long and colourful history the destroyer suddenly stood all alone.

If frigates were being constructed to take on the duties of anti-submarine and radar-picket patrols, the destroyer's role was thrown wide open to speculation and expansion.

It was no use continuing in the old style and merely substituting bulk for increased efficiency. That idea merely raised them to the dying status of cruisers. As Sir Winston Churchill once commented, 'By steadily increasing the size and cost of destroyers we transfer them gradually from the class of the hunters to that of the hunted.' A shrewd observation.

One thing was certain. The new destroyer would still have to be a *maid of all work*, but she would be expected to operate, if need be, entirely alone.

Fast and manœuvrable, able to outpace and detect the latest nuclear-powered submarines, yet able to stand and fight even the heaviest opponent, they were just some of the problems which faced the designers. And so from the lessons learned in the Korean War, and from studying the practical advances made in the United States Navy as well as Russia's growing naval power, the first true step into the missile age for destroyers was planned and taken.

They were called the 'County' class, and between 1962 and 1970 eight vessels were completed. Quite apart from their impressive performance, the ships carried on the tradition of lithe grace and smooth design which made their predecessors so famous and admired.

There the comparison must end. The Guided Missile Armed Destroyers are a far cry from the old 'V's' and 'W's' for instance, which served so splendidly in two world wars. Gone are the days when men off watch had no room to sling their hammocks. Gone too is the necessity for men to carry food from a primitive galley to arrive cold and wet on their mess-decks and the meal partly awash. The old 'V' and 'W' destroyers were in my opinion the very stuff of the destroyer tradition, their companies unmatched. But times have changed, and so must conditions for the men who serve the new navy, if our world is to survive.

The 'County' class are airconditioned throughout, with the latest accommodation and amenities to ease the lot of the most dedicated sea-lawyer.

At full load they have a displacement of 6,200 tons and carry a complement of 471, including 33 officers.

They are the first destroyers to be fitted with COSAG (combined steam and gas) turbine machinery. This has a double advantage. It is a small compact unit of light design so that there is more space available in the hull for the weapons systems and storage. More to the point, COSAG enables a ship to develop full power from *cold* in minutes, so that a vessel lying in port without steam up can get under way immediately in an emergency.

In the last war a chief engineer, watching his reluctant gauges and fretting at the delay in getting enough steam, would have imagined such an advance something of a miracle.

Apart from their impressive array of Seaslug and Seacat missile launchers, the 'County' class destroyers also carry four 115 millimetre guns in twin mountings. Radar-controlled. fully automatic, these rapid firing weapons can be used both for attack and defence against ships and aircraft.

In addition to their other, more conventional weapons, the ships each carry a Wessex helicopter fitted with anti-submarine *dipping* Sonar, which increases the range of operations even when working without additional support.

The class embodies three main roles. Firstly, escort duties with a larger task group with the ability to supply guided-missile anti-aircraft defence and to back up the anti-submarine capability of the group. Next, they can act as part of a task unit, with the ability to bombard the shore in support of land forces and to attack with gunfire. Finally, but in these uncertain times no less important, they can perform police duties and show the flag in any part of the world.

They are designed to operate in 'fall-out' areas, and their smooth lines and clean hull design facilitates 'washing down' in the event of a nuclear attack.

The undoubted success of the 'County' class was quickly recognised and further plans were put in motion to design and launch more missile destroyers.

It was not difficult to find examples of what could happen to the unprepared in the event of war. Around the embattled coastline of Viet Nam there had been several bitter incidents where small, fast-moving craft had savaged larger ships and then vanished before any real chance of hitting-back had been gained.

In the swift Six Days War in 1965 fought between Israel and the Arab bloc the lesson was driven home with a vengeance. A mere handful of small, missile-armed craft reduced the Egyptian navy to a shambles. In the twinkling of an eye, or so it seemed at the time, the whole balance of naval power in one sea area was altered. It was like history repeating itself. In the Second World War, off the coast of Malaya, two British capital ships, the *Prince of Wales* and *Repulse* were sent to the bottom in the space of an hour. Not merely two great ships and many hundreds of men perished on that day. The balance of naval power was tipped by a few determined and persistent airmen, and the grim consequences are too well known to be recounted here. But it is fair to say that but for a total inability to accept that huge capital ships were helpless without air cover, the military catastrophe in Malaya and Singapore might have been averted. The Six Days War in a similar fashion proved beyond doubt that the missile had come to stay, and with ship design, quality was far more important than quantity and size.

These facts are of particular importance to the Royal Navy. No longer having the burden it once carried, the need to police from one end of the world to the other, the navy has been able to concentrate its attention on the production of smaller and more effective warships. The massive powers of America and Russia, and the emerging strength of the

Chinese nation, have made the Royal Navy more conscious of its new role in world affairs, and the old concept of standing alone against all comers is now a part of history. Each new ship is as much a floating test-bed and training vessel as it is a naval unit. Ideas, mistakes, experiments and day-to-day trials with weapons and machinery have done much to make the best use of the facilities and the money available.

1973 sees the first of a new class, the 'Type 42' Guided Missile Armed Destroyer. H.M.S. *Sheffield* has incorporated many of the 'County' class ideas, but she has some extra ones of her own. For instance, although she is of some 3,500 tons displacement and is crammed with all the latest mechanical equipment, she will have, when in commission, twenty-five per cent reduction in technical manpower. This is largely due to her new gas-turbine installation which requires only a small number of personnel compared with destroyers of a similar size.

With a speed of over 30 knots she will carry Seadart surface to surface missiles, fully automatic 115 millimetre guns, and a twin-engined Lynx helicopter armed with anti-submarine torpedoes. Her agility, endurance and hitting-power will place her well in the vanguard of destroyer design.

Economy of building costs and in manpower, the maximum cruising range with the minimum use of fuel and supplies, the capability to stand alone if so required and live off her own resources, all these matters must be considered. The question of technical personnel is one of pressing importance. To avoid cramming a destroyer's hull and thereby abusing the limited space available, each part of the ship's mechanical equipment must be sited and used with the minimum of manpower.

This latter fact is well displayed in H.M.S. *Bristol*, the new 'Type 82' destroyer and a project running almost parallel to *Sheffield*.

Built by the famous Swan Hunter group (Wallsend), *Bristol* has the impressive displacement of 6,750 tons, full load, but still retains the ability to perform at over 30 knots.

For some while to come she must surely be the most

advanced of her breed. Her machinery is remotely controlled from a ship control centre, which enables commands to be obeyed, alterations of course to be executed with minimum delay, and keeps the personnel down to manageable proportions.

Automatic steering has done away even with the need for a quartermaster, that familiar figure on every bridge I have known, and it will enable the captain or the officer of the watch to make fast changes of course and speed even when in close company with other craft. This will be particularly useful when fuelling at sea, transferring stores and similar manœuvres.

Sleek and extremely seaworthy, she will be comfortable for her people even when 'shut down' for nuclear fall-out.

Bristol's weapons system is equally advanced and sophisticated. She carries the latest radar and sonar which will provide all the necessary information and data to her Seadart missiles and her Ikara anti-submarine launcher.

She is also designed to carry a Wasp helicopter for reconnaissance and anti-submarine operations.

And what of the men who will serve, maintain, and command these ships of the future? How will they compare with all those who have gone before them, who straddled their legs to remain upright in a pitching, open bridge, while the narrow hull bucked and plunged beneath them? In the ships where it was not uncommon for officers to be marooned aft in the wardroom because of heavy weather and great seas making the iron-deck unusable. And those who hunted *Bismarck* and harried the mighty *Scharnhorst*, who burst into Narvik and raised the heart of a nation with the cry 'The Navy's here!' as they swept alongside the prison-ship *Altmark*. And all those others, too numerous to mention, whose deeds now read like a roll of honour.

Will it make any difference for the captain of tomorrow to know he is commanding a ship costing millions, carrying weapons and equipment upon which the very survival of his country may depend?

The questions are answered already. The fact that such men are available and willing to dare, to tackle any job thrown their way, is proof enough for me.

As an old destroyer hand myself I know the feeling when it comes up in conversation.

'Destroyers?' A pause and it all comes flooding back. 'I used to serve in them.' And for that I am grateful.

D.R.

May, 1972

Bibliography

C. Aspinall-Oglander: *Roger Keyes.*

Battle of Jutland. Official dispatches (HM Stationery Office).

Commander Carlyon Bellairs, RN: *The Battle of Jutland.*

Keble Chatterton: *Danger Zone.*

Sir Julian Corbett: *History of the Great War*: Vol. III.

H. W. Fawcett and G. W. Hooper: *The Fighting at Jutland.*

Commander Holloway H. Frost, USN: *The Battle of Jutland.*

Commander P. K. Kemp, RN: *H.M. Destroyers.*

E. F. Knight: *Harwich Naval Forces.*

Captain Donald Macintyre, DSO, DSC, RN: *Jutland.*

Kenneth Poolman: *Kelly.*

Captain S. W. Roskill, RN: *The War at Sea*, Vols. I, II, III.

Commander L. A. Woollard, RN: *Harwich Command.*

Index